College Football Records

College Football Records

Division I-A and the Ivy League, 1869–1984

by
Robert Baldwin

McFarland & Company, Inc., Publishers
Jefferson, North Carolina, and London

Library of Congress Cataloguing-in-Publication Data

Baldwin, Robert, 1963–
  College football records.

  Includes index.
    1. Football — United States — History.   2. Football —
  United States — Records.   I. Title.
  GV950.B35   1987   796.332'63'0973   87-42500

ISBN 0-89950-246-6 (acid-free natural paper)

Manufactured in the United States of America.

McFarland & Company, Inc., Publishers
  Box 611, Jefferson, North Carolina 28640

Table of Contents

Introduction

It was in 1869 that Princeton and Rutgers participated in the very first collegiate football game. Over the next 115 years, college football has evolved into the most exciting American sport being played today. Unfortunately, a recap of the great years of past competition is not always available to the devoted fan. This book has been compiled in an attempt to capture some of that missing rich tradition and to allow the college football fan to reflect back on the history of this tradition-laden game. Despite the phenomenal growth of the game and all the good and bad qualities it has brought, the essence of college football is still what it was in the beginning—a match between two schools, a match between student bodies and school prides.

The overall record of a school's varsity football team is a summation of this history. That is why this compilation of past records is presented. The records on the following pages, in both the composite and in the broken-down form against every opposition team, give the fan the history of each school's records against arch rivals, league competitors, brief or chance intersectional opposition, and obscure opponents.

The schools presented in this book are the remaining division I-A or "big time" teams still playing collegiate football, as classified by the National Collegiate Athletic Association, the governing body of college athletics. These are the only colleges still competing among themselves for the pride of their institution and not for a formalized national championship, as the NCAA does not recognize a division I-A football champion. Also included because of their immense interest and contribution to the game are the eight Ivy League schools. For each school, the overall series record against every opposing team in its football history is listed. They are separated by conference opponents, division I opponents (including division I-A and division I-AA schools), and all other opposition, including division II and division III schools, those schools that no longer play football, disbanded institutions, and other organized teams.

The 111 schools covered in this book are grouped together within their respective athletic conferences, with independent schools listed last. Historical data about each conference is included to provide the fan with a sense of the competition and tradition involved with league play. The conference title is, after all, the only formalized championship division I-A college football teams vie for.

Individual records are listed in the order of wins, losses, and ties. Opposition is grouped alphabetically within three categories: conference competition (if applicable), division I competition, and

1

other opponents. Division I competition includes all division I-A schools listed in this book and division I-AA schools. A list of schools which competed within division I-AA football as of 1984 can be found in a separate appendix at the end of the book. I gratefully appreciate the aid of the sports information directors of each individual school listed who provided me with the necessary information to compile this book. It is with their cooperation that this retrospective look at college football has been achieved.

Explanation of Abbreviations

The following abbreviations are frequently found throughout the book.

A.A.	Athletic Association
A.A.F.	Army Air Field
A.B.	Air Base
A.C.	Athletic Club
A.F.B.	Air Force Base
(B)	Second Team
C.C.	City College
C.G.	Coast Guard
Col.	College
H.S.	High School
Inst.	Institute
J.C.	Junior College
J.V.	Junior Varsity
N.A.S.	Naval Air Station
Y.	Y.M.C.A.

Atlantic Coast Conference

Formed: 1953
Charter Members: Clemson, Duke, Maryland, North Carolina, North
Carolina State, South Carolina, Virginia, Wake Forest.

Overall Records

	Years	W	L	T	Pct.
Georgia Tech	92	496	326	40	.599
North Carolina	94	497	346	52	.584
Duke	72	373	264	29	.582
Clemson	89	449	329	42	.573
Maryland	92	466	397	39	.538
Virginia	95	439	417	47	.512
North Carolina State	93	369	401	52	.481
Wake Forest	83	286	430	31	.404

Conference Records

	Years	W	L	T	Pct.
Clemson	32	124	60	4	.670
Maryland	32	119	66	3	.641
North Carolina	32	112	86	4	.564
Georgia Tech	2	6	5	1	.542
Duke	32	97	83	7	.537
North Carolina State	32	98	87	7	.529
Wake Forest	32	59	138	5	.304
Virginia	31	40	132	3	.237
South Carolina (see Chapter 11)	18	52	58	4	.474
Combined bowl game record		41	39	1	.512

Total Championships

1. Clemson	9	6. Wake Forest	1
2. Maryland	7	South Carolina	1
3. Duke	6	8. Virginia	0
North Carolina State	6	Georgia Tech	0
5. North Carolina	5		

Past Champions

1984 Maryland	1982 Clemson
1983 Maryland	1981 Clemson

5

1980 North Carolina	North Carolina State
1979 North Carolina State	1964 North Carolina State
1978 Clemson	1963 North Carolina
1977 North Carolina	1962 Duke
1976 Maryland	1961 Duke
1975 Maryland	1960 Duke
1974 Maryland	1959 Clemson
1973 North Carolina State	1958 Clemson
1972 North Carolina	1957 North Carolina State
1971 North Carolina	1956 Clemson
1970 Wake Forest	1955 Maryland
1969 South Carolina	Duke
1968 North Carolina State	1954 Duke
1967 Clemson	1953 Duke
1966 Clemson	Maryland
1965 Clemson	

CLEMSON

Nickname: Tigers
Colors: Purple and orange
Location: Clemson, South
Carolina
Stadium: Memorial (73,900)

First year of football: 1896
Year entered conference: 1953
Conference championships: 9

Atlantic Coast Conference Competition

Duke	16-12-1	North Carolina State	34-18-1
Georgia Tech	12-35-2	Virginia	24-0
Maryland	14-18-1	Wake Forest	38-11-1
North Carolina	20-12-1		

Division I Competition

Alabama	3-11	Mississippi	0-2
Appalachian State	1-0	Mississippi State	1-0-1
Army	0-1	Missouri	2-0
Auburn	11-31-2	Navy	1-0
Baylor	0-1	Nebraska	1-0
Boston College	7-5-2	Notre Dame	1-1
Citadel	27-5-1	Ohio State	1-0
Colorado	0-1	Oklahoma	0-2
Davidson	11-5-4	Pacific	0-1
Florida	3-9-1	Pittsburgh	0-1
Florida State	1-2	Rice	4-3
Furman	34-10-4	South Carolina	48-31-3
Georgia	14-35-4	Southern California	0-1
Kentucky	3-6	Tennessee	5-11-2
Louisiana State	0-1	Texas A&M	0-2
Miami (Fla.)	1-4	Texas Christian	2-1

Tulane	4-6	Virginia Tech	13-6-1
Vanderbilt	1-3	Western Carolina	3-0
Virginia Military	5-5-2		

Other Opponents

Bingham	1-0	Howard	3-0
Camp Gordon	4-0	Jacksonville N.A.S.	0-1
Camp Hancock	0-1	Maryville	1-0
Camp Sevier	1-0	Mercer	4-3
Centre	0-3	Newberry	6-0
Charlotte Y.	1-0	Oglethorpe	0-1
Cumberland	0-0-1	Pensacola N.A.S.	1-0
Duquesne	4-0	Port Royal	1-0
Elon	1-0	Presbyterian	32-3-4
Erskine	7-1	Riverside	1-0
Fordham	0-0-1	Sewanee	0-1
George Washington	3-1-1	Southwestern (Tenn.)	1-0-1
Georgia Pre-Flight	0-1	Villanova	1-1
Guilford	1-0	Wofford	9-3

Total Overall Record	449-329-42	.573
Total Conference Record	124-60-4	.670
Overall Bowl Game Record	6-5-0	.545

DUKE

Nickname: Blue Devils	First year of football: 1888
Colors: Blue and white	Year entered conference: 1953
Location: Durham, North Carolina	Conference championships: 6
Stadium: Wallace Wade (33,950)	

Atlantic Coast Conference Competition

Clemson	12-16-1	North Carolina State	36-20-4
Georgia Tech	25-26-1	Virginia	23-13
Maryland	14-14	Wake Forest	45-18-2
North Carolina	31-36-4		

Division I Competition

Alabama	1-1	Colgate	7-0
Arkansas	1-0	Columbia	0-1
Army	4-8-1	Davidson	16-4-1
Auburn	2-3	East Carolina	2-2
Baylor	1-0	Florida	2-3
Boston College	1-2	Furman	1-2
California	1-0-1	Illinois	1-1

Indiana	1-2	Richmond	9-1
Kentucky	4-0	South Carolina	24-14-2
Louisiana State	1-1	South Dakota	1-0
Miami (Fla.)	1-1	Southern California	0-3
Michigan	0-6	Southern Methodist	2-0
Missouri	0-1	Stanford	1-1
Navy	9-14-5	Syracuse	2-0
Nebraska	1-0	Tennessee	12-11-2
Notre Dame	1-2	Tulane	0-2
Ohio State	1-3	UCLA	0-1
Oklahoma	0-1	Virginia Military	7-1
Oregon State	0-1	Virginia Tech	7-4
Pennsylvania	1-1	Washington	1-1
Pittsburgh	8-9	West Virginia	3-0
Purdue	2-1-1	William and Mary	1-6
Rice	3-0		

Other Opponents

Bogue Field	1-0	Mercer	2-0
Camp Lejeune	1-0	Newberry	1-0
Elon	5-0-1	New York	0-0-1
Emory and Henry	2-0	North Carolina Pre-Flight	1-1
George Washington	2-0	Oglethorpe	1-0
Georgetown	0-1	Presbyterian	0-0-1
Georgia Navy	0-1	Randolph-Macon	3-0
Guilford	7-0	Villanova	2-1
Hampden-Sydney	1-0	Washington and Lee	7-1
Jacksonville N.A.S.	0-1	Wofford	6-0-1
Lynchburg	2-0		

Total Overall Record	373-264-29	.582
Total Conference Record	97-83-7	.537
Overall Bowl Game Record	3-3-0	.500

GEORGIA TECH

Nickname: Yellow Jackets
Colors: Gold and white
Location: Atlanta, Georgia
Stadium: Grant Field (58,120)

First year of football: 1892
Year entered conference: 1983
Conference championships: 0

Atlantic Coast Conference Competition

Clemson	35-12-2	North Carolina State	3-1
Duke	26-25-1	Virginia	6-0-1
Maryland	0-0	Wake Forest	7-0
North Carolina	10-8-2		

Division I Competition

Air Force	3-0	Missouri	1-1
Alabama	21-28-3	Navy	13-8
Arkansas	1-1	Notre Dame	4-25-1
Army	2-1	Penn State	3-3
Auburn	39-44-4	Pennsylvania	1-2
Baylor	2-0	Pittsburgh	2-5
Boston College	1-0	Purdue	0-1
California	3-4	Rice	2-0-1
Citadel	7-0	Rutgers	1-0
Davidson	12-2	South Carolina	10-7
Florida	24-9-6	Southern California	1-2
Florida State	9-0-1	Southern Methodist	8-2-1
Furman	7-2-2	Tennessee	16-23-1
Georgia	32-42-5	Tennessee-Chattanooga	4-0
Iowa State	1-0	Texas	0-1
Kansas	1-0	Texas A&M	1-1
Kentucky	11-7-1	Texas Christian	2-0
Louisiana State	12-5	Texas Tech	2-0
Memphis State	2-1	Tulane	35-13
Miami (Fla.)	6-2	Tulsa	1-1
Michigan	0-1	Vanderbilt	16-15-3
Michigan State	2-0	Virginia Military	12-1
Mississippi	2-1	West Virginia	1-0
Mississippi State	2-0	William and Mary	1-0

Other Opponents

Camp Gordon	1-0	Howard	5-0
Carlisle	1-0	Maryville	0-0-1
Carnegie Tech	0-2	Mercer	12-1-1
Centre	1-0	Mooney School	3-0
Cumberland	3-0	Nashville	0-2
Dahlonega	3-0	Oglethorpe	8-1
11th Cavalry	2-0-1	Presbyterian	3-0
5th Division	1-0	St. Albans	0-2
Fort Benning	0-1	St. Mary's (Tx.)	1-0
Fort McPherson	2-1	Savannah A.A.	0-1
Georgetown	5-0	Sewanee	5-7-1
Georgia Pre-Flight	2-0	Transylvania	1-0
Gordon	5-0	Washington and Lee	4-1-1
Grant	1-0	Wofford	1-0

Total Overall Record   496-326-40   .599
Total Conference Record   6-5-1   .542
Overall Bowl Game Record   14-8-0   .636

MARYLAND

Nickname: Terrapins
Colors: Red and white
Location: College Park,
    Maryland
Stadium: Byrd (45,000)

First year of football: 1892
Year entered conference: 1953
Conference championships: 7

Atlantic Coast Conference Competition

Clemson	18-14-1	North Carolina State	20-17-4
Duke	14-13	Virginia	32-15-2
Georgia Tech	0-0	Wake Forest	24-8-1
North Carolina	22-25-1		

Division I Competition

Air Force	2-0	Missouri	6-0
Alabama	1-2	Navy	5-14
Auburn	1-2	Ohio	1-0
Baylor	1-1	Oklahoma	0-4
Boston College	0-0	Penn State	1-27
Boston University	2-0	Pennsylvania	1-4
Cincinnati	2-0	Pittsburgh	1-1
Connecticut	1-0	Princeton	0-2
Delaware	3-5-1	Richmond	11-5-2
Florida	6-11	Rutgers	4-3
Florida State	0-2	South Carolina	17-11
Georgia	3-2-1	Southern Methodist	2-0
Houston	0-1	Syracuse	13-14-2
Indiana	0-2	Tennessee	2-5
Indiana State	1-0	Texas	0-3
Kentucky	3-2-2	Texas A&M	0-2
Louisiana State	3-0	Tulane	2-2
Louisville	2-0	UCLA	1-1
Miami (Fla.)	7-5	Vanderbilt	3-7
Miami (of Ohio)	0-1	Virginia Military	14-9-2
Michigan State	1-4	Virginia Tech	14-10
Minnesota	1-0	West Virginia	9-10-2
Mississippi	1-1	William and Mary	1-2
Mississippi State	1-0	Yale	2-8-1

Other Opponents

Alexandria H.S.	1-0	Bethel	1-0
American	0-1	Business H.S.	1-0
Bainbridge Training	1-1	Carnegie Tech	0-1
Baltimore C.C.	2-0	Catholic	8-1-2
Baltimore Med. Col.	0-1	Central H.S.	6-2
Baltimore Poly	3-1	Charlotte Hall Mil.	1-0

Chicago	0-1	Marine Barracks	1-0
Clifton A.C.	1-0	Merchant Marine	1-0
Columbia A.C.	0-1	Mt. of St. Joseph's	2-0
Curtis Bay C.G.	0-1	Mt. St. Mary's	2-2-1
Dickinson	1-0	Mt. Washington Club	0-1
Duquesne	1-0	New York	2-0
Eastern H.S.	4-0	Old Univ. of Maryland	3-2-1
Episcopal H.S.	0-3	Olympia A.C.	1-0
Fort Monroe	0-0-1	Orient A.C.	1-0
Fredericksburg	2-0	Penn Military	3-1
Gallaudet	9-6-1	Randolph-Macon	0-2-1
George Washington	10-3	Richmond A.A.B.	1-0
Georgetown	6-9	Rock Hill	3-1
Georgetown Prep	1-1	St. Johns (Md.)	18-11
Gibraltar A.C.	0-1	Swarthmore	0-1
Gonzaga H.S.	1-1	Tech. H.S.	5-2
Greenville A.A.B.	1-0	Third Army Corps	1-0
Guilford	1-0	Villanova	8-2
Gunton Temple Bapt. Ch.	1-0	Walbrook A.C.	0-1
Hampden-Sydney	2-2	Washington (Md.)	18-3-1
Haverford	0-2	Washington and Lee	13-5-2
Johns Hopkins	16-11-5	Western H.S.	0-0-1
Lakehurst N.A.S.	1-0	Western Maryland	18-13-1

Total Overall Record   466-397-39   .538
Total Conference Record   119-66-3   .641
Overall Bowl Game Record   5-9-1   .367

NORTH CAROLINA

Nickname: Tar Heels
Colors: Blue and white
Location: Chapel Hill, North
        Carolina
Stadium: Kenan (49,500)

First year of football: 1888
Year entered conference: 1953
Conference championships: 5

Atlantic Coast Conference Competition

Clemson	12-20-1	North Carolina State	50-18-6
Duke	37-30-4	Virginia	51-34-4
Georgia Tech	8-10-2	Wake Forest	53-26-2
Maryland	25-22-1		

Division I Competition

Air Force	1-4	Auburn	3-0
Appalachian State	1-0	Boston College	1-1
Arizona State	0-1	Bowling Green	1-0
Arkansas	1-0	Cincinnati	1-0
Army	4-1	Citadel	2-0

Davidson	31-4-4	Notre Dame	1-15
East Carolina	6-1-1	Ohio	1-0
Florida	7-2-1	Ohio State	1-3
Florida State	0-1	Oklahoma	0-4
Furman	3-0	Penn State	1-0
Georgia	12-16-2	Pennsylvania	2-4
Harvard	0-2	Pittsburgh	2-2
Illinois	1-0	Princeton	0-2
Kansas	1-0	Rice	0-1
Kentucky	4-4	Richmond	12-2
Lafayette	0-1	Rutgers	0-2
Lehigh	0-2	South Carolina	33-13-4
Louisiana State	1-3	Southern California	1-0
Memphis State	2-0	Tennessee	10-20-1
Miami (Fla.)	4-3	Texas	3-3
Miami (of Ohio)	3-1	Texas Christian	1-0
Michigan	2-1	Texas Tech	2-1
Michigan State	1-2	Tulane	3-9-2
Mississippi State	0-1	Vanderbilt	8-5
Missouri	0-2	Virginia Military	14-6-1
Navy	2-4	Virginia Tech	8-11-6
Nebraska	0-1	William and Mary	10-0-2
Northwestern	2-0	Yale	0-7

Other Opponents

Bingham	4-0	Mercer	1-0
Camp Lee	1-0	Morganton D.D.I.	1-0
Charlotte Y.	0-1	N.A.T.T.C.	1-0
Cherry Point Marines	2-0	New York	4-0
Duquesne	1-0	Norfolk A.C.	1-0
Fordham	0-3-2	Oak Ridge	6-0
Georgetown	4-7-2	Riverside	1-0
Greensboro A.A.	3-0	Sewanee	2-1-2
Guilford	9-0	Transylvania	0-1
Hampton A.C.	0-1	USS Franklin	1-0
Horner Academy	1-0	Virginia Medical	2-0
Lenoir-Rhyne	1-0	Washington and Lee	5-3-2

Total Overall Record	497-346-52	.584
Total Conference Record	112-86-4	.564
Overall Bowl Game Record	6-9-0	.400

NORTH CAROLINA STATE

Nickname: Wolfpack
Colors: Red and White
Location: Raleigh, North
         Carolina
Stadium: Carter-Finley
         (45,600)

First year of football: 1892
Year entered conference: 1953
Conference championships: 6

Atlantic Coast Conference Competition

Clemson	18-34-1	North Carolina	18-50-6
Duke	20-36-4	Virginia	25-8-1
Georgia Tech	1-3	Wake Forest	44-28-6
Maryland	17-20-4		

Division I Competition

Alabama	0-3	Miami (Fla.)	3-5-1
Appalachian State	3-0	Michigan State	1-4-1
Arizona State	1-1	Mississippi State	2-2
Army	0-1	Navy	2-6
Auburn	1-1	Nebraska	0-2
Boston College	1-1	Ohio	1-0
Boston University	1-0	Oklahoma	0-2
Bucknell	1-0	Penn State	2-17
Citadel	4-0	Pittsburgh	1-2
Davidson	30-9-6	Richmond	16-1-1
East Carolina	11-4	South Carolina	20-23-4
Florida	4-8-1	Southern Methodist	0-1
Florida State	4-8	Southern Mississippi	3-4
Furman	4-7-4	Syracuse	4-0
Georgia	1-6-1	Tennessee	1-0
Holy Cross	0-1	Texas Tech	0-1
Houston	1-1-1	Tulane	0-1
Indiana	2-0	UCLA	0-2
Iowa	1-0	Vanderbilt	0-1
Iowa State	1-0	Virginia Military	7-11-1
Kansas	1-0	Virginia Tech	16-20-3
Kent State	0-1	West Virginia	4-5
Kentucky	1-2	William and Mary	10-8
Louisville	0-1	Wyoming	0-2

Other Opponents

Bingham	1-0	Manhattan	1-3
Buffalo	1-0	Maryland A.C.	1-0
Camp Davis	0-1	Maryville	1-0
Carnegie Tech	0-1	Milligan	2-0
Catawba	4-0	Newberry	1-0
Catholic	0-3	Newport News	1-0
Dayton	1-0	North Carolina All-Stars	0-0-1
Detroit	0-2	North Carolina Pre-Flight	0-2
Duquesne	1-1	Presbyterian	0-1
Eastern	1-0	Raleigh Academy	2-0
Elon	4-0	Randolph-Macon	4-0
Gallaudet	1-0	Roanoke	6-0-1
George Washington	0-2	St. Albans	1-0
Georgetown	2-6-2	USS Franklin	4-0
Greenville A.B.	1-0	Villanova	1-3-1
Guilford	7-0	Virginia Medical	2-0
Hampton Road	1-0	Washington and Lee	5-11-1
High Point	1-0	Wofford	1-0
Lenoir-Rhyne	1-0		

Total Overall Record   369-401-52   .481
Total Conference Record   98-87-7   .529
Overall Bowl Game Record   5-3-1   .611

VIRGINIA

Nickname: Cavaliers
Colors: Orange and blue
Location: Charlottesville,
             Virginia
Stadium: Scott (45,000)

First year of football: 1888
Year entered conference: 1954
Conference championships: 0

Atlantic Coast Conference Competition

Clemson	0-24	North Carolina	35-50-4
Duke	13-23	North Carolina State	8-25-1
Georgia Tech	0-6-1	Wake Forest	15-11
Maryland	15-32-2		

Division I Competition

Army	3-5	Ohio State	0-1
Boston College	0-1	Penn State	0-3
Bucknell	1-1	Pennsylvania	1-15
Citadel	2-0	Pittsburgh	0-2
Colgate	1-0	Princeton	1-9-1
Columbia	0-4	Purdue	1-1
Dartmouth	0-1	Richmond	21-2-2
Davidson	8-0-2	Rutgers	3-2
East Carolina	0-1	South Carolina	11-18-1
Florida	0-1	Syracuse	0-2
Furman	0-1	Tennessee	1-2
Georgia	6-6-3	Texas	0-1
Harvard	1-8	Tulane	2-4
James Madison	2-1	Vanderbilt	7-12-2
Kentucky	2-1	Virginia Military	52-23-3
Lafayette	2-1-1	Virginia Tech	28-33-5
Lehigh	6-3	Washington	0-1
Miami (of Ohio)	1-0-1	West Virginia	10-10-1
Michigan	0-2	William and Mary	20-4-1
Missouri	0-1	Yale	2-3-1
Navy	6-25		

Other Opponents

Apprentice School	0-1	Chicago	1-0
Baltimore C.C.	1-0	Coast Guard	1-0
Buffalo	1-0	Dickinson	1-0
Carlisle	1-5-1	Episcopal	2-0
Centre	0-1	Fort Monroe	1-0

Franklin and Marshall	1-0	Oceana N.A.S.	1-0
Gallaudet	7-1	Pantops	2-0
George Washington	12-2-1	Princeton J.V.	1-0
Georgetown	7-7-2	Randolph-Macon	21-0-1
Hampton A.C.	0-0-2	Richmond A.B.	0-0-1
Hampden-Sydney	17-1-2	Roanoke	6-1
Johns Hopkins	8-1	St. Albans	8-0
Lynchburg	1-0	St. Johns (Md.)	17-0
Maryland A.C.	1-0	Schuylkill Navy	0-0-1
Maryland Med. Col.	1-0-1	Sewanee	3-2-1
Miller	2-0	Swarthmore	2-1
Nashville	1-0	Washington and Lee	21-13-1
Norfolk Blues	1-0	Washington Y.	1-0
North Carolina Pre-Flight	0-0-1	West Philadelphia A.C.	1-0

Total Overall Record	439-417-47	.512
Total Conference Record	40-132-3	.237
Overall Bowl Game Record	1-0-0	1.000

WAKE FOREST

Nickname: Demon Deacons
Colors: Gold and black
Location: Winston-Salem,
      North Carolina
Stadium: Groves (31,500)

First year of football: 1888
Year entered conference: 1953
Conference championships: 1

Atlantic Coast Conference Competition

Clemson	11-38-1	North Carolina	26-53-2
Duke	18-45-2	North Carolina State	28-44-6
Georgia Tech	0-7	Virginia	11-15
Maryland	8-24-1		

Division I Competition

Appalachian State	5-2	Kansas State	1-1
Army	0-3	Louisiana State	0-3
Auburn	2-6	Marshall	2-1
Baylor	0-4	Memphis State	2-2
Boston College	3-5-2	Miami (Fla.)	3-3
Citadel	2-1	Michigan	0-1
Davidson	11-15-4	Minnesota	0-1
Delaware	1-0	Navy	0-1
East Carolina	1-1	Nebraska	0-1
Florida	0-4	Oklahoma	0-1
Florida State	2-7-1	Penn State	0-1
Furman	7-11	Purdue	0-3
Georgia	2-1	Richmond	8-7-1
Houston	0-2	South Carolina	20-32-2

Southern Methodist	0-3	Tulsa	2-0
Temple	0-1	Vanderbilt	1-3
Tennessee	3-5	Virginia Military	3-2-2
Tennessee-Chattanooga	1-0	Virginia Tech	11-20-1
Texas	0-1	West Virginia	0-2
Texas Christian	0-1	Western Carolina	2-0
Texas Tech	0-2	William and Mary	9-9-1
Tulane	0-1		

Other Opponents

Asheville A.C.	1-0	Lynchburg	2-1
Atlantic Christian	1-0	Maryville	1-0
Baltimore C.C.	1-0	Mercer	2-2
Camp Davis	1-1	Norfolk Blues	0-1
Carson-Newman	1-0	North Carolina Med. Col.	1-1
Catawba	1-0	North Carolina Pre-Flight	1-0
Catholic	0-2	Oglethorpe	0-1
Duquesne	3-0	Presbyterian	5-4-1
Elon	8-0-1	Quantico Marines	0-1
Emory and Henry	0-1	Randolph-Macon	1-0
Erskine	3-0	Richmond Blues	1-0
Florence Y.	1-0	Roanoke	2-0
Gallaudet	1-1	Sewanee Club (Va.)	1-0
George Washington	9-3	USS Franklin	2-1
Georgetown	2-1	Villanova	1-2
Greensboro A.A.B.	0-1	Virginia Med Col.	0-1
Guilford	11-0-1	Warrenton Prep.	2-0
Hampden-Sydney	1-1-1	Washington and Lee	2-7
High Point	1-0	Western Maryland	1-1
Horner Academy	2-0	William Jewell	1-0
Lenoir-Rhyne	1-0	Wofford	5-0-1

Total Overall Record	286-430-31	.404
Total Conference Record	59-138-5	.304
Overall Bowl Game Record	1-2-0	.333

Big Eight Conference

Formed: 1907*
Charter Members: Iowa, Kansas, Missouri, Nebraska, Washington (Mo.).
Former Members: Drake, Grinnell.

Overall Records

	Years	W	L	T	Pct.
Oklahoma	90	576	220	50	.710
Nebraska	95	592	271	39	.678
Colorado	95	483	318	32	.599
Missouri	94	482	354	48	.572
Kansas	95	435	394	56	.523
Oklahoma State	83	358	371	44	.492
Iowa State	93	383	400	43	.490
Kansas State	89	315	500	47	.393

*The Big Eight Conference has changed its name several times during its existence.

Conference Records

	Years	W	L	T	Pct.
Oklahoma	65	285	86	19	.755
Nebraska	78	285	109	14	.716
Missouri	78	254	167	30	.596
Colorado	37	113	125	7	.476
Kansas	78	179	235	28	.448
Oklahoma State	28	77	100	9	.438
Iowa State	77	146	259	21	.367
Kansas State	72	102	291	18	.270
Drake	19	30	43	4	.416
Iowa	4	5	8	1	.393
Grinnell	9	9	23	3	.300
Washington (Missouri)	20	10	53	6	.188
Combined bowl game record		50	46	1	.521

Total Championships

1.	Nebraska	34	4.	Kansas	4
2.	Oklahoma	30	5.	Colorado	2
3.	Missouri	12		Iowa State	2

	Oklahoma State	2	Iowa	1
8.	Kansas State	1		

Past Champions

1984	Oklahoma	1946	Oklahoma
	Nebraska		Kansas
1983	Nebraska	1945	Missouri
1982	Nebraska	1944	Oklahoma
1981	Nebraska	1943	Oklahoma
1980	Oklahoma	1942	Missouri
1979	Oklahoma	1941	Missouri
1978	Nebraska	1940	Nebraska
	Oklahoma	1939	Missouri
1977	Oklahoma	1938	Oklahoma
1976	Colorado	1937	Nebraska
	Oklahoma State	1936	Nebraska
	Oklahoma	1935	Nebraska
1975	Oklahoma	1934	Kansas State
1974	Oklahoma	1933	Nebraska
1973	Oklahoma	1932	Nebraska
1972	Oklahoma	1931	Nebraska
1971	Nebraska	1930	Kansas
1970	Nebraska	1929	Nebraska
1969	Missouri	1928	Nebraska***
	Nebraska	1927	Missouri
1968	Kansas	1926	Oklahoma State
	Oklahoma	1925	Missouri
1967	Oklahoma	1924	Missouri
1966	Nebraska	1923	Nebraska
1965	Nebraska	1922	Nebraska
1964	Nebraska	1921	Nebraska
1963	Nebraska	1920	Oklahoma
1962	Oklahoma	1919	Missouri
1961	Colorado	1918	(No Standings)
1960	Missouri*	1917	Nebraska
1959	Oklahoma	1916	Nebraska
1958	Oklahoma	1915	Nebraska
1957	Oklahoma	1914	Nebraska
1956	Oklahoma	1913	Nebraska
1955	Oklahoma		Missouri
1954	Oklahoma	1912	Nebraska
1953	Oklahoma		Iowa State
1952	Oklahoma	1911	Nebraska
1951	Oklahoma		Iowa State
1950	Oklahoma	1910	Nebraska
1949	Oklahoma	1909	Missouri
1948	Oklahoma**	1908	Kansas
1947	Oklahoma	1907	Nebraska****
	Kansas		Iowa

*Big Eight Conference
**Big Seven Conference
***Big Six Conference
****Old Missouri Valley Conference

COLORADO

Nickname: Buffaloes
Colors: Silver, gold and blue
Location: Boulder, Colorado
Stadium: Folsom Field (51,941)

First year of football: 1890
Year entered conference: 1948
Conference championships: 2

Big Eight Conference Competition

Iowa State	27-11-1	Nebraska	11-31-1
Kansas	23-18-3	Oklahoma	8-30-1
Kansas State	28-12	Oklahoma State	14-12-1
Missouri	13-33-3		

Division I Competition

Air Force	12-4	New Mexico	6-3
Alabama	1-0	Northwestern	1-1
Arizona	11-0	Notre Dame	0-2
Army	1-1	Ohio State	1-1
Auburn	0-1	Oregon	5-4
Baylor	3-2	Oregon State	1-3
Brigham Young	8-2-1	Penn State	1-1
California	2-2	Rice	0-1
Cincinnati	1-0	San Jose State	2-0
Clemson	1-0	Southern California	0-3
Colorado State	44-14-2	Stanford	1-1
Drake	2-2	Texas	0-4
Fresno State	1-0	Texas Tech	1-2
Hawaii	0-1	Tulane	0-1
Houston	1-0	Tulsa	1-0
Indiana	3-1	UCLA	0-4
Kent State	1-0	Utah	30-24-3
Louisiana State	1-5	Utah State	10-6-1
Miami (Fla.)	5-1	Washington	2-2-1
Michigan	0-1	Washington State	1-1
Michigan State	0-3	Wichita State	1-0
Minnesota	1-0	Wisconsin	2-0-1
Montana State	1-2	Wyoming	21-2-1

Other Opponents

Alumni	11-0-2	Denver East H.S.	5-0
Chadron State	2-1	Denver Manual H.S.	5-0
Chicago	0-1	Denver North H.S.	2-0
Colorado College	32-14-3	Denver West H.S.	4-0
Colorado Mines	36-14-1	Denver Wheel Club	5-1
Creighton	1-0	Ft. Warren (Wyo.)	1-2
Denver	26-14-4	George Washington	0-1
Denver A.C.	3-13	Haskell	1-0

Hawaiian Navy	1-0	Peru State	1-0
Lieutenants	1-0	Regis	4-0
Littleton A.C.	1-0	Salt Lake City A.F.B.	1-0
Longmont H.S.	1-0	Second A.F.B.	0-1
Lowry A.F.B.	1-0	State Prep School	11-0-1
Missouri Mines	1-0	Washburn (Kan.)	1-0-1
Northern Colorado	9-2	Western State	4-0

Total Overall Record	483-318-32	.599
Overall Conference Record	113-125-7	.476
Overall Bowl Game Record	4-6-0	.400

IOWA STATE

Nickname: Cyclones
Colors: Cardinal and gold
Location: Ames, Iowa
Stadium: Cyclone (50,000)

First year of football: 1892
Year entered conference: 1908
Conference championships: 2

Big Eight Conference Competition

Colorado	11-27-1	Nebraska	14-63-2
Kansas	24-35-5	Oklahoma	4-51-2
Kansas State	40-24-4	Oklahoma State	10-15-1
Missouri	23-46-9		

Division I Competition

Air Force	2-0	North Carolina State	0-1
Arizona	1-4-1	Northeast Louisiana	1-0
Arkansas	0-1	Northwestern	1-6
Army	0-1	Ohio	1-0
Boston College	0-1	Oregon State	0-1
Bowling Green	2-0	Pacific	2-1
Brigham Young	4-0	Purdue	0-1
California	0-1	Rice	1-1
Colorado State	4-1	San Diego State	3-3
Drake	48-16-4	San Jose State	3-0
Florida State	1-0	South Carolina	0-1
Georgia Tech	0-1	South Dakota	8-0
Idaho	2-0	Syracuse	0-1-1
Illinois	2-3-1	Tennessee	0-1
Iowa	12-20	Texas	0-1
Kent State	4-0	Texas A&M	0-2
Louisiana State	0-1	Texas Tech	0-2
Michigan State	0-2	Tulsa	1-0
Minnesota	2-8-1	UCLA	1-1
Montana	1-0	Utah	4-0
New Mexico	5-1	Vanderbilt	0-1
New Mexico State	0-1	Virginia Military	1-0

Washington	1-0	Wichita State	1-0
West Texas State	2-0	Wisconsin	0-5

Other Opponents

Alumni	0-0-1	Iowa Pre-Flight	0-1
Buffalo	1-0	Iowa Teachers	10-1-3
Camp Dodge	0-1	Loyola (La.)	0-1
Central Iowa	1-0	Luther	3-0
Central Oklahoma	0-1	Marquette	2-8-1
Coe	16-2	Morningside	8-1
Cornell College	14-3-1	Nebraska Wesleyan	1-0
Creighton	1-0	Omaha Guards	1-0
Dayton	1-0	Ottumwa N.A.S.	0-1
Denver	7-3	Panora	1-0
Des Moines	4-0	Rush Medical	1-0
Des Moines Y.	4-0	Simpson	15-1-1
Detroit	1-1	South Dakota State	2-0
Doane	1-0	State Center	0-0-1
Dubuque	1-0	Still	2-0
Eldora	1-0	Upper Iowa	1-0
Ellsworth College	1-0	Villanova	0-2
G. Adolphus	1-0	Washington (Mo.)	6-1
Grinnell	20-10-3	Wayne State	1-0
Highland Park	2-0	William Penn	2-0
Iowa Falls	1-0		

Total Overall Record	383-400-43	.490
Total Conference Record	146-259-21	.367
Overall Bowl Game Record	0-4	.000

KANSAS

Nickname: Jayhawks	First year of football: 1890
Colors: Crimson and blue	Year entered conference: 1907
Location: Lawrence, Kansas	Conference championships: 4
Stadium: Memorial (55,000)	

Big Eight Conference Competition

Colorado	18-23-3	Nebraska	21-67-3
Iowa State	35-24-5	Oklahoma	23-53-6
Kansas State	55-23-4	Oklahoma State	22-18-3
Missouri	41-43-9		

Division I Competition

Arizona	3-2-1	Army	0-1
Arkansas	2-0	Baylor	1-0
Arkansas State	1-0	Boston	2-0

California	2-1	Pennsylvania	0-1
Colorado State	3-0	Pittsburgh	0-3
Drake	10-7-1	Rice	1-0
Florida State	1-3	San Diego State	1-0
Georgia Tech	0-1	South Dakota	1-0
Illinois	2-3	Southern California	1-0
Indiana	1-1	Southern Methodist	1-3
Iowa	6-4	Stanford	0-1
Kentucky	3-0-1	Syracuse	4-4
Louisville	0-1	Temple	0-1
Miami (Fla.)	0-3	Tennessee	0-2
Michigan	0-3	Texas	2-0
Michigan State	0-4	Texas A&M	1-2
Minnesota	3-3	Texas Christian	5-15-4
Mississippi State	0-1	Texas Tech	0-4
New Mexico	2-1	Tulane	1-0
North Carolina	0-1	Tulsa	1-5
North Carolina State	0-1	UCLA	1-4
North Texas State	1-0	Utah	2-0
Northern Illinois	0-1	Vanderbilt	0-1
Notre Dame	1-3-1	Washington	0-1
Ohio	0-1	Washington State	7-2
Oregon	1-0-1	West Virginia	0-1
Oregon State	2-2	Wichita State	4-2
Pacific	0-0-1	Wisconsin	2-4
Penn State	0-1	Wyoming	2-1-1

Other Opponents

Abilene	1-0	Kansas City Y.M.C.A.	1-1
Baker	6-3-1	Kirksville	1-0
Beloit	0-0-1	Knox	0-1
Creighton	3-0	Loyola (La.)	1-0
Denver	6-2-1	Marquette	0-4
Denver A.C.	2-1	Midland	3-0
Doane	3-0	Olathe Navy	1-0
Drury	1-0	Ottawa	4-1-1
Emporia College	5-0	Pittsburg State	1-0
Emporia State	16-1-1	St. Benedict's	2-0
Ensworth Med.	1-0	St. Louis	1-2
Fort Riley	0-1	St. Mary's (Kan.)	8-0
George Washington	3-3	Santa Clara	1-0
Glasco	1-0	Villanova	0-1
Grinnell	2-2	Warrensburg	5-0
Haskell	6-5	Washburn	28-5-4
Iowa Pre-Flight	0-1	Washington (Mo.)	12-0-3
James Milliken	1-0	William Jewell	6-0
Kansas City Medical	4-3		

Total Overall Record	435-394-56	.523
Total Conference Record	179-235-28	.448
Overall Bowl Game Record	1-5-0	.167

KANSAS STATE

Nickname: Wildcats
Colors: Purple and white
Location: Manhattan, Kansas
Stadium: KSU (42,000)

First year of football: 1896
Year entered conference: 1913
Conference championships: 1

Big Eight Conference Competition

Colorado	12-28	Nebraska	10-57-2
Iowa State	24-40-4	Oklahoma	11-55-4
Kansas	23-55-4	Oklahoma State	12-27
Missouri	16-49-5		

Division I Competition

Air Force	3-0	Northwestern	0-2
Arizona	1-5-1	Oregon State	1-0
Arizona State	0-4	Pacific	1-0-1
Arkansas	3-1	Penn State	0-2
Arkansas State	2-0	Purdue	0-2
Army	0-1	San Jose State	0-1
Auburn	0-2	South Carolina	1-2
Baylor	1-0	South Dakota	3-0
Boston College	0-3	Tennessee Tech	1-0
Brigham Young	4-3	Texas	1-3
Cal State-Long Beach	0-1	Texas A&M	2-2
Cincinnati	0-4	Texas Christian	2-1
Colorado State	4-1	Texas-El Paso	0-1
Drake	2-3	Texas Tech	0-2
Florida	0-2	Tulsa	6-9-1
Florida State	0-3	Utah State	1-2
Illinois	0-1	Vanderbilt	0-1
Indiana	2-3	Virginia Tech	1-1
Iowa	0-3	Wake Forest	1-0
Kentucky	1-3	Washington	0-3
Memphis State	2-1	West Virginia	1-1
Michigan State	0-5-1	Wichita State	17-3-2
Minnesota	0-1	Wisconsin	0-2
Mississippi State	0-2	Wyoming	3-4
New Mexico	0-4		

Other Opponents

Baker	6-1	Clyde H.S.	1-0
Bethany (Okla.)	2-4	Colorado College	0-1
Bradley	1-0	Creighton	8-1
Camp Funston	2-0	Drury	1-0
Centre	1-0	Duquesne	1-1
Chapman H.S.	2-0-3	Emporia College	6-2

Emporia State	13-8-3	North Dakota State	1-0
Fort Hays State	8-1-1	Olathe N.A.S.	0-1-1
Fort Riley	3-3-1	Ottawa	3-3
Grinnell	2-0	Pittsburg State	1-0
Haskell	6-3	St. Mary's (Kan.)	1-3
Junction City	1-0	San Francisco	0-1
Kansas City Medical	0-1	South Dakota State	2-0
Kansas City Vets	1-0	Southwestern (Kan.)	6-1-1
Kansas Wesleyan	7-0	Tampa	2-0
Manhattan (N.Y.)	1-0	Washburn	18-10-2
Manhattan H.S.	1-1	Washington (Mo.)	4-2
Marquette	6-7	Washington H.S.	0-0-1
Missouri Mines	1-0	William Jewell	1-1

Total Overall Record	315-500-47	.393
Total Conference Record	102-291-18	.270
Overall Bowl Game Record	0-1-0	.000

MISSOURI

Nickname: Tigers	First year of football: 1890
Colors: Gold and black	Year entered conference: 1907
Location: Columbia, Missouri	Conference championships: 12
Stadium: Faurot Field	
(62,000)	

Big Eight Conference Competition

Colorado	33-13-3	Nebraska	32-43-3
Iowa State	46-22-9	Oklahoma	22-48-5
Kansas	43-41-9	Oklahoma State	20-11
Kansas State	49-16-5		

Division I Competition

Air Force	4-2	Florida	1-0
Alabama	2-1	Georgia	0-1
Arizona	3-0	Georgia Tech	1-1
Arizona State	2-1	Idaho	2-0
Arkansas	2-1	Illinois	9-5
Army	3-1	Indiana	2-0
Auburn	1-0	Iowa	7-5
Baylor	2-1	Kentucky	1-2
Brigham Young	0-1	Louisiana State	1-0
California	2-3-1	Louisville	1-0
Clemson	0-2	Maryland	0-6
Colorado State	1-0	Miami (Fla.)	0-1
Drake	14-4	Michigan	2-2
Duke	1-0	Michigan State	3-3
East Carolina	1-1	Minnesota	4-3-1

Mississippi	3-1	Southern California	1-2
Mississippi State	2-0	Southern Methodist	7-13-1
Navy	2-0	Southern Mississippi	1-0
New Mexico	1-0	Stanford	0-1
North Carolina	2-0	Temple	0-1
Northwestern	3-3	Texas	4-8
Notre Dame	2-2	Texas A&M	0-2
Ohio State	1-8-1	Tulane	0-0-2
Oregon	1-0	UCLA	0-2-1
Oregon State	0-1	Utah	1-1
Penn State	1-3	Utah State	1-0
Pittsburgh	0-1	Vanderbilt	2-1-1
Purdue	2-6	Virginia	1-0
Rice	1-0	Washington State	1-0
San Diego State	2-0	West Virginia	2-0
South Carolina	1-0	Wisconsin	1-4

Other Opponents

Amity	2-0	Kirksville	1-1
Austin Mutes	1-0	Kirksville Teachers	3-1
Baker	0-1	Missouri Mines	10-1-1
Cape Girardeau	1-0	Missouri Valley	2-0
Christian Brothers	2-0	Missouri Wesleyan	2-0
Central Missouri	5-0	Monmouth	2-0
Centre	1-0	New York	3-3
Chicago	1-1	North Dakota State	1-0
Dallas A.C.	1-0	Ottawa	0-1-1
Denver A.C.	0-2	Pastime A.C.	1-0
DePauw	1-0	St. Louis	10-10-1
Drury	4-0	San Antonio A.C.	1-0
Engineers	1-0	Sedalia A.C.	2-0
Fordham	0-3	Simpson	3-2
Fort Riley	1-0	Springfield Teachers	1-0
Great Lakes	0-1	Tarkio	4-1
Grinnell	1-1	Warrensburg	8-1
Haskell	2-5	Washburn	2-2
Iowa Pre-Flight	1-2	Washington (Mo.)	25-11-2
Iowa Wesleyan	1-0	Wentworth Military	2-0-1
Kansas City Med.	1-3	Westminster (Mo.)	2-0
Kansas City Y.M.C.A.	1-0	William Jewell	5-0

Total Overall Record   482-354-48   .572
Total Conference Record   254-167-30   .596
Overall Bowl Game Record   8-11-0   .421

NEBRASKA

Nickname: Cornhuskers
Colors: Scarlet and cream
Location: Lincoln, Nebraska
Stadium: Memorial (73,650)

First year of football: 1890
Year entered conference: 1907
Conference championships: 34

Big Eight Conference Competition

Colorado	31-11-1	Missouri	43-32-3
Iowa State	64-13-2	Oklahoma	27-35-3
Kansas	67-21-3	Oklahoma State	22-2-1
Kansas State	57-10-2		

Division I Competition

Air Force	1-1	North Carolina	1-0
Alabama	2-3	North Carolina State	2-0
Arizona	0-0-1	North Dakota	1-0
Arizona State	0-1	Northwestern	2-1
Arkansas	0-1	Notre Dame	6-7-1
Army	3-2	Ohio State	0-2
Auburn	3-0	Oregon	3-1
Baylor	2-1	Oregon State	7-2
California	1-0	Penn State	5-6
Cincinnati	1-0	Pittsburgh	4-15-3
Clemson	0-1	Purdue	0-1
Colgate	1-0	Rutgers	1-0
Colorado State	3-0	South Carolina	1-0
Drake	6-2	South Dakota	14-1-2
Duke	0-1	Southern California	0-1-1
Florida	1-0	Southern Methodist	1-0-1
Florida State	1-1	Stanford	0-1
Georgia	1-0	Syracuse	5-7
Hawaii	5-1	Texas	3-1
Houston	0-1	Texas /A&M	4-1
Illinois	5-2-1	Texas Christian	5-1
Indiana	7-9-3	Texas Tech	1-0
Iowa	24-12-3	UCLA	3-3
Louisiana State	4-0-1	Utah	2-0
Miami (Fla.)	4-2	Utah State	3-0
Michigan	1-2-1	Wake Forest	1-0
Michigan State	2-0	Washington	1-1-1
Minnesota	18-29-2	Washington State	0-3
Mississippi State	1-0	Wisconsin	3-2
Montana State	2-0	Wyoming	4-0
New Mexico State	2-0		

Other Opponents

Adrian	1-0	Kirksville	1-0
Baker	0-0-1	Knox	5-0
Bellevue	3-0	Lincoln H.S.	8-0
Butte	0-2	Lincoln Medics	1-0
Camp Dodge	0-1	Morningside	1-0
Carlisle	0-1	Nebraska Wesleyan	8-0
Chicago	1-1	New York	2-0
Creighton	3-0	Omaha Balloon	1-0
Denver	4-0	Omaha U. Club	1-0
Denver A.C.	3-1	Omaha Y.	3-0
Doane	16-2	Peru State	3-0
Grand Island	3-0	St. Louis	0-1
Grinnell	7-2	Sioux City A.C.	1-0
Haskell	7-2	South Dakota State	1-0
Hastings	2-0	Tarkio	3-0
Iowa Pre-Flight	0-1	Wabash	1-0
Kansas City Med.	1-2-2	Washington (Mo.)	1-1
Kearney State	1-0	William Jewell	0-1

Total Overall Record	592-271-39	.678
Total Conference Record	285-109-14	.716
Overall Bowl Game Record	13-10-0	.565

OKLAHOMA

Nickname: Sooners
Colors: Crimson and cream
Location: Norman, Oklahoma
Stadium: Owen Field (75,000)

First year of football: 1895
Year entered conference: 1920
Conference championships: 30

Big Eight Conference Competition

Colorado	30-8-1	Missouri	47-23-5
Iowa State	51-4-2	Nebraska	35-27-3
Kansas	53-23-6	Oklahoma State	61-12-6
Kansas State	55-11-4		

Division I Competition

Alabama	0-1-1	Drake	3-2
Arizona State	0-1	Duke	1-0
Arkansas	8-4-1	Florida State	3-1
Army	2-1	Hawaii	2-0
Auburn	1-0	Houston	1-0
Baylor	4-0	Illinois	0-1
Boston College	2-0	Indiana	0-1
California	2-0	Iowa	1-0
Clemson	2-0	Kentucky	2-1

Louisiana State	1-0	Syracuse	2-0
Maryland	4-0	Temple	1-1
Miami (Fla.)	2-0	Tennessee	1-1
Michigan	1-0	Texas	28-47-4
Navy	0-1	Texas A&M	7-5
New Mexico	2-0	Texas Christian	4-2
North Carolina	4-0	Tulsa	8-6-1
North Carolina State	2-0	Utah	1-0
Northwestern	1-2	Utah State	2-0
Notre Dame	1-7	Vanderbilt	2-0-1
Ohio State	1-1	Wake Forest	1-0
Oregon	4-0	Washington	0-1
Oregon State	1-1	Washington State	2-0
Penn State	1-0	West Virginia	2-1
Pittsburgh	8-1-1	Wichita State	3-0
Rice	6-0	William and Mary	1-1
Southern California	2-3-1	Wisconsin	2-0
Southern Methodist	3-1-1	Wyoming	2-0
Stanford	3-1		

Other Opponents

Arkansas City	2-1	Marquette	1-0
Bethany (Okla.)	1-2	Missouri Mines	1-0
Camp Doniphan	0-1	Norman H.S.	2-0
Centenary	1-0	Norman N.A.S.	1-1
Central Oklahoma	17-1-1	Northwest Oklahoma	5-0
Chicago	1-0	Oklahoma Christian	1-0
Chilocco Indians	3-0	Oklahoma City	3-1-1
Creighton	2-0-1	Oklahoma City Military	1-0
Dallas A.C.	0-1	Oklahoma City Team	2-1
Detroit	1-0	Paul's Valley	1-0
Emporia College	1-0-1	Pawhuska	0-0-1
Fort Reno	1-0	Phillips	2-0
Ft. Worth	1-0	Post Field	1-0
George Washington	0-1-1	St. Louis	2-0
Guthrie	1-0	Santa Clara	2-2
Haskell	2-0	Shawnee Normal	1-0
Hondo A.A.F.	1-0	Southwest Oklahoma	2-0
Honolulu	0-1	Sulphur	1-0
Kansas City Medics	1-0	Washburn	2-2-2
Kingfisher	19-0-3	Washington (Mo.)	7-0-1
Lawton	2-0		

Total Overall Record	576-220-50	.710
Total Conference Record	285-86-19	.755
Overall Bowl Game Record	16-8-1	.660

OKLAHOMA STATE

Nickname: Cowboys
Colors: Orange and black
Location: Stillwater, Oklahoma
Stadium: Lewis Field (50,440)

First year of football: 1901
Year entered conference: 1960.
(OS was member of Old Mis-
souri Valley Conf. 1925-1927.)
Conference championships: 2

Big Eight Conference Competition

Colorado	12-14-2	Missouri	11-20
Iowa State	15-10-1	Nebraska	2-22-1
Kansas	18-22-3	Oklahoma	12-61-6
Kansas State	27-12		

Division I Competition

Air Force	0-1-1	San Diego State	2-2
Arizona	3-3	South Carolina	1-1
Arizona State	1-0	Southern Illinois	1-0
Arkansas	15-30-1	Southern Methodist	1-6-2
Army	1-0	Temple	2-0
Baylor	3-10	Texas	1-9
Bowling Green	1-0	Texas A&M	3-7
Brigham Young	2-0	Texas-Arlington	2-0
Cincinnati	2-1	Texas Christian	10-6-2
Colorado State	1-0	Texas-El Paso	3-0
Drake	7-2-1	Texas Tech	7-11-3
Florida State	1-2	Tulsa	27-22-5
Georgia	0-2	Utah	1-0
Houston	7-7-1	Virginia Tech	1-1
Iowa	1-1	Washington	0-1
Louisiana State	0-1	Washington State	0-2
Louisville	1-1	West Texas State	1-1
Michigan	0-1	West Virginia	0-2
Minnesota	0-2	Wichita State	20-5-1
Mississippi State	1-1	William and Mary	0-1
North Texas State	8-1	Wyoming	3-0
Rice	2-0-1		

Other Opponents

Baker	2-0	Creighton	11-6-1
Bethany (Okla.)	1-0	Denver	8-1
Blackwell	2-0	Detroit	6-7
Camp McArthur	0-1	Duquesne	0-2
Centenary	0-2	Emporia State	1-1-1
Central Missouri State	2-0	Grinnell	2-1
Central Oklahoma	14-5-2	Hardin-Simmons	2-1
Chilocco Indians	1-3-1	Haskell	5-4

Jefferson	0-1	Phillips	6-2-1
Kingfisher	3-3-1	Regis	1-0
Logan County H.S.	0-1	St. Louis	3-0-1
Marquette	2-1	St. Mary's (Tex.)	1-0
Missouri Mines	1-2	San Francisco	1-0
Northeast Oklahoma	1-0	Southeast Oklahoma	2-0
Northwest Oklahoma	8-0	Southwest Oklahoma	8-1
Oklahoma Baptist	1-0	Southwestern (Kan.)	1-2-1
Oklahoma City	8-9-2	Tonkawa Preps	2-1-1
Oklahoma N.A.S.	0-1	Tulsa B.C.	0-1
Oklahoma Tech	0-1	Washburn	6-1
Pawnee Indians	1-0	Washington (Mo.)	5-6-1

Total Overall Record	358-371-44	.492
Total Conference Record	77-100-9	.438
Overall Bowl Game Record	7-2-0	.778

Big Ten Conference

Formed: 1896
Charter Members: Chicago, Illinois, Michigan, Minnesota, Northwestern, Purdue, Wisconsin.

Overall Records

	Years	W	L	T	Pct.
Michigan	105	648	222	31	.736
Ohio State	95	589	233	48	.705
Minnesota	101	508	301	40	.625
Michigan State	88	463	284	40	.614
Wisconsin	96	443	336	49	.565
Purdue	97	442	338	44	.563
Illinois	95	437	362	43	.545
Iowa	96	394	397	33	.498
Northwestern	96	350	447	40	.442
Indiana	97	327	443	41	.428

Conference Records

	Years	W	L	T	Pct.
Ohio State	72	309	114	20	.720
Michigan	89	317	130	14	.703
Michigan State	32	124	100	6	.552
Minnesota	89	253	221	26	.532
Purdue	89	227	233	28	.494
Illinois	89	246	260	26	.487
Wisconsin	89	229	252	38	.478
Iowa	85	173	262	21	.402
Northwestern	87	174	326	20	.354
Indiana	85	130	306	23	.308
Chicago	44	120	99	14	.545
Combined bowl game record		32	36	0	.471

Total Championships

1. Michigan	26		Chicago	6
2. Ohio State	24	8.	Purdue	5
3. Minnesota	14	9.	Michigan State	4
4. Illinois	12		Northwestern	4
5. Wisconsin	7	11.	Indiana	2
6. Iowa	6			

Past Champions

1984	Ohio State	1947	Michigan
1983	Illinois	1946	Illinois
1982	Michigan	1945	Indiana
1981	Iowa	1944	Ohio State
	Ohio State	1943	Michigan
1980	Michigan		Purdue
1979	Ohio State	1942	Ohio State
1978	Michigan	1941	Minnesota
	Michigan State	1940	Minnesota
1977	Michigan	1939	Ohio State
	Ohio State	1938	Minnesota
1976	Michigan	1937	Minnesota
	Ohio State	1936	Northwestern
1975	Ohio State	1935	Minnesota
1974	Ohio State		Ohio State
	Michigan	1934	Minnesota
1973	Ohio State	1933	Michigan
	Michigan	1932	Michigan
1972	Ohio State	1931	Northwestern
	Michigan		Michigan
1971	Michigan		Purdue
1970	Ohio State	1930	Northwestern
1969	Michigan		Michigan
	Ohio State	1929	Purdue
1968	Ohio State	1928	Illinois
1967	Indiana	1927	Illinois
	Purdue	1926	Michigan
	Minnesota		Northwestern
1966	Michigan State	1925	Michigan
1965	Michigan State	1924	Chicago
1964	Michigan	1923	Illinois
1963	Illinois	1922	Iowa
1962	Wisconsin	1921	Iowa
1961	Ohio State	1920	Ohio State
1960	Minnesota	1919	Illinois
	Iowa	1918	Illinois
1959	Wisconsin	1917	Ohio State
1958	Iowa	1916	Ohio State
1957	Ohio State	1915	Minnesota
1956	Iowa	1914	Illinois
1955	Ohio State	1913	Chicago
1954	Ohio State	1912	Wisconsin
1953	Illinois	1911	Minnesota
	Michigan State	1910	Illinois
1952	Wisconsin	1909	Minnesota
	Purdue	1908	Chicago
1951	Illinois	1907	Chicago
1950	Michigan	1906	Wisconsin
1949	Michigan	1905	Chicago
	Ohio State	1904	Minnesota
1948	Michigan	1903	Michigan

	Minnesota		1899	Chicago
1902	Michigan		1898	Michigan
1901	Michigan		1897	Wisconsin
1900	Minnesota		1896	Wisconsin

ILLINOIS

Nickname: Fighting Illini
Colors: Orange and blue
Location: Champaign, Illinois
Stadium: Memorial (66,480)

First year of football: 1890
Year entered conference: 1896
Conference championships: 12

Big Ten Conference Competition

Indiana	29-15-2	Northwestern	41-32-5
Iowa	30-17-2	Ohio State	20-49-4
Michigan	19-51	Purdue	32-28-6
Michigan State	12-11-1	Wisconsin	26-23-6
Minnesota	20-24-2		

Division I Competition

Air Force	1-0-1	Ohio	2-2
Alabama	0-1	Oklahoma	1-0
Army	3-3-1	Oregon	1-0
Baylor	0-1	Oregon State	0-1
California	5-1	Penn State	1-3
Colgate	1-1	Pennsylvania	2-0
Drake	4-0	Pittsburgh	6-2
Duke	1-1	South Dakota	2-0
Florida	0-1	Southern California	1-7
Iowa State	3-2-1	Southern Methodist	1-1
Kansas	3-2	Stanford	4-6
Kansas State	1-0	Syracuse	9-1
Kentucky	1-1	Texas A&M	0-2
Miami (of Ohio)	2-0	Tulane	0-1
Mississippi State	1-1	UCLA	5-3
Missouri	5-9	Washington	4-5
Nebraska	2-5-1	Washington State	2-1
North Carolina	0-1	West Virginia	1-1
Notre Dame	0-11-1	Western Michigan	1-0

Other Opponents

Alumni	1-1-1	Camp Grant	1-1
Baker	1-0	Carlisle	0-2
Beloit	1-0	Chanute Field	1-0
Bradley	6-0-1	Chicago	23-17-4
Butler	7-1	Chicago A.A.	0-1
Camp Funston	1-0	Chicago A.C.	0-2

Chicago Dental	1-0	Lombard	2-0
Chicago P&S	6-1	Marion-Sims	1-0
Christian Brothers	1-0	Marquette	0-0-1
Coe	3-0	Millikin	3-0
DePaul	2-0-1	Missouri Mines	1-0
DePauw	6-0	Monmouth	2-0
Doane	1-0	Municipal Pier	0-1
Englewood H.S.	4-0	North Central	1-0
Eureka	2-0	North Division H.S.	1-0
Great Lakes	0-3-1	Northwestern Col.	1-0
Haskell	2-0	Oberlin	1-1
Illinois Col.	1-0	Osteopaths	2-0
Illinois Normal	3-0	Pastime A.C.	2-0
Illinois Wesleyan	6-1	Rose Poly	1-0
Indianapolis L.A.	0-1	Rush-Lake Forest	2-0
Iowa Pre-Flight	0-1	St. Louis	4-0
Kansas City A.C.	1-0	Wabash	7-0-1
Knox	8-0	Washington (Mo.)	9-0
Lake Forest	3-1-1		

Total Overall Record	437-362-43	.545
Total Conference Record	246-260-26	.487
Overall Bowl Game Record	3-2-0	.600

INDIANA

Nickname: Hoosiers
Colors: Cream and crimson
Location: Bloomington, Indiana
Stadium: Memorial (52,350)

First year of football: 1887
Year entered conference: 1900
Conference championships: 2

Big Ten Conference Competition

Illinois	15-29-2	Northwestern	22-34-1
Iowa	19-29-4	Ohio State	10-48-4
Michigan	8-33	Purdue	27-54-6
Michigan State	9-24-2	Wisconsin	11-24-2
Minnesota	15-28-3		

Division I Competition

Arizona	2-2	Florida	1-0
Baylor	1-1	Harvard	0-2
Boston College	0-1	Kansas	1-1
Brigham Young	1-0	Kansas State	3-2
California	0-2	Kent State	1-0
Cincinnati	6-3-2	Kentucky	11-5-1
Colgate	0-1	Louisiana State	1-2
Colorado	1-3	Maryland	2-0
Duke	2-1	Miami (Fla.)	1-1

Miami (of Ohio)	7-3-1	Pittsburgh	7-2
Mississippi State	3-0	Southern California	0-4
Missouri	0-2	Southern Methodist	0-1
Nebraska	9-7-3	Syracuse	4-3
North Carolina State	0-2	Temple	1-0-1
Notre Dame	5-22-1	Texas	0-3
Ohio	4-1	Texas Christian	0-4
Oklahoma	1-0	Tulsa	1-0
Oklahoma State	0-0-1	Utah	1-0
Oregon	0-2	Vanderbilt	2-0
Oregon State	1-2	Washington	2-0
Pacific	1-0	Washington State	1-2

Other Opponents

Alumni	5-0-1	Indiana Training Sch.	1-0
Bedford	1-0	Iowa Seahawks	0-1
Butler	5-5	Kalamazoo	1-0
Camp Taylor	0-1	Knightstown	1-0
Centre	3-1	Lake Forest	1-0
Chicago	5-20-1	Louisville A.C.	3-0
Cornell Col.	1-0	Manual Training	1-0
Danville A.C.	1-0	Marquette	6-0
DePauw	23-7-3	Millikin	1-0
Detroit	0-1	Noblesville	1-1
Earlham	3-0	Rose Poly	7-0-1
Fordham	0-1	St. Louis	2-0
Fort Harrison	1-0	Transylvania	0-1
Fort Knox	2-0	Tufts	0-1
Franklin	5-1	Villanova	2-0
Great Lakes	0-1	Vincennes	2-0
Hanover	1-0	Wabash	14-6
Indiana Lt. Art	0-1	Washington (Mo.)	3-0
Indiana Medical	1-0	Washington and Lee	0-0-1
Indiana Normal	1-0	Xavier	0-1

Total Overall Record	327-443-41	.428
Total Conference Record	130-306-23	.308
Overall Bowl Game Record	1-1-0	.500

IOWA

Nickname: Hawkeyes	First year of football: 1889
Colors: Black and gold	Year entered conference: 1900
Location: Iowa City, Iowa	Conference championships: 6
Stadium: Kinnick (60,200)	

Big Ten Conference Competition

Illinois	17-30-2	Michigan	6-27-3
Indiana	29-19-4	Michigan State	10-11-1

Minnesota	24-52-2	Purdue	19-40-2
Northwestern	31-14-3	Wisconsin	26-34-2
Ohio State	11-30-2		

Division I Competition

Air Force	0-0-1	Oklahoma	0-1
Arizona	3-5	Oklahoma State	1-1
Arkansas	1-0	Oregon	1-0
Boston	1-0	Oregon State	7-5
California	3-0	Penn State	3-6
Colgate	1-1	Pittsburgh	1-2
Colorado State	1-0	South Dakota	8-0
Drake	11-3	Southern California	2-6
Florida	0-1	Syracuse	1-1
Hawaii	2-0	Temple	1-0
Idaho	1-0	Tennessee	1-0
Iowa State	20-12	Texas	1-0
Kansas	4-6	Texas A&M	0-1
Kansas State	3-0	Texas Christian	2-1
Miami (Fla.)	0-2	UCLA	2-6
Missouri	5-7	Utah	0-1
Montana	1-0	Utah State	1-0
Nebraska	12-24-3	Washington	2-2
North Carolina State	0-1	Washington State	3-1-1
North Dakota	1-0	Wyoming	1-0
Notre Dame	8-13-3	Yale	1-0

Other Opponents

Augustana	2-1	Iowa Pre-Flight	0-2
Bergstron A.A.F.	1-0	Iowa Teachers	10-1
Bradley	5-0	Iowa Wesleyan	1-0
Butler	1-0	Knox	6-0-1
Camp Grant	1-0	Lawrence	1-0
Carleton	1-0	Luther	1-0
Carroll	2-0	Marquette	1-1
Centenary	0-1	Monmouth	4-0
Chicago	3-9-2	Morningside	4-0
Chicago P&S	0-1	Parsons	1-0
Coe	9-0	Ripon	1-0
Cornell Col.	13-1	Rush	1-1
Denver	1-0	St. Louis	2-1
Denver A.C.	0-1	Simpson	4-0
Des Moines	1-0	Southeast Oklahoma	1-0
Des Moines Y.	1-0	Upper Iowa	2-0
Detroit	1-0	Wabash	2-0
Doane	0-1	Washington (Mo.)	4-0
George Washington	1-1	William Penn	2-0
Great Lakes	0-4	Wilton	1-0
Grinnell	11-5-1		

Total Overall Record	394-397-33	.498
Total Conference Record	173-262-21	.402
Overall Bowl Game Record	4-2-0	.667

MICHIGAN

Nickname: Wolverines
Colors: Maize and blue
Location: Ann Arbor, Michigan
Stadium: Michigan (101,700)

First year of football: 1879
Year entered conference: 1896
Conference championships: 26

Big Ten Conference Competition

Illinois	51-19	Northwestern	40-11-2
Indiana	33-8	Ohio State	44-32-5
Iowa	27-6-3	Purdue	26-10
Michigan State	50-22-5	Wisconsin	35-8-1
Minnesota	50-22-3		

Division I Competition

Air Force	1-0	North Carolina	1-2
Arizona	2-0	Notre Dame	11-5
Army	4-5	Oklahoma	0-1
Auburn	0-1	Oklahoma State	1-0
Baylor	0-0-1	Oregon	3-0
Brigham Young	0-1	Oregon State	3-0
California	6-2	Pennsylvania	11-8-2
Central Michigan	1-0	Pittsburgh	2-0
Colorado	1-0	Princeton	2-1
Columbia	3-0	South Carolina	0-1
Cornell	6-12	South Dakota	1-0
Dartmouth	1-0	Southern California	3-3
Drake	2-0	Southern Methodist	1-0
Duke	6-0	Stanford	6-3-1
Eastern Michigan	5-0	Syracuse	5-4-1
Georgia	0-1	Texas A&M	2-0
Georgia Tech	1-0	Tulane	3-0
Harvard	4-4	UCLA	4-2
Kansas	3-0	Vanderbilt	9-0-1
Kentucky	1-0	Virginia	2-0
Lehigh	1-0	Wake Forest	1-0
Miami (Fla.)	1-0	Washington	5-3
Miami (of Ohio)	1-0	Washington State	1-0
Missouri	2-2	West Virginia	1-0
Navy	12-5-1	Western Michigan	2-0
Nebraska	2-1-1	Yale	2-2

Other Opponents

Adrian	1-0	Kenyon	1-0
Albion	16-1	Lake Forest	2-0
American Medical	1-0	Lawrence	1-0
Beloit	3-0	Marietta	2-0
Buffalo	1-0	Marquette	2-0
Butler	1-0	Michigan A.A.	2-0
Camp Grant	1-0	Michigan M.A.	1-0
Carlisle	1-0	Mount Union	7-0
Carroll	1-0	Oberlin	9-0
Case Tech	26-0-1	Ohio Northern	3-0
Chicago	20-8	Ohio Wesleyan	2-1-1
Chicago P&S	2-0	Olivet	2-0
Chicago U. Club	1-3	Orchard Lake	1-0-1
Cleveland A.A.	0-1	Peninsulars	1-0
Denison	1-0	Quantico Marines	1-0
DePauw	3-0	Racine Col.	2-0
Detroit	1-0	Stevens Tech	1-0
Detroit A.C.	4-0	Toronto	1-0-1
Ferris State	1-0	Wabash	1-0
Grand Rapids	1-0	Washington (Mo.)	1-0
Great Lakes	2-0	Wesleyan	0-1
Harvard (Chi.)	1-0	Western Reserve	3-0
Hillsdale	2-0	Windsor Club	2-0
Iowa Pre-Flight	1-1	Wittenberg	2-0
Kalamazoo	5-0		

Total Overall Record	648-222-31	.736
Total Conference Record	317-130-14	.703
Overall Bowl Game Record	6-10-0	.375

MICHIGAN STATE

Nickname: Spartans
Colors: Green and white
Location: East Lansing,
        Michigan
Stadium: Spartan (76,000)

First year of football: 1896
Year entered conference: 1953
Conference championships: 4

Big Ten Conference Competition

Illinois	11-12-1	Northwestern	21-8
Indiana	24-9-2	Ohio State	8-15
Iowa	11-10-1	Purdue	18-19-2
Michigan	22-50-5	Wisconsin	15-12
Minnesota	14-11		

Division I Competition

Akron	2-0	Nebraska	0-2
Arizona	3-0	North Carolina	2-1
Army	0-2	North Carolina State	4-1-1
Auburn	0-1	Notre Dame	17-32-1
Baylor	1-0	Ohio	1-0
Boston College	0-2-1	Oregon	1-1
Bowling Green	1-0	Oregon State	6-2-1
California	2-0	Penn State	8-1-1
Cincinnati	1-1	Pittsburgh	4-0-1
Colgate	1-4	South Dakota	5-0-1
Colorado	3-0	Southern California	1-4
Cornell	0-1	Southern Methodist	1-0
Eastern Michigan	3-0	Stanford	3-1
Georgia Tech	0-2	Syracuse	9-3
Hawaii	2-0	Temple	7-1-2
Houston	0-1	Texas A&M	2-1
Iowa State	2-0	Texas Christian	1-0
Kansas	4-0	Toledo	1-0
Kansas State	5-0-1	UCLA	3-3
Kentucky	2-2	Washington	1-1
Maryland	4-1	Washington State	5-2
Miami (Fla.)	0-3	West Virginia	4-0
Miami (of Ohio)	2-0	Western Michigan	5-2
Mississippi State	2-1-1	William and Mary	2-0
Missouri	3-3	Wyoming	2-0

Other Opponents

Adrian	4-0	Great Lakes	1-1
Albion	11-4-3	Grinnell	4-0
Alma	22-4-4	Haskell	0-1
Armour Inst.	1-0	Hillsdale	7-0
Butler	1-1	Illinois Wesleyan	5-0
Camp MacArthur	0-1	Kalamazoo	9-8
Carnegie Tech	3-0-1	Lake Forest	3-1-1
Carroll	2-0	Lansing H.S.	2-0
Case Tech	2-0	Loyola (Ca.)	1-0
Centre	2-0	Manhattan	1-1
Chicago	0-1	Marietta	0-1
Chicago Y.	3-0	Marquette	18-6-1
Cornell Col.	1-1	Massachusetts State	1-0
Creighton	0-2	Michigan Deaf School	4-0
Culver Mil. Acad.	1-0	Michigan Frosh	4-0
DePaul	1-0-1	Mount Union	4-0
DePauw	5-1	North Central	1-0
Detroit	7-6-1	North Dakota State	2-0
Detroit A.C.	3-4-1	Ohio Northern	1-0
Detroit Y.	1-0	Ohio Wesleyan	2-2
Fordham	1-0	Olivet	18-4-1
Georgetown	1-1	Port Huron Y.	2-0

Ripon	1-0	Scranton	1-0
Saginaw Naval Brig.	1-0	South Dakota State	1-0
St. Louis	0-1-1	Wabash	5-1-1
San Francisco	1-0	Washington (Mo.)	1-0
Santa Clara	1-3-2	Wayne State	9-0

Total Overall Record	463-284-40	.614
Total Conference Record	124-100-6	.552
Overall Bowl Game Record	2-3-0	.400

MINNESOTA

Nickname: Golden Gophers
Colors: Maroon and Gold
Location: Minneapolis,
    Minnesota
Stadium: Humphrey Metrodome
    (62,345)

First year of football: 1882
Year entered conference: 1896
Conference championships: 14

Big Ten Conference Competition

Illinois	24-20-2	Northwestern	39-23-4
Indiana	28-15-3	Ohio State	6-22
Iowa	52-24-2	Purdue	22-18-3
Michigan	22-50-3	Wisconsin	50-36-8
Michigan State	11-14		

Division I Competition

Arizona	1-0	Oregon State	2-1
Arizona State	0-1	Pittsburgh	9-1
Army	1-0	Rice	2-0
California	1-2	South Dakota	8-1
Colorado	0-1	Southern California	1-4-1
Drake	1-0	Southern Methodist	1-0
Iowa State	8-2-1	Stanford	1-1-1
Kansas	3-3	Texas	1-0
Kansas State	1-0	Texas Christian	1-0
Maryland	0-1	Toledo	1-0
Mississippi	1-0	Tulane	1-0
Missouri	3-4-1	UCLA	2-1
Navy	1-0	Utah	1-0
Nebraska	29-18-2	Vanderbilt	2-2
North Dakota	18-0	Wake Forest	1-0
Notre Dame	0-4-1	Washington	11-7
Ohio	6-0-1	Washington State	1-2
Oklahoma State	2-0	Western Michigan	3-0
Oregon	2-0	Wyoming	1-0

Other Opponents

All-Stars	0-1	Hamline	6-1
Alumni	2-2	Haskell	4-0
Ames	11-0	High Schools	12-0-1
Beloit	3-0-1	Iowa Seahawks	0-3
Boat Club	1-0	Lawrence	6-0
Butler	2-0	MacAlester	4-0
Camp Grant	1-0	Municipal Pier	1-0
Carleton	10-1	North Dakota State	6-0
Carlisle	1-2	Overland Aviation	1-0
Chicago	13-5-1	Pillsbury	1-0
Coe	1-0	Ripon	2-0
Cornell Col.	1-0	Rush Med.	1-0
Creighton	1-0	St. Thomas	3-0
Ex-Collegiates	6-1-1	Shattuck	5-5-1
Fort Warren	1-0	South Dakota State	7-0
Grinnell	12-2-2	Wabash	2-0

Total Overall Record	508-301-40	.625
Total Conference Record	253-221-26	.532
Overall Bowl Game Record	1-2-0	.333

NORTHWESTERN

Nickname: Wildcats
Colors: Purple and white
Location: Evanston, Illinois
Stadium: Dyche (49,300)

First year of football: 1886
Year entered conference: 1896
Conference championships: 4

Big Ten Conference Competition

Illinois	32-41-5	Minnesota	23-39-4
Indiana	34-22-1	Ohio State	13-42-1
Iowa	14-31-3	Purdue	19-34-1
Michigan	11-40-2	Wisconsin	22-45-5
Michigan State	8-21		

Division I Competition

Arizona	0-2	Florida	0-2
Arizona State	0-2	Iowa State	7-1
Arkansas	0-1	Kansas State	2-0
Army	2-0	Kentucky	1-0
Boston College	1-0	Miami (Fla.)	2-2
California	1-0	Miami (of Ohio)	1-3
Cincinnati	2-0	Missouri	3-3
Colgate	1-0	Navy	2-0
Colorado	1-1	Nebraska	1-2
Dartmouth	1-0	North Carolina	0-2
Drake	2-0	North Dakota	1-0

Northern Illinois	2-0	Southern California	0-4
Notre Dame	7-34-2	Southern Methodist	0-1
Ohio	0-1	Stanford	1-2-1
Oklahoma	2-1	Syracuse	3-4
Oregon	1-0	Texas	1-0
Oregon State	3-1	Tulane	1-3
Pacific	1-0	UCLA	3-2
Pittsburgh	3-3	Utah	1-1
Rice	0-1	Vanderbilt	0-1-1
Rutgers	0-1	Washington	0-3
South Carolina	1-0	Washington State	1-0
South Dakota	4-0	Wyoming	1-0

Other Opponents

Alumni	3-3	Hyde Park H.S.	1-0
Armour Inst.	2-0	Illinois Wesleyan	1-1-1
Beloit	12-3-4	Iowa Pre-Flight	0-1
Butler	2-0	Knox	3-1
Carleton	2-0	Lake Forest	17-4-3
Carlisle	0-1	Lombard	3-0
Centre	1-0	Marquette	2-0
Chicago	8-26-3	Monmouth	2-0
Chicago A.C.	1-0	Municipal Pier	0-1
Chicago Dental	0-1	North Central	5-0
Chicago P&S	3-1	North Division H.S.	3-0
Chicago Wanderers	1-0	Northwest Division H.S.	1-0
Chicago Y.	2-0	Northwestern Dental	1-0
Cornell Col.	1-0	Ohio Northern	1-0
Denver A.C.	0-1	Oshkosh Normal	1-0
DePaul	2-0	Rush Medical	4-1
DePauw	3-0	St. Viator	1-0
Dixon	1-0	South Division H.S.	0-0-1
Englewood H.S.	4-0	Transylvania	0-0-1
Evanston H.S.	4-0	Wabash	2-0
Fort Sheridan	4-0	Washington (Mo.)	1-0
Great Lakes	1-2-1	West Division H.S.	1-0
Harvard Prep	0-1		

Total Overall Record	350-447-40	.442
Total Conference Record	174-326-20	.354
Overall Bowl Game Record	1-0-0	1.000

OHIO STATE

Nickname: Buckeyes
Colors: Scarlet and gray
Location: Columbus, Ohio
Stadium: Ohio (85,340)

First year of football: 1890
Year entered conference: 1913
Conference championships: 24

Big Ten Conference Competition

Illinois	49-20-4	Minnesota	22-6
Indiana	48-10-4	Northwestern	42-13-1
Iowa	30-11-2	Purdue	22-9-2
Michigan	32-44-5	Wisconsin	40-10-4
Michigan State	15-8		

Division I Competition

Akron	4-1	North Carolina	3-1
Alabama	0-1	Notre Dame	0-2
Arizona	0-1	Ohio	4-0
Arizona State	1-0	Oklahoma	1-1
Auburn	0-0-1	Oregon	6-0
Baylor	2-0	Oregon State	2-0
Brigham Young	1-0	Penn State	2-6
California	5-1	Pennsylvania	3-0
Cincinnati	9-2	Pittsburgh	14-4-1
Clemson	0-1	Princeton	0-1-1
Colgate	1-0-1	Southern California	9-9-1
Colorado	1-1	Southern Methodist	7-1-1
Columbia	2-0	Stanford	2-3
Cornell	0-2	Syracuse	2-1
Drake	1-0	Texas A&M	2-0
Duke	3-1	Texas Christian	4-1-1
Florida State	0-2	UCLA	3-3-1
Kentucky	3-0	Vanderbilt	3-1
Miami (Fla.)	1-0	Virginia	1-0
Miami (of Ohio)	2-0	Washington	4-1
Missouri	8-1-1	Washington State	5-0
Navy	3-0	West Virginia	3-1
Nebraska	2-0		

Other Opponents

Antioch	1-0	Kenyon	17-6
Camp Sherman	1-0	Marietta	6-2
Carlisle	0-1	Mount Union	1-0
Case Tech	11-10-2	Muskingum	7-0
Central Kentucky	0-1	New York	2-0
Chicago	10-2-2	Oberlin	13-9-3
Columbus Barracks	2-1	Ohio Medical	5-2-1
Dayton Y.	1-0	Ohio Wesleyan	26-2-1
Denison	14-1-2	Otterbein	13-2-3
DePauw	1-0	17th Regiment	1-0
Fort Knox	1-0	Western Reserve	5-6-1
Great Lakes	1-1	Wilmington	1-0
Heidelberg	3-0	Wittenberg	12-3
Iowa Seahawks	1-1	Wooster	4-2-2

Total Overall Record	589-233-48	.705
Total Conference Record	309-114-20	.720
Overall Bowl Game Record	9-10-0	.474

PURDUE

Nickname: Boilermakers
Colors: Black and gold
Location: West Lafayette,
    Indiana
Stadium: Ross-Ade (69,200)

First year of football: 1887
Year entered conference: 1896
Conference championships: 5

Big Ten Conference Competition

Illinois	28-32-6	Minnesota	18-22-3
Indiana	54-27-6	Northwestern	34-19-1
Iowa	40-19-2	Ohio State	9-22-2
Michigan	10-26	Wisconsin	22-31-7
Michigan State	19-18-2		

Division I Competition

Baylor	1-0	Ohio	8-0
Boston	1-0	Oregon	1-0
Bowling Green	0-1	Oregon State	0-1
Duke	1-2-1	Pacific	1-0
Georgia Tech	1-0	Penn State	1-0-1
Harvard	1-0	Pittsburgh	4-1
Illinois State	1-0	Rice	1-1
Indiana State	1-0	Southern California	1-2
Iowa State	1-0	Southern Methodist	1-0-1
Kansas State	2-0	Stanford	3-1
Kentucky	2-1	Tennessee	1-0
Miami (Fla.)	1-5	Texas	0-2
Miami (of Ohio)	7-3-1	Texas A&M	1-0
Mississippi	1-0	Texas Christian	2-0
Missouri	6-2	UCLA	0-3-2
Montana State	1-0	Vanderbilt	0-2
Navy	0-2	Virginia	1-1
Nebraska	1-0	Wake Forest	3-0
Notre Dame	20-34-2	Washington	1-2-1

Other Opponents

Alumni	1-2-1	Case Tech	3-0
Armour Inst.	1-0	Centenary	1-0
Beloit	4-0	Chicago	14-27-1
Butler	9-3	Chicago All-Univ.	0-1
Camp Grant	1-0	Coe	1-0
Carnegie Tech	5-1	Culver	1-0

DePauw	26-1	Marquette	5-0
Detroit	1-0	Millikin	1-0
Earlham	4-0	Monmouth	1-0
Engelwood H.S.	1-0	New York	1-0
Fordham	2-5-1	North Division H.S.	1-0
Franklin	6-0-1	Oberlin	1-3
Great Lakes	2-3	Rose Poly	7-0
Greer	2-0	Rush Medical	1-0
Haskell	2-0	Santa Clara	0-1
Illinois Wesleyan	1-0	Wabash	19-8-2
Indiana Medical	1-0	Wendell Phillips H.S.	1-0
Iowa Pre-Flight	0-1	Western Reserve	2-0
Light Artillery	1-0	Wilmington	1-0

Total Overall Record	442-338-44	.563
Total Conference Record	227-233-28	.494
Overall Bowl Game Record	4-1-0	.800

WISCONSIN

Nickname: Badgers
Colors: Red and white
Location: Madison, Wisconsin
Stadium: Camp Randall (77,280)

First year of football: 1889
Year entered conference: 1896
Conference championships: 7

Big Ten Conference Competition

Illinois	23-26-6	Minnesota	36-50-8
Indiana	24-11-2	Northwestern	45-22-5
Iowa	34-26-2	Ohio State	10-40-4
Michigan	8-35-1	Purdue	31-22-7
Michigan State	12-15		

Division I Competition

Air Force	1-0	Kentucky	0-1
Alabama	1-0	Louisiana State	1-0
Arizona State	0-2	Miami (Fla.)	1-0
Arkansas	1-0	Missouri	4-1
Auburn	0-0-1	Navy	1-1
Brigham Young	0-1	Nebraska	2-3
California	1-3	New Mexico State	1-0
Cincinnati	1-0	North Dakota	3-0
Colgate	1-0	Northern Illinois	5-0
Colorado	0-2-1	Notre Dame	6-8-2
Columbia	0-1	Oklahoma	0-2
Drake	1-0	Oregon	2-0
Iowa State	5-0	Oregon State	1-0
Kansas	4-2	Penn State	2-0
Kansas State	2-0	Pennsylvania	2-2

Pittsburgh	0-3	Toledo	1-0
Richmond	1-0	UCLA	1-7
San Diego State	1-1	Utah	1-0
South Dakota	1-0	Utah State	0-1
Southern California	0-6	Washington	0-3
Stanford	2-0	Washington State	1-0
Syracuse	1-2-1	West Virginia	2-0
Tennessee	0-1	Western Michigan	2-0
Texas	0-1	Wyoming	1-0
Texas Christian	0-0-1	Yale	1-2

Other Opponents

Alumni	3-1	Haskell	1-0
Armour Inst.	1-0	Hyde Park H.S.	2-0
Beloit	16-1	Knox	2-0
Bradley	1-0	Lake Forest	7-1
Calumet Club	0-1	Lawrence	17-0-1
Camp Grant	1-2	Madison H.S.	4-0
Carleton	2-0	Marquette	32-4
Carlisle	0-1	Milwaukee Medical	1-0
Chicago	19-16-5	North Central	1-0
Chicago A.A.	1-2	North Dakota State	2-0
Chicago P&S	1-0	Northwestern Col.	1-0
Coe	2-0-1	Osteopaths	1-0
Colorado College	1-0	Rice Institute	2-0
Company I	1-0	Ripon	5-0
Cornell Col.	3-0	Rush Medical	4-0
Dixon	1-0	South Dakota State	8-1
Fort Sheridan	1-0	Upper Iowa	1-0
Franklin	1-0	Wisconsin-Oshkosh	1-0
Freshmen	1-0	Wisconsin-Platteville	1-0
Great Lakes	1-1-1	Wisconsin-Whitewater	2-0
Grinnell	4-0		

Total Overall Record	443-336-49	.565
Total Conference Record	229-252-38	.478
Overall Bowl Game Record	1-5-0	.167

Ivy League

(Officially Classified NCAA As Division I-AA)

Formed: 1956*
Charter members: Brown, Columbia, Cornell, Dartmouth, Harvard, Pennsylvania, Princeton, Yale.

Overall Records

	Years	W	L	T	Pct.
Yale	112	729	221	53	.753
Princeton	115	654	254	48	.709
Harvard	110	660	277	46	.695
Dartmouth	103	545	284	41	.650
Pennsylvania	108	630	375	41	.622
Cornell	97	498	338	33	.592
Brown	99	449	414	36	.519
Columbia	94	312	425	41	.427

*Informal league competition existed prior to 1956 where no champion was officially recognized.

Conference Records

	W	L	T	Pct.
Dartmouth	142	56	5	.712
Yale	131	66	6	.660
Harvard	121	74	8	.616
Princeton	114	85	4	.571
Cornell	84	114	5	.426
Pennsylvania	79	120	4	.399
Brown	73	125	5	.372
Columbia	47	151	5	.244
Combined bowl game record	2	2	0	.500

Total Championships

1.	Dartmouth	13	5. Pennsylvania	4
2.	Yale	11	6. Brown	1
3.	Harvard	7	Columbia	1
4.	Princeton	5	Cornell	1

Past Champions

1984	Pennsylvania	1969	Dartmouth
1983	Harvard		Princeton
	Pennsylvania		Yale
1982	Dartmouth	1968	Harvard
	Harvard		Yale
	Pennsylvania	1967	Yale
1981	Dartmouth	1966	Dartmouth
	Yale		Harvard
1980	Yale		Princeton
1979	Yale	1965	Dartmouth
1978	Dartmouth	1964	Princeton
1977	Yale	1963	Dartmouth
1976	Brown		Princeton
	Yale	1962	Dartmouth
1975	Harvard	1961	Columbia
1974	Harvard		Harvard
	Yale	1960	Yale
1973	Dartmouth	1959	Pennsylvania
1972	Dartmouth	1958	Dartmouth
1971	Cornell	1957	Princeton
	Dartmouth	1956	Yale
1970	Dartmouth		

BROWN

Nickname: Bruins
Colors: Brown and white
Location: Providence, Rhode
          Island
Stadium: Brown (20,000)

First year of football: 1878
Conference championships: 1

Ivy League Competition

Columbia	27-20-2	Pennsylvania	12-39-2
Cornell	15-16-1	Princeton	15-36
Dartmouth	16-43-3	Yale	21-64-4
Harvard	21-61-2		

Division I Competition

Army	2-6	Lehigh	7-1
Boston College	5-0	Maine	3-1
Boston University	7-1-1	Massachusetts	7-0
Bucknell	0-1	New Hampshire	14-1
Colgate	19-25-7	Penn State	0-1
Connecticut	6-1	Rhode Island	56-12-2
Holy Cross	18-22-2	Rutgers	5-6
Lafayette	5-3	Syracuse	3-9-3

| Temple | 0-3 | William and Mary | 1-0 |
| Washington State | 0-1 | | |

Other Opponents

Albright	1-0	Lebanon Valley	0-1
Amherst	6-4-1	M.I.T.	8-5-1
Andover	4-1	Manhattan	1-0
Bates	5-0	Needham	1-0
Boston A.C.	1-3	New York	1-0
Bowdoin	6-2	Newton A.A.	4-0
Camp Devens	1-1	Norwich	8-0
Camp Kilmer	1-0	Ohio Wesleyan	1-0
Campello	1-0	Orange A.A.	1-0
Canisius	1-0	Pawtucket C.C.	1-0
Carlisle	6-3	Providence H.S.	1-0
Chicago	1-2	St. Bonaventure	2-0
Coast Guard	2-1	Springfield	7-2-1
Colby	16-1	Trinity (Ct.)	2-2-3
Crescent A.C.	0-1	Tufts	25-2
Dayton	1-0	Union	1-0
Fall Rivers	2-1	USN Reserves	0-1
Fort Adams	1-0	Ursinus	1-0
Harvard Frosh	1-0	Vermont	15-0-1
Haskell	0-1	W.P.I.	7-1
Haverford	1-0	Washington & Jefferson	0-1
Homestead	0-1	Wesleyan	12-2
Johns Hopkins	1-0	Western Reserve	2-0
League 1, Navy Yard	0-1	Williams	4-1

Total Overall Record	449-414-36	.519
Total Conference Record	73-125-5	.372
Overall Bowl Game Record	0-1-0	.000

COLUMBIA

Nickname: Lions
Colors: Blue and white
Location: New York City, New York
Stadium: Baker Field (20,000)

First year of football: 1870
Conference championships: 1

Ivy League Competition

Brown	20-27-2	Pennsylvania	17-46-1
Cornell	23-46-3	Princeton	8-45-1
Dartmouth	11-43-1	Yale	14-46-2
Harvard	10-32-1		

Division I Competition

Army	4-14-3	Ohio	0-1
Bucknell	1-1-2	Ohio State	0-2
Colgate	4-16-1	Penn State	2-0
Connecticut	1-0	Rutgers	21-23-5
Duke	1-0	Stanford	2-0-1
Georgia	1-1	Syracuse	9-11-4
Holy Cross	1-5	Tulane	0-1
Lafayette	8-11-1	Virginia	4-0
Lehigh	5-3	Virginia Military	4-0
Maine	3-0	William and Mary	1-0
Michigan	0-3	Wisconsin	1-0
Navy	9-13-1		

Other Opponents

Alfred	1-0	Merritt	1-0
Alumni	1-0	Middlebury	6-0
Amherst	7-4-3	New York	8-3-1
Berkeley	1-0	New York C.C.	4-0
Buffalo	2-2	St. Lawrence	2-0
Carlisle	2-1	Seton Hall	1-0
Crescent A.C.	0-3	Stevens	9-5-2
Fordham	3-0	Swarthmore	3-2
Fort Monmouth	1-0	Trinity (Ct.)	1-2
Franklin and Marshall	1-0	Tufts	1-0
Georgetown	1-0	Union	13-1-1
Hamilton	3-1	USS Arizona	0-0-1
Haverford	3-0	Ursinus	2-0
Hobart	2-0	Vermont	5-0
Johns Hopkins	2-0-1	Wesleyan	16-5-1
Manhattan A.C.	1-1	Williams	14-5-2

Total Overall Record	312-425-41	.427
Total Conference Record	47-151-5	.244
Overall Bowl Game Record	1-0-0	1.000

CORNELL

Nickname: Big Red   First year of football: 1887
Colors: Red and white   Conference championships: 1
Location: Ithaca, New York
Stadium: Schoellkopf (27,000)

Ivy League Competition

Brown	16-15-1	Pennsylvania	35-51-5
Columbia	46-23-3	Princeton	23-42-2
Dartmouth	26-41-1	Yale	14-31-2
Harvard	18-29-2		

Division I Competition

Army	2-3	Navy	1-9
Boston	0-2	New Hampshire	1-0
Bucknell	27-4	Ohio State	2-0
Cincinnati	0-1	Penn State	8-4-2
Colgate	43-25-3	Pittsburgh	4-2
Holy Cross	3-0	Rice	0-2
Lafayette	9-5-1	Richmond	4-1
Lehigh	12-3-2	Rutgers	5-6
Michigan	12-6	Syracuse	23-11
Michigan State	1-0	Virginia Tech	1-0

Other Opponents

Albright	2-0	Merchant Marine	1-0
Alfred	3-0	New London Sub Base	1-0
Allegheny	1-0	New York	2-0
Amherst	1-1	Niagara	13-0
Bowdoin	1-0	Oberlin	13-1
Buffalo	3-0-1	Palmyra	1-0
Canisius	1-0	Rensselaer Poly	2-0
Carlisle	3-2	Rochester	9-0
Carnegie Tech	3-0	St. Bonaventure	7-0-2
Chicago	1-2-2	St. John's (NY)	1-0
Chicago U. Club	1-1	St. Lawrence	2-1
Clarkson	5-0	Spring	1-0
Crescent A.C.	1-0	Stevens	2-0
Detroit A.C.	1-0	Susquehanna	3-0
Dickinson	1-0	Swarthmore	2-1
Fordham	0-2	Syracuse A.C.	1-0
47th Infantry	0-1	Trinity (Ct.)	3-0
Franklin and Marshall	2-0	Tufts	2-2
Geneva	1-0	U.S.N.T.S. (Sampson)	2-0
Gettysburg	3-0	Union	8-1
Hamilton	8-0	Ursinus	2-0
Hampden-Sydney	3-0	Vermont	5-0
Haverford	1-0	Washington & Jefferson	4-0
Hobart	6-0	Washington & Lee	1-0
Johns Hopkins	1-0	Wesleyan	0-1
M.I.T.	1-0	Western Reserve	5-1
Manhattan A.C.	1-0	Williams	13-5-3
Massachusetts State	1-0		

Total Overall Record	498-338-33	.592
Total Conference Record	84-114-5	.426
Overall Bowl Game Record	0-0-0	.000

DARTMOUTH

Nickname: Big Green
Colors: Green and white
Location: Hanover, New
          Hampshire
Stadium: Memorial Field
          (20,416)

First year of football: 1881
Conference championships: 13

Ivy League Competition

Brown	43-16-3	Pennsylvania	26-24-2
Columbia	43-11-1	Princeton	31-30-3
Cornell	41-26-1	Yale	24-39-5
Harvard	38-46-4		

Division I Competition

Army	1-6	New Hampshire	13-3-1
Boston College	2-1	Northwestern	0-1
Boston University	8-1	Notre Dame	0-2
Bucknell	1-0	Penn State	2-1
Cincinnati	0-1	Rutgers	1-0
Colgate	3-6-1	Stanford	0-4
Georgia	1-1	Syracuse	6-3-1
Holy Cross	28-20-4	Temple	1-0
Lafayette	3-1	Tennessee	1-0
Lehigh	0-1	Virginia	1-0
Maine	7-0	Virginia Tech	1-0
Massachusetts	5-3	Washington	1-0
Miami (of Ohio)	1-0	West Virginia	1-0-1
Michigan	0-1	William and Mary	1-6
Navy	0-3-1		

Other Opponents

Allegheny	4-0	Fordham	0-1
Amherst	24-3-3	Franklin and Marshall	0-1
Andover	5-2	Georgetown	0-1
Bates	8-0	Hampden-Sydney	1-0
Boston A.A.	0-1	Hobart	5-0
Bowdoin	9-0-1	Lebanon Valley	2-0
Buffalo	1-0	M.I.T.	5-1
Carlisle	0-2	McGill	2-0
Chicago	1-1	Massachusetts Agr. Col.	15-0-1
Chicago A.C.	0-2	Middlebury	4-0
Coast Guard	1-1	New Hampshire State	4-0
Colby	4-0	Newton A.C.	2-0
Dickinson	1-0	Norwich	26-0
Exeter	6-1	St. Lawrence	3-0

Sewanee	1-0	U.S. Marines	1-0
South Berwick	1-0	Union	1-0-1
Springfield	5-0	Vermont	24-1-3
Stevens	2-1-1	Wesleyan	5-3
Trinity (Ct.)	3-0	Williams	20-4-2
Tufts	13-1-1	Worcester A.A.	1-0

Total Overall Record	545-284-41	.650
Total Conference Record	142-56-5	.712
Overall Bowl Game Record	0-0-0	.000

HARVARD

Nickname: Crimson	First year of football: 1874
Colors: Crimson	Conference championships: 7
Location: Cambridge,	
Massachusetts	
Stadium: Harvard (37,290)	

Ivy League Competition

Brown	61-21-2	Pennsylvania	35-18-2
Columbia	32-10-1	Princeton	28-42-7
Cornell	29-18-2	Yale	38-55-8
Dartmouth	46-38-4		

Division I Competition

Army	19-16-2	Navy	1-1-3
Boston College	3-1	New Hampshire	7-0
Boston University	8-3	North Carolina	2-0
Bucknell	2-1-1	Northeastern	2-0
Colgate	3-2	Ohio	3-0
Connecticut	1-0	Oregon	1-0
Davidson	3-0	Penn State	3-2
Florida	2-0	Purdue	0-1
Georgia	1-0	Rhode Island	1-0
Holy Cross	25-12-2	Rutgers	2-3
Indiana	2-0	Stanford	0-1
Lafayette	2-0	Texas	1-0
Lehigh	4-1	Vanderbilt	1-0
Maine	11-0	Virginia	8-1
Massachusetts	10-6-1	William and Mary	4-0-2
Michigan	4-4		

Other Opponents

All Canada	3-0	B.A.A.	5-1-1
Amherst	24-1	Bates	23-0
Andover	6-0	Bowdoin	17-0

Britannia	2-1-1	Newtowne A.C.	2-0
Buffalo	1-1	North Carolina Pre-Flight	0-1
Camp Edwards	2-0	Orange A.A.	2-0
Carlisle	12-2	Ottawa (Ont.)	3-0
Centre	2-1	Rensselaer Poly	1-0
Chicago	2-0	Rochester	1-0
Chicago A.C.	3-0	Springfield	12-0
Coast Guard	3-0	Stagg's Team	2-0
Colby	3-0	Stevens	4-0
Exeter	11-0	Trinity (Ct.)	3-0
Geneva	0-1	Tufts	17-5
Graduates	2-1	Valparaiso	1-0
King's Point Acad.	1-0	Vermont	2-0
M.I.T.	15-0	Washington (Mo.)	1-0
McGill	5-0-2	Washington & Jefferson	1-0
Melville PT Boat	0-1	Wesleyan	17-1
Middlebury	4-0-1	Western Maryland	1-0
Montreal	1-0-1	Williams	30-0
New London Sub Base	0-1	Worcester Tech	3-1
Newton A.C.	2-0		

Total Overall Record   660-277-46   .695
Total Conference Record   121-74-8   .616
Overall Bowl Game Record   1-0-0   1.000

PENNSYLVANIA

Nickname: Quakers
Colors: Red and blue
Location: Philadelphia,
           Pennsylvania
Stadium: Franklin Field
         (60,546)

First year of football: 1876
Conference championships: 4

Ivy League Competition

Brown	39-12-2	Harvard	18-35-2
Columbia	46-17-1	Princeton	21-54-1
Cornell	51-35-5	Yale	15-36-1
Dartmouth	24-26-2		

Division I Competition

Alabama	0-1	Duke	1-1
Army	5-11-2	Georgia	0-1
Bucknell	16-2	Georgia Tech	2-1
California	0-7	Illinois	0-2
Colgate	1-1	Kansas	1-0
Davidson	1-0	Lafayette	51-16-4
Delaware	3-2	Lehigh	42-8

Maryland	1-0	Richmond	0-1
Michigan	8-11-2	Rutgers	10-6
Navy	21-20-4	Vanderbilt	1-0
North Carolina	4-2	Virginia	15-1
Notre Dame	0-5-1	Virginia Military	1-1
Ohio State	0-3	Virginia Tech	1-1
Oregon	0-1	West Virginia	5-0
Penn State	25-18-4	William and Mary	1-2
Pittsburgh	1-10-1	Wisconsin	2-2

Other Opponents

A.C.S.N.	2-0	Lakehurst	1-0
Albright	2-0	Mansfield	1-0
All-Philadelphia	4-0-1	Medico Chirurgical	1-0
Amherst	1-0	Navy Yard	1-0
Carlisle	13-6-2	Orange A.A.	1-0
Carnegie Tech	1-0	Pennsylvania Military	3-0
Centre	1-0	St. Joseph	1-0
Chicago	6-1-1	Sewanee	1-0
Chicago A.C.	2-0	Stevens	4-0-1
Columbia A.C.	2-0	Swarthmore	30-4-1
Crescent A.C.	7-0	Tioga	3-0
Dickinson	8-0	Trinity (Ct.)	1-0
Drexel	1-0	U.S. Marines	0-1
Duquesne A.C.	1-0	Ursinus	8-2
Falls of Schuylkill	1-0	Villanova	5-1
Franklin and Marshall	34-1	Vineland	1-0
George Washington	0-2	Volunteers	1-0
Georgetown	3-0-1	Washington and Jefferson	1-0
Georgia N.A.C.	0-1	Washington and Lee	1-0
Gettysburg	18-0-1	Wesleyan	9-3
Graduates	6-0-1	West Virginia Wesleyan	1-0
Haverford	8-0	Williams	2-0
Johns Hopkins	5-0		

Total Overall Record	630-375-41	.622
Total Conference Record	79-120-4	.399
Overall Bowl Game Record	0-1-0	.000

PRINCETON

Nickname: Tigers
Colors: Orange and black
Location: Princeton, New
        Jersey
Stadium: Palmer (45,725)

First year of football: 1869
Conference championships: 5

Ivy League Competition

Brown	36-15	Harvard	43-28-6
Columbia	45-8-1	Pennsylvania	54-21-1
Cornell	42-23-2	Yale	38-59-10
Dartmouth	30-31-3		

Division I Competition

Army	6-4-3	North Carolina	2-0
Bucknell	9-0	Notre Dame	0-2
Colgate	19-14-1	Ohio State	1-0-1
Delaware	0-2	Penn State	5-0
Holy Cross	4-0	Rutgers	53-17-1
Lafayette	27-2-3	Syracuse	5-0-1
Lehigh	33-2-2	Vanderbilt	1-1
Maine	1-1	Virginia	9-1-1
Maryland	2-0	Virginia Tech	3-0
Michigan	1-2	West Virginia	1-1
Navy	18-12-6	William and Mary	1-0

Other Opponents

Amherst	11-0	Muhlenberg	1-0
Atlantic City N.A.S.	0-1	Navy Pay School	1-0
Baltimore Medical	1-0	New York	4-0
Camp Upton	1-0	New York A.C.	2-0
Carlisle	6-0	Orange A.A.	6-0-2
Chicago	2-2-1	Princeton Seminary	1-0
Chicago A.C.	1-0	Rochester	1-0
Columbia A.C.	2-0	Sewanee	1-0
Columbia Law School	1-0	Springfield	1-0
Crescent A.C.	5-0	Stevens	23-0
Dickinson	3-0	Swarthmore	9-1
Elizabeth A.C.	2-0	307th Field Artillery	1-0
Fordham	3-0	Trinity (Ct.)	1-0
Franklin and Marshall	4-0	Tufts	1-0
Georgetown	5-0	Union	1-0
Gettysburg	1-0	Vermont	1-0
Government Aeronautical	1-0	Villanova	8-1
Graduates	1-0	Volunteers	1-0
Haverford	2-0	Washington and Jefferson	6-0
Johns Hopkins	5-0	Washington and Lee	6-1-1
Lakehurst Naval	1-0	Wesleyan	13-0
Lawrenceville School	3-0	Williams	9-1-1
Manhattan A.C.	2-0	Wissahickon Barracks	1-0
Maryland A.C.	2-0		

Total Overall Record	654-254-48	.709
Total Conference Record	114-85-4	.571
Overall Bowl Game Record	0-0-0	.000

YALE

Nickname: Elis, Bulldogs
Colors: Blue and white
Location: New Haven,
        Connecticut
Stadium: Yale Bowl (70,896)

First year of football: 1872
Conference championships: 11

Ivy League Competition

Brown	64-21-4	Harvard	55-38-8
Columbia	46-14-2	Pennsylvania	36-15-1
Cornell	31-14-2	Princeton	59-38-10
Dartmouth	39-24-5		

Division I Competition

Air Force	1-0	Michigan	2-2
Army	21-12-8	Navy	5-3-1
Boston College	0-4	New Hampshire	1-0
Boston University	2-0	North Carolina	7-0
Bucknell	2-0	Notre Dame	1-0
Colgate	21-7-3	Penn State	7-0
Connecticut	30-6	Rutgers	11-2
Georgia	5-6	Syracuse	11-0
Holy Cross	14-3	Temple	1-0
Iowa	0-1	Vanderbilt	0-1-1
Lafayette	4-0	Virginia	3-2-1
Lehigh	11-0	Virginia Tech	2-0
Maine	7-0-1	West Virginia	1-0
Maryland	8-2-1	William and Mary	0-1
Miami (of Ohio)	0-1	Wisconsin	2-1

Other Opponents

Alfred	1-0	King's Point Acad.	3-0
Amherst	22-0-1	Loomis Inst.	1-0
Bates	6-0-1	M.I.T.	4-0
Boston A.C.	2-0-1	Manhattan A.C.	1-0
Bowdoin	3-0	Massachusetts Agri. Col.	1-0
Carlisle	5-0	Middlebury	1-0
Carnegie Tech	3-0	Morgan State	1-0
Chicago	1-0-1	Muhlenberg	1-0
Chicago A.C.	3-0	New Hampshire Naval Base	1-0
Coast Guard	4-0	New Jersey A.C.	1-0
Crescent A.C.	13-0	Newton A.C.	2-0
Elizabeth A.C.	1-0	New York A.C.	2-0
Eton	1-0	New York	1-0
Fordham	1-0	Orange A.A.	9-0
Graduates	1-0	Rochester	1-1

St. John's (Md.)	1-0	Villanova	1-0
Springfield	11-0	Volunteers	1-0
Stevens	8-0	Washington and Jefferson	4-2-1
Trinity (Ct.)	18-0	Washington and Lee	1-0
Tufts	10-0	Wesleyan	46-0
Union	1-0	Williams	16-0
Vermont	4-0		

Total Overall Record	729-221-53	.753
Total Conference Record	131-66-6	.660
Overall Bowl Game Record	0-0-0	.000

Mid-American Conference

Formed: 1947
Charter Members: Butler, Cincinnati, Ohio, Western Reserve.
Other Former Members: Marshall

Overall Records

	Years	W	L	T	Pct.
Central Michigan	81	426	217	29	.655
Miami (of Ohio)	96	502	258	36	.653
Bowling Green	66	330	202	48	.610
Western Michigan	79	360	265	21	.574
Ball State	60	269	215	28	.553
Northern Illinois	83	373	299	50	.551
Ohio	89	405	328	43	.550
Toledo	65	293	277	20	.514
Eastern Michigan	92	324	321	43	.502
Kent State	62	226	283	28	.447

Conference Records

	Years	W	L	T	Pct.
Central Michigan	10	63	17	4	.774
Miami (of Ohio)	37	143	57	5	.710
Bowling Green	33	126	74	8	.625
Ball State	10	43	31	0	.581
Ohio	38	123	110	7	.527
Toledo	33	97	115	3	.458
Northern Illinois	10	31	41	2	.432
Western Michigan	37	95	132	7	.421
Kent State	34	81	132	4	.382
Eastern Michigan	9	11	58	4	.178
Cincinnati	6	19	3	0	.864
Western Reserve	8	10	23	2	.314
Marshall	15	23	63	1	.270
Butler	3	1	10	0	.091
Combined bowl game record		11	5	0	.688

Total Championships

1. Miami (of Ohio)	12	4. Ohio	5
2. Bowling Green	7	Cincinnati	5
3. Toledo	6	6. Central Michigan	2

Ball State	2	Kent State	1
8. Northern Illinois	1	11. Eastern Michigan	0
Western Michigan	1		

Past Champions

1984	Toledo	1965	Bowling Green
1983	Northern Illinois		Miami (of Ohio)
1982	Bowling Green	1964	Bowling Green
1981	Toledo	1963	Ohio
1980	Central Michigan	1962	Bowling Green
1979	Central Michigan	1961	Bowling Green
1978	Ball State	1960	Ohio
1977	Miami (of Ohio)	1959	Bowling Green
1976	Ball State	1958	Miami (of Ohio)
1975	Miami (of Ohio)	1957	Miami (of Ohio)
1974	Miami (of Ohio)	1956	Bowling Green
1973	Miami (of Ohio)	1955	Miami (of Ohio)
1972	Kent State	1954	Miami (of Ohio)
1971	Toledo	1953	Ohio
1970	Toledo	1952	Cincinnati
1969	Toledo	1951	Cincinnati
1968	Ohio	1950	Miami (of Ohio)
1967	Toledo	1949	Cincinnati
	Ohio	1948	Miami (of Ohio)
1966	Miami (of Ohio)	1947	Cincinnati

BALL STATE

Nickname: Cardinals
Colors: Cardinal and white
Location: Muncie, Indiana
Stadium: Ball State (16,300)

First year of football: 1924
Year entered conference: 1975
Conference championships: 2

Mid-American Conference Competition

Bowling Green	3-8	Northern Illinois	11-7-2
Central Michigan	5-12	Ohio	2-4
Eastern Michigan	15-9-2	Toledo	5-5
Kent State	5-3	Western Michigan	5-7
Miami (of Ohio)	2-4-1		

Division I Competition

Akron	3-6-1	Louisiana Tech	1-1
Appalachian State	2-0	McNeese State	1-1
Eastern Illinois	3-3	Massachusetts	0-1
Eastern Kentucky	0-3	Middle Tennessee State	4-2
Illinois State	9-5	Rhode Island	1-0
Indiana State	30-22-1	Richmond	2-0

Southeastern Louisiana	1-0	Western Illinois	0-2
Southern Illinois	4-3-1	Western Kentucky	0-1
Tennessee State	0-0-1	Wichita State	1-1
Washington State	0-1	Youngstown State	1-0

Other Opponents

Anderson	3-0	Huntington	1-0
Bradley	1-1	Indiana (B)	0-1
Buffalo	2-0	Indiana (Pa.)	4-0
Butler	14-22-2	Indiana Central	2-3-2
Cal Poly-Pomona	1-0	Manchester	10-7-2
Cedarville	1-0	Merom	1-0
Central Missouri State	1-0	Millikin	2-0
Central Normal	15-6-1	Notre Dame (B)	0-1
Concordia	1-0	Oakland City	7-0
Dayton	2-1	Ohio Northern	0-1
Defiance	1-0	St. Joseph's (Ind.)	13-8-3
DePauw	14-12-1	Slippery Rock	1-0
DeSales	1-0	Valparaiso	14-19-1
Earlham	7-2	Villanova	0-1
Evansville	14-5-1	Wabash	1-6-1
Franklin	7-4-3	Wittenberg	1-0
Grand Rapids	1-0	Wooster	1-0
Hanover	9-4-2		

Total Overall Record	269-215-28	.553
Total Conference Record	43-31-0	.581
Overall Bowl Game Record	0-0-0	.000

BOWLING GREEN

Nickname: Falcons
Colors: Orange and brown
Location: Bowling Green, Ohio
Stadium: Doyt Perry Field
   (30,500)

First year of football: 1919
Year entered conference: 1952
Conference championships: 7

Mid-American Conference Competition

Ball State	8-3	Northern Illinois	6-2
Central Michigan	11-10	Ohio	19-17-1
Eastern Michigan	12-7-1	Toledo	26-19-4
Kent State	35-12-6	Western Michigan	23-6-2
Miami (of Ohio)	11-28-3		

Division I Competition

| Akron | 0-1 | Baylor | 0-1 |
| Arkansas State | 1-0 | Brigham Young | 1-1 |

Cal State-Long Beach	0-3	Purdue	1-0
Delaware	2-0	Richmond	1-1
Drake	1-0	San Diego State	0-2-1
East Carolina	1-1	Southern Illinois	8-0
Eastern Kentucky	0-3	Southern Mississippi	3-1
Fresno State	1-2	Syracuse	2-0
Hawaii	0-1	Temple	1-1
Iowa State	0-2	Tennessee-Chattanooga	0-2
Kentucky	0-2	Texas-Arlington	1-1
Marshall	18-3	Texas-El Paso	1-0
Michigan State	0-1	Utah State	0-2
North Carolina	0-1	West Texas State	1-4
North Texas State	1-0	Wichita State	1-0
Northern Iowa	1-0	William and Mary	0-1
Oklahoma State	0-1	Youngstown State	3-1

Other Opponents

Adrian	0-1	Huntington	1-0
Albion	1-0	John Carroll	1-2-1
Alma	3-0	Lockbourne A.F.B.	1-0
Ashland	5-1	Marietta	0-1
Baldwin-Wallace	8-10-3	Miami Naval	1-0
Bluffton	9-2-1	Morningside	1-0
Bradley	4-0	Morris Harvey	1-1
Bunker Hill Navy	0-2	Mount Union	3-3
Cal Poly-San Luis Obispo	1-0	Oberlin	1-1
Cal State-Los Angeles	2-0	Ohio Northern	3-5-3
Canisius	1-0	Ohio Wesleyan	5-0-2
Capital	2-4-5	Otterbein	2-0-2
Case Tech	2-0	Patterson Field	1-0
Cedarville	2-0	Quantico Marines	1-0
Dayton	16-3-1	St. Bonaventure	0-2
Defiance	10-5-1	Tampa	0-2
Detroit	1-0	Villanova	0-1
Findlay	10-2-5	Wayne State	8-1-1
Grand Valley State	2-0	Waynesburg	0-1
Grosse Isle Navy	1-0	Western Reserve	0-1-1
Heidelberg	2-3-1	Wittenberg	5-2
Hiram	4-1-2	Wooster	1-0-1
Hope	1-0	Xavier	6-2

Total Overall Record	330-202-48	.610
Total Conference Record	126-74-8	.625
Overall Bowl Game Record	0-2-0	.000

CENTRAL MICHIGAN

Nickname: Chippewas
Colors: Maroon and gold

First year of football: 1896
Year entered conference: 1975

Location: Mt. Pleasant,   Conference championships: 2
         Michigan
Stadium: Perry Shorts
        (20,000)

Mid-American Conference Competition

Ball State	12-5	Northern Illinois	19-11-1
Bowling Green	10-11	Ohio	8-2-1
Eastern Michigan	39-18-5	Toledo	9-3-1
Kent State	9-5	Western Michigan	19-34-2
Miami (of Ohio)	4-3		

Division I Competition

Akron	2-3	Louisville	0-2
Alcorn State	1-1	Marshall	2-0
Arkansas State	0-1	Michigan	0-1
Boise State	1-0	Morehead State	1-0
Delaware	1-0	Northern Iowa	4-0
Drake	1-0	Northern Michigan	26-12-1
East Carolina	1-1	Northwestern Louisiana	2-0
Eastern Illinois	20-2	Pacific	0-1
Eastern Kentucky	5-1	San Jose State	1-0
Illinois State	25-4	Southern Illinois	7-7
Indiana State	9-0	Western Illinois	11-15
Kentucky	0-1	Youngstown State	4-6-2
Louisiana Tech	1-0		

Other Opponents

Adrian	1-1	Detroit	0-5
Albion	1-3-1	Detroit (B)	1-0-1
Alma (B)	1-0	Detroit Tech	2-1
Alma College	18-13-1	Elsie Giants	4-0
Alma H.S.	1-1	Ferris State	28-6
Assumption (Ont.)	3-0	Flint M.S.D.	3-1
Baldwin-Wallace	0-1	Grand Rapids	2-1
Battle Creek Col.	0-0-1	Grand Rapids J.C.	2-0-2
Bay City H.S.	2-0	Great Lakes	1-2
Bay City J.C.	1-0	Hillsdale	8-7-1
Bay City Western H.S.	2-1	Hofstra	2-0
Bluffton	1-0	Hope	1-0
Bolling A.F.B.	0-1	Ithaca H.S.	4-0
Bradley	3-3	John Carroll	0-0-1
Cadillac H.S.	2-0	Kalamazoo	4-0
Carrolton A.C.	1-0	Lawrence Tech	1-0
Central State (Ohio)	2-0	McBain H.S.	1-0
Clare H.S.	1-0	Marion H.S.	1-0
Dayton	2-0	Michigan (B)	3-0-2
Defiance	1-0	Mich. Military Acad.	1-0
DePauw	1-0	Michigan State (B)	0-5-1
DeSales	2-0	Michigan Tech	2-0

Midland A.C.	1-0	Saginaw H.S.	1-0
Mt. Pleasant H.S.	2-2	St. Ambrose	1-0
Mt. Pleasant Indians	3-0	St. Mary's (Mich.)	4-0
Ohio Wesleyan	0-1	Traverse City H.S.	1-0
Olivet	4-0	Valparaiso	3-0
Pittsburg State	1-0	Wayne State	20-6-4
Purdue (B)	0-1	West Branch H.S.	5-0
Sag. Art'r Hills H.S.	1-0	Whitewater State	1-2
Sag. Eastern H.S.	0-1-1	Wisconsin-Milwaukee	6-1
Saginaw All Stars	0-1		

Total Overall Record	426-217-29	.655
Total Conference Record	63-17-4	.774
Overall Bowl Game Record	0-0-0	.000

EASTERN MICHIGAN

Nickname: Hurons	First year of football: 1892
Colors: Green and white	Year entered conference: 1976
Location: Ypsilanti,	Conference championships: 0
Michigan	
Stadium: Rynearson (19,280)	

Mid-American Conference Competition

Ball State	9-15-2	Northern Illinois	9-12-2
Bowling Green	7-12-1	Ohio	1-8
Central Michigan	18-39-5	Toledo	3-9
Kent State	3-7	Western Michigan	7-11-2
Miami (of Ohio)	0-5		

Division I Competition

Akron	4-8	Montana State	1-0
Arkansas State	1-2	Murray State	0-1
Eastern Illinois	10-4	North Carolina A&T	1-0
Eastern Kentucky	0-3-1	Northern Iowa	1-1
Idaho State	1-1	Northeastern	2-0
Illinois State	12-12-6	Northeastern Louisiana	1-1-1
Indiana State	9-2	Northwestern Louisiana	1-1
Kentucky State	2-1	Southern Illinois	6-6
Louisiana Tech	1-3	Weber State	1-1
McNeese State	2-1-1	Western Illinois	4-10-1
Marshall	1-1	Western Kentucky	1-1
Michigan	0-5	Youngstown State	2-5

Other Opponents

Adrian	13-3-2	Michigan Alumni	1-0
Albion	4-12	Michigan Deaf School	6-1
Allegheny	2-0	Michigan Frosh	0-7-2
Alma	12-12-2	Michigan Jr. Laws	1-0
Alumni	3-0	Michigan Lits.	1-0
Ann Arbor H.S.	2-2	Michigan Mil. Acad.	1-0
Ashland	0-1	Michigan Reserves	1-0
Assumption	9-1	Mich. Univ. Army Corps	0-1
Baldwin-Wallace	3-4	Morningside	1-0
Battle Creek Col.	1-0	Mt. Clements	0-1
Battle Creek Training	1-0	New Mexico Highlands	1-0
Case Tech	2-0	North Dakota State	0-0-1
Cleary Bus. Col.	1-1	Northern Michigan	13-7
Culver Mil. Acad.	0-1	Notre Dame (B)	2-0-1
DeKalb	1-0	Ohio Northern	0-3
DePaul	1-0	Ohio State (B)	1-0
Detroit	3-6-1	Olivet	6-3
Detroit A.C.	0-1	Orchard Lake	0-2
Detroit Bus. School	4-0	Polish Seminary	1-0
Detroit Central H.S.	0-0-1	Quantico Marines	3-0
Detroit Frosh	2-0	St. Joseph's (Ind.)	0-2
Detroit H.S.	1-0	St. Norbert	1-0
Ferris State	7-0	St. Viator	2-0
Findlay	1-2	So. Connecticut	1-0
Flint	1-0-1	South Dakota State	2-1
Fort Wayne	1-0	Tampa	0-3
Georgetown (Ky.)	1-0	Toledo A.A.	1-0
Grand Rapids J.C.	2-0	Toledo Y.	1-1-1
Great Lakes	1-0	Valparaiso	3-2
Hillsdale	15-19-1	Wayne State	21-14-3
Hope	8-6-2	Waynesburg	2-0
Iowa Teachers	4-2	Western Reserve	3-0-1
John Carroll	2-3-1	Wisconsin-Milwaukee	2-0
Kalamazoo	9-9	Wisconsin-Oshkosh	2-0
Lit. Students '96	1-0	Wittenberg	1-0
MSNC Alumni	0-0-1	Wyandotte	1-0
Michigan (B)	2-1	Ypsilanti	1-0
Michigan Agric. Col.	0-1	Ypsilanti H.S.	1-0
Michigan Agric. Col. Frosh	0-1		

Total Overall Record   324-321-43 .502
Total Conference Record   11-58-4 .178
Overall Bowl Game Record   0-0-0 .000

KENT STATE

Nickname: Golden Flashes
Colors: Blue and gold
Location: Kent, Ohio
Stadium: Dix (30,400)

First year of football: 1920
Year entered conference: 1951
Conference championships: 1

Mid-American Conference Competition

Ball State	3-5	Northern Illinois	6-10
Bowling Green	12-35-6	Ohio	13-23-1
Central Michigan	5-9	Toledo	17-14
Eastern Michigan	7-3	Western Michigan	15-18-1
Miami (of Ohio)	6-26		

Division I Competition

Air Force	1-1	Marshall	18-9
Akron	13-13-2	Navy	0-1
Bucknell	0-1	New Hampshire	0-3
Cincinnati	0-1	North Carolina State	1-0
Colorado	0-1	Northeastern Louisiana	1-0
Connecticut	2-0	Penn State	0-2
Delaware	0-1	Pittsburgh	0-1
Eastern Kentucky	0-1	San Diego State	0-2
Hawaii	1-0	Syracuse	1-1
Illinois State	2-0	Utah State	1-1
Indiana State	0-1	Virginia Tech	1-1
Iowa State	0-4	West Virginia	0-1
Kentucky	0-1	Youngstown State	0-2
Louisville	9-8		

Other Opponents

Albion	1-0	Lawrence Tech	1-0
Ashland	2-7-3	Marietta	2-1
Assumption	1-0	Morris Harvey	0-1-1
Baldwin-Wallace	9-13	Mount Union	6-6-2
Bluffton	3-0	Muskingum	0-1-1
Buffalo State	3-4	Oberlin	0-2
Capital	3-0-1	Ohio Wesleyan	1-0
Case Tech	0-2	Otterbein	4-1
Cedarville	2-0	Patterson Field	1-0
Dayton	1-0-1	Rio Grande	2-0
Defiance	1-0-1	St. Ignatius	1-1
Edinboro	1-1-1	Slippery Rock	0-2
Findlay	6-3	Tampa	0-1
Fort Belvoir	0-1	Washington & Jefferson	1-0
Heidelberg	2-5	Waynesburg	5-0
Hiram	7-3-2	West Liberty	1-3-1
Hobart	1-0	Western Reserve	4-4-1
Holbrook	1-0	Wilmington	1-1
Indiana (Pa.)	1-4-1	Wittenberg	0-1
John Carroll	4-7	Wooster	1-2
Kalamazoo	2-0	Xavier	8-5-1
Kenyon	1-1-1		

Total Overall Record	226-283-28	.447
Total Conference Record	81-132-4	.382
Overall Bowl Game Record	0-1-0	.000

MIAMI (of Ohio)

Nickname: Redskins
Colors: Red and white
Location: Oxford, Ohio
Stadium: Yager (25,500)

First year of football: 1888
Year entered conference: 1948
Conference championships: 12

Mid-American Conference Competition

Ball State	4-2-1	Northern Illinois	3-2
Bowling Green	28-11-3	Ohio	34-26-1
Central Michigan	3-4	Toledo	21-11
Eastern Michigan	5-0	Western Michigan	33-9
Kent State	26-6		

Division I Competition

Akron	2-1-1	North Carolina	1-3
Arizona State	1-0	Northwestern	3-1
Army	0-1	Notre Dame	0-1
Cincinnati	49-34-6	Ohio State	0-2
Dartmouth	0-1	Pittsburgh	0-2
Eastern Kentucky	2-0	Purdue	3-7-1
Florida	1-0	South Carolina	3-2
Georgia	1-0	Syracuse	0-1
Houston	0-2	Tennessee Tech	1-0
Illinois	0-2	Texas Tech	1-0
Indiana	3-7-1	Tulane	1-0
Kentucky	4-5-1	Vanderbilt	0-1
Marshall	28-4-1	Virginia	0-1-1
Maryland	1-0	Washington	0-1
Miami (Fla.)	0-2	Wichita State	6-0
Michigan	0-1	William and Mary	2-0
Michigan State	0-2	Yale	1-0
Murray State	2-0		

Other Opponents

Adrian	1-0	Central	0-2
Alma	2-0	Central Normal	1-0
Antioch	3-0	Centre	3-5
Arkansas A&M	0-1	Dayton	29-10-3
Ashland	1-0	Defiance	1-0
Baldwin-Wallace	1-0	Denison	15-7-2
Bethany	1-0	DePauw	3-6-1
Bradley	2-0	Detroit Tech	0-1
Buffalo	1-0	Findlay	1-0
Butler	3-3-1	George Washington	0-1
Carnegie Tech	0-1	Georgetown	8-0
Case Tech	4-1-1	Hanover	4-0

Heidelberg	1-0	Rochester	1-0
John Carroll	1-1	St. Louis	0-2
Kentucky Wesleyan	2-0	Transylvania	3-0
Kenyon	4-0	Villanova	2-1
Marietta	3-2	Wabash	4-0
Marquette	2-1	Western Reserve	6-6-1
Mount Union	11-2	Wilmington	7-0
Oberlin	9-5	Wittenberg	12-9-1
Ohio Northern	9-0	Wooster	2-2-1
Ohio Wesleyan	17-15-1	Wright Field	1-0
Otterbein	5-0	Xavier	19-10-3
Quantico Marines	1-0		

Total Overall Record	502-258-36	.653
Total Conference Record	143-57-5	.710
Overall Bowl Game Record	5-1-0	.833

NORTHERN ILLINOIS

Nickname: Huskies
Colors: Cardinal and black
Location: DeKalb, Illinois
Stadium: Huskie (30,437)

First year of football: 1899
Year entered conference: 1975
Conference championships: 1

Mid-American Conference Competition

Ball State	7-11-2	Miami (of Ohio)	2-3
Bowling Green	2-6	Ohio	7-4
Central Michigan	11-19-1	Toledo	3-13
Eastern Michigan	12-9-2	Western Michigan	3-14
Kent State	10-6		

Division I Competition

Akron	1-0	Montana	0-1
Boston College	0-1	New Mexico State	0-1
Cal State-Fullerton	1-0	North Dakota	0-1
Cal State-Long Beach	5-4	Northeast Louisiana	0-2
East Tennessee State	1-0	Northern Arizona	0-1
Eastern Illinois	23-9-1	Northern Iowa	1-2
Eastern Kentucky	0-2	Northwestern	0-2
Fresno State	1-1	San Diego State	0-4
Idaho	2-2	Southern Illinois	24-13-1
Illinois State	22-22-9	Southwest Missouri State	1-0
Indiana State	3-5	West Texas State	4-3
Kansas	1-0	Western Illinois	17-13-1
Louisville	0-1	Western Kentucky	0-1
McNeese State	0-1	Wichita State	1-1
Marshall	4-1	Wisconsin	0-5

Other Opponents

Adams State	0-1	Mankato State	1-0
American Col. of PE	1-0	Millikin	2-3
Aurora	2-0-1	Milton	2-0
Beloit	3-8	Mt. Morris	8-2-1
Belvidere	2-0	Nebraska-Omaha	7-6
Bradley	4-3	Nebraska-Peru	1-0
Buffalo	1-1	North Central	11-4-2
Butler	2-0	North Dakota State	0-2
Chicago C.C.	1-0	Northeast Missouri State	3-1
Chicago Teachers	1-0	Northwest Missouri State	1-0
Chicago Y.	0-2	St. Ambrose	0-2
Concordia	2-0	St. Bede	1-0-1
Cornell Col.	0-1	St. Joseph (Ind.)	1-0
Crane J.C.	3-0	St. Viator	3-4
Dayton	0-2	Shurtleff	0-2
DePaul	0-1	Sterling	2-1
Dixon	3-2	Valparaiso	2-1
Dubuque	1-2-1	Washburn	2-0
Elmhurst	15-0-1	Wheaton	28-10-3
Eureka	3-3	Wilson J.C.	1-0
Evansville	0-2	Winona State	2-0
Gary J.C.	0-1	Wisconsin-LaCrosse	2-0
German Pres. Sem.	0-1	Wisconsin-Milwaukee	4-4-2
Hillsdale	4-0	Wisconsin-Oshkosh	2-0
Illinois College	2-0	Wisconsin-Platteville	6-2-1
Illinois Wesleyan	2-4-1	Wisconsin-Stevens Point	4-0-1
LaSalle-Peru J.C.	1-0	Wisconsin-Whitewater	12-6-1
Lewis	1-2	Xavier	3-2
Lombard	0-1		

Total Overall Record	373-299-50	.551
Total Conference Record	31-41-2	.432
Overall Bowl Game Record	1-0-0	1.000

OHIO

Nickname: Bobcats
Colors: Green and white
Location: Athens, Ohio
Stadium: Peden (17,550)

First year of football: 1894
Year entered conference: 1947
Conference championships: 5

Mid-American Conference Competition

Ball State	4-2	Miami (of Ohio)	26-34-1
Bowling Green	23-19-1	Northern Illinois	4-7
Central Michigan	2-8-1	Toledo	18-16-1
Eastern Michigan	8-1	Western Michigan	23-17-1
Kent State	23-13-1		

Division I Competition

Akron	4-2-1	Murray State	1-1
Boston College	1-0	Navy	1-0
Boston University	1-0	North Carolina	0-1
Cincinnati	23-23-4	North Carolina State	0-1
Columbia	1-0	Northwestern	1-0
Delaware	1-1	Ohio State	0-4
Eastern Kentucky	0-1	Penn State	0-5
Florida State	0-1	Pittsburgh	0-1
Furman	1-0	Purdue	0-6
Harvard	0-3	Richmond	2-1
Idaho	1-1	Rutgers	1-0
Illinois	2-2	South Carolina	0-2
Indiana	1-4	Southern Illinois	1-0
Iowa State	0-1	Syracuse	0-2
Kansas	1-0	Tulane	1-1
Kentucky	1-0	Virginia Tech	0-2
Louisville	2-2	West Texas State	1-2
Marshall	27-7-6	West Virginia	4-10
Maryland	0-1	Western Kentucky	1-1
Michigan State	0-1	William and Mary	2-2
Minnesota	0-6-1	Youngstown State	4-1
Morehead State	1-0		

Other Opponents

Athens H.S.	1-0	Marietta	13-16-3
Bethany (W.V.)	1-3-1	Mercer Bus. Col.	2-0
Buchtel	0-1	Morris Harvey	7-0
Buckhannon	1-1	Mount Union	1-2
Buffalo	2-2	Muskingum	13-0-3
Butler	8-2-1	Nelsonville	1-0
Camp Sherman	1-0	Oberlin	1-3
Carnegie Tech	0-1	Ohio Medical	1-2
Chillicothe	1-0	Ohio Northern	6-5-1
Chillicothe Y.	1-0	Ohio State Frosh	1-0
Columbia East H.S.	1-0	Ohio Wesleyan	16-12-5
D&D Institute	2-0	Otterbein	9-7-2
Dayton	14-8	Parker H.S.	1-0-1
Dayton Y.	1-0	Parkersburg A.A.	0-1
Denison	13-8-1	Parkersburg A.C.	0-1
DePauw	1-0	Parkersburg H.S.	1-1-1
Duquesne	1-0	Parkersburg Y.	1-0-1
Franklin	2-0	Portsmouth	1-0
Gallipolis	1-0	Rio Grande	9-0
Georgetown	2-0	Simpson	1-0
Heidelberg	0-2-1	Transylvania	2-0
Indiana (Pa.)	1-0	Washington and Jefferson	0-2
John Carroll	2-0	Washington and Lee	0-1
Kentucky State	0-1	Wayne State	1-0
Kenyon	6-0-1	West Liberty	2-0-1
Lancaster	1-0	West Reston	0-1

West Virginia Wesleyan	0-2	Wittenberg	7-9-1
Western Pennsylvania	0-1	Wooster	2-2
Western Reserve	9-6-1	Xavier	11-8
Wilmington	3-1		

Total Overall Record	405-328-43	.550
Total Conference Record	123-110-7	.527
Overall Bowl Game Record	0-2-0	.000

TOLEDO

Nickname: Rockets
Colors: Blue and gold
Location: Toledo, Ohio
Stadium: Glass Bowl (18,500)

First year of football: 1917
Year entered conference: 1952
Conference championships: 6

Mid-American Conference Competition

Ball State	5-5	Miami (of Ohio)	11-21
Bowling Green	19-26-4	Northern Illinois	13-3
Central Michigan	3-9-1	Ohio	16-18-1
Eastern Michigan	9-3	Western Michigan	20-19
Kent State	14-17		

Division I Competition

Akron	2-6	New Hampshire	3-0
Arizona State	0-1	North Dakota	2-0
Boston	0-2	Richmond	3-0
Cincinnati	0-3	San Jose State	1-0
Colorado State	1-1	South Dakota	1-1
Davidson	1-0	Southern Illinois	2-0
East Carolina	2-2	Temple	2-1
Eastern Illinois	1-0	Texas-Arlington	2-0
Eastern Kentucky	3-2-2	Tulsa	1-1
Louisville	3-5	West Virginia	0-1
McNeese State	0-1	Western Carolina	1-0
Marshall	19-14-1	Wichita State	0-2
Massachusetts	1-1	William and Mary	1-0
Michigan State	0-1	Wisconsin	0-1
Minnesota	0-1	Youngstown State	4-2-1
Nevada-Las Vegas	1-0		

Other Opponents

Adrian	0-2	Bluffton	4-2
Alma	0-2-1	Bradley	7-1
Assumption	1-1	Brandeis	0-0-1
Baldwin-Wallace	6-2-1	Buffalo	3-2
Bates	2-0	Butler	1-2

Camp Shelby	1-0	Marietta	1-0
Canisius	0-2	Michigan (B)	0-1
Capital	2-2	Muskingum	4-0
Carnegie Tech	0-2	Notre Dame Reserves	0-1
Case Tech	3-1	Ohio Northern	0-3
Coast Guard	0-1	Ohio State (B)	0-1
Davis and Elkins	2-0	Ohio Wesleyan	2-0
Dayton	10-13	Oklahoma City	2-0
Defiance	6-4	Otterbein	3-0
Detroit	1-4	Pittsburg State	1-0
Detroit Tech	3-0	Quantico Marines	1-0-1
Findlay	8-2	St. Bonaventure	0-1
Fort Belvoir	0-1	St. Joseph (Ind.)	1-1
Georgetown	1-0	St. Mary's (Tex.)	2-0
Grand Rapids	1-0	Scranton	0-2
Great Lakes	1-0	Springfield	2-0
Haskell	0-0-1	Tampa	0-3
Heidelberg	1-3-1	Valparaiso	1-0
Hillsdale	3-4	Villanova	5-5
Illinois Wesleyan	2-0	Wayne State	13-8-1
Jefferson Barracks	1-0	West Liberty	1-0
John Carroll	7-6-2	Western Reserve	2-7-1
Kenyon	2-0	Wittenberg	0-1
Long Island	0-2	Wooster	0-1
Loras	0-1	Xavier	4-9

Total Overall Record	293-277-20	.514
Total Conference Record	97-115-3	.458
Overall Bowl Game Record	5-0-0	1.000

WESTERN MICHIGAN

Nickname: Broncos	First year of football: 1906
Colors: Brown and gold	Year entered conference: 1948
Location: Kalamazoo, Michigan	Conference championships: 1
Stadium: Waldo (25,000)	

Mid-American Conference Competition

Ball State	7-5	Miami (of Ohio)	9-33
Bowling Green	6-23-2	Northern Illinois	14-3
Central Michigan	34-19-2	Ohio	17-23-1
Eastern Michigan	11-7-2	Toledo	19-20
Kent State	18-15-1		

Division I Competition

Akron	1-2	Cal State-Long Beach	2-1
Arkansas State	1-1	Cincinnati	0-2
Brigham Young	2-3	Fresno State	0-1

Idaho	1-0	Northern Iowa	11-4-2
Illinois	0-1	Notre Dame	0-2
Illinois State	5-0	Pacific	1-1
Lamar	1-0	South Carolina	0-1
Louisville	2-2	Texas-Arlington	2-2
Marshall	21-7	Utah State	0-1
Michigan	0-2	West Texas State	1-3
Michigan State	2-5	Western Kentucky	11-3-1
Minnesota	0-3	Wisconsin	0-2
Montana	1-0	Youngstown State	1-0
New Mexico	0-1		

Other Opponents

Adrian	1-0	Illinois Wesleyan	2-0
Albion	14-6	Indiana (Pa.)	1-1
Alma	5-0	John Carroll	1-0-1
Baldwin-Wallace	0-0-1	Kalamazoo	3-1
Battle Creek H.S.	1-0	Lombard	1-2
Battle Creek Training	2-0	McFadden's School	1-0
Beloit	2-0	Manchester	2-0
Benton Harbor Bus. Col.	1-0	Marquette	0-1
Bradley	0-2	Michigan (B)	2-2
Bunker Hill Navy	0-1	Michigan State Frosh	1-0
Butler	10-3	Milwaukee Engineers	1-0
Camp Custer	1-0	North Central	1-1
Chicago	0-1	Notre Dame (B)	1-1
Chicago Y.	5-2-1	Notre Dame Frosh	6-2
Culver Mil. Acad.	4-1	Notre Dame Reserves	1-1
Dayton	0-1	Ohio Northern	1-0
Defiance	1-0	Oklahoma City	0-1
DePaul	1-4-1	Olivet	4-2
Detroit	0-10	Otsego Independents	1-0
Dowagiac H.S.	1-0	Ripon	2-0
Earlham	4-0	St. Thomas	0-1
Ferris State	6-0-1	St. Viator	4-1-1
Fort Sheridan	1-0	Valparaiso	7-0
Grand Rapids H.S.	1-0	Wabash	2-1
Grand Rapids Veterinary	1-0	Washington (Mo.)	9-4
Grand Valley State	2-0	Wayland H.S.	1-0
Great Lakes	0-4-1	Wayne State	7-2
Grosse Isle Navy	1-0	West Chester State	2-0
Hillsdale	2-2-2	Western Reserve	8-3-1
Hope	8-0	Wisconsin-Oshkosh	4-0
Illinois (B)	1-0	Wooster	2-0
Illinois College	3-0	Xavier	2-3

Total Overall Record	360-265-21	.574
Total Conference Record	95-132-7	.421
Overall Bowl Game Record	0-0-0	.000

Pacific Coast Conference

Formed: 1969
Charter Members: California-Santa Barbara, Fresno State, Cal
State-Long Beach, Los Angeles State, Pacific, San Diego State,
San Jose State.

Overall Records

	Years	W	L	T	Pct.
Nevada-Las Vegas	17	109	77	3	.585
Fresno State	63	348	255	26	.574
Cal State-Long Beach	30	168	134	4	.556
Utah State	87	364	301	28	.545
San Jose State	67	324	270	35	.543
New Mexico State	88	342	344	32	.499
Pacific	66	306	312	23	.495
Cal State-Fullerton	15	79	88	2	.473

Conference Records

	Years	W	L	T	Pct.
San Jose State	16	52	22	3	.695
Utah State	7	23	15	1	.603
Cal State-Long Beach	16	44	36	0	.550
Fresno State	16	37	42	0	.468
Pacific	16	29	48	1	.378
Cal State-Fullerton	10	18	34	0	.346
New Mexico State	1	2	5	0	.286
Nevada-Las Vegas	3	5	14	0	.263
San Diego State	7	27	6	1	.809
California-Santa Barbara	3	4	11	0	.267
Los Angeles State	3	0	11	0	.000
Combined bowl game record		9	10	3	.477

Total Championships

1. San Diego State	5	Utah State	2
2. San Jose State	4	7. Pacific	0
3. Cal State-Long Beach	3	Nevada-Las Vegas	0
4. Fresno State	2	New Mexico State	0
Cal State-Fullerton	2		

74

Past Champions

1984 Cal State-Fullerton*	1976 San Jose State
1983 Cal State-Fullerton	1975 San Jose State
1982 Fresno State	1974 San Diego State
1981 San Jose State	1973 San Diego State
1980 Cal State-Long Beach	1972 San Diego State
1979 Utah State	1971 Cal State-Long Beach
1978 Utah State	1970 Cal State-Long Beach
San Jose State	San Diego State
1977 Fresno State	1969 San Diego State

*Regular season champion Nevada-Las Vegas was forced to forfeit its title by special PCAA ruling.

CAL STATE-FULLERTON

Nickname: Titans
Colors: Blue, orange, and white
Location: Fullerton, California
Stadium: Santa Ana (12,000)

First year of football: 1970
Year entered conference: 1975
Conference championships: 2

Pacific Coast Conference Competition

Cal State-Long Beach	4-9	Pacific	4-6
Fresno State	7-5	San Jose State	3-8
Nevada-Las Vegas	2-7	Utah State	2-4
New Mexico State	1-0		

Division I Competition

Arizona	0-2	Northeast Louisiana	1-1
Boise State	3-4	Northern Arizona	3-2
Colorado State	1-0	Northern Illinois	0-1
Eastern Kentucky	0-1	San Diego State	0-3
Grambling State	0-2	Southern Mississippi	0-1
Hawaii	1-7	Utah	0-1
Idaho	1-0	Weber State	0-2
Idaho State	1-1	Wyoming	1-1
Nevada-Reno	5-3		

Other Opponents

Cal Poly-Pomona	5-3-1	Northridge State	9-1
Cal Poly-San Luis Obispo	5-6	Sacramento State	2-0
California-Davis	1-1	San Francisco State	1-0
California Lutheran	0-1-1	Santa Clara	2-0
California-Riverside	4-2	Southern Utah	2-0
Hayward State	2-0	U.S. International	1-1
Los Angeles State	3-2	Whittier	2-0

Total Overall Record	79-88-2	.473
Total Conference Record	18-34-0	.346
Overall Bowl Game Record	0-1-0	.000

CAL STATE-LONG BEACH

Nickname: 49ers
Colors: Brown and gold
Location: Long Beach,
    California
Stadium: Veterans (12,500)

First year of football: 1955
Year entered conference: 1969
Conference championships: 3

Pacific Coast Conference Competition

Cal State-Fullerton	9-4	Pacific	11-9
Fresno State	13-14	San Jose State	3-12
Nevada-Las Vegas	3-1	Utah State	6-2
New Mexico State	1-0		

Division I Competition

Arizona	0-1	Northern Arizona	3-3
Boise State	2-1	Northern Illinois	5-4
Bowling Green	3-0	Oregon	0-1
Brigham Young	0-5	Oregon State	1-0
Cincinnati	0-1	San Diego State	10-13
Drake	7-1	Southern Illinois	2-0
Grambling State	1-1	Southwestern Louisiana	1-1
Hawaii	4-2	Tennessee State	0-1
Kansas State	1-0	Texas-El Paso	1-1
Lamar	2-1	UCLA	0-2
Louisville	0-1-1	Utah	0-1
Mississippi	0-1	Weber State	1-0
Montana	1-0	Western Michigan	1-2
Montana State	1-0	Wichita State	3-1
Nevada-Reno	2-0	Wyoming	0-1
North Texas State	2-0-1		

Other Opponents

Cal Poly-Pomona	6-1	Northridge State	8-3
Cal Poly-San Luis Obispo	12-6	Occidental	1-1
California Baptist	1-0	Pepperdine	5-1
California-Davis	2-0	Pomona	0-1
California-Riverside	0-1	Sacramento State	6-3
California-Santa Barbara	12-5	San Diego	1-0
California Tech	1-0	San Diego Marines	0-2
Chico State	1-1	San Francisco State	3-8
Eastern Washington	0-1	Santa Clara	1-1
LaVerne	2-0	Texas A&I	1-2
Los Angeles State	6-8-2		

Total Overall Record   168-134-4 .556
Total Conference Record   44-36-0 .550
Overall Bowl Game Record   0-0-1 .000

FRESNO STATE

Nickname: Bulldogs
Colors: Cardinal and blue
Location: Fresno, California
Stadium: Bulldog (30,000)

First year of football: 1921
Year entered conference: 1969
Conference championships: 2

Pacific Coast Conference Competition

Cal State-Fullerton	6-6	Pacific	33-25-2
Cal State-Long Beach	14-13	San Jose State	20-29-3
Nevada-Las Vegas	3-3	Utah State	4-7
New Mexico State	4-0		

Division I Competition

Arizona	2-0	North Texas State	0-2
Arizona State	0-3	Northern Arizona	7-1-1
Arkansas State	2-1	Northern Illinois	1-1
Boise State	2-0	Oregon	2-0
Bowling Green	2-1	Oregon State	0-1
Brigham Young	3-1	San Diego State	15-23-4
Colorado	0-1	Southern Illinois	1-1
Colorado State	1-0	Southwestern Louisiana	1-2
Drake	0-1	Stanford	0-3
Hawaii	13-9	Texas-El Paso	2-1
Idaho	4-3	Utah	0-1
Idaho State	1-2	Washington	0-1
McNeese State	0-1-1	Weber State	2-0
Montana State	10-16	West Texas State	2-0
Nevada-Reno	16-10-1	Western Michigan	1-0
New Mexico	1-2	Wichita State	1-3

Other Opponents

Abilene Christian	2-2	Hayward State	1-1
Adams State	1-0	Humboldt State	0-1
Cal Poly-Pomona	2-2	LaVerne	4-1
Cal Poly-San Luis Obispo	29-10-2	Los Angeles State	15-3
California Christian	2-0	Loyola (Ca.)	4-2
California-Davis	11-5-1	Northridge State	8-1
California-Santa Barbara	15-4-1	Occidental	3-1
California Tech	5-0	Oklahoma City	0-2
Chico State	3-4	Olympic Club	0-1
Fresno H.S.	0-1	Pepperdine	4-2
Hardin-Simmons	0-2	Portland	1-0-1

Portland State	2-0	Santa Clara	2-9-1
Redlands	2-0	South Dakota State	1-0
Reedley H.S.	1-0	Tulare H.S.	1-0
Sacramento State	1-0	Washburn	2-1
St. Mary's (Ca.)	0-3	Whittier	7-0
San Francisco	1-5	Whitworth	1-0
San Francisco State	9-1	Willamette	3-0-1

Total Overall Record	348-255-26	.574
Total Conference Record	37-42-0	.468
Overall Bowl Game Record	2-1-0	.667

NEVADA-LAS VEGAS

Nickname: Rebels
Colors: Scarlet and gray
Location: Las Vegas, Nevada
Stadium: Silver Bowl (32,000)

First year of football: 1968
Year entered conference: 1982
Conference championships: 0

Pacific Coast Conference Competition

Cal State-Fullerton	7-2	Pacific	0-4
Cal State-Long Beach	1-3	San Jose State	1-3
Fresno State	3-3	Utah State	1-3
New Mexico State	0-1		

Division I Competition

Air Force	1-0	Northeast Louisiana	1-0
Akron	0-1	Northern Arizona	4-2
Alcorn State	1-0	Northern Iowa	1-0
Boise State	3-3	Oregon	0-1
Brigham Young	1-3	Oregon State	1-0
Colorado State	3-0-1	Prairie View A&M	1-0
Delaware	0-1	San Diego State	2-4
Hawaii	3-7	South Dakota	1-0
Idaho	2-1	Southern Methodist	0-1
Idaho State	3-3	Tennessee State	1-0
Jackson State	1-0	Texas-El Paso	4-1
Lamar	0-0-1	Toledo	0-1
Marshall	1-0	Utah	1-3
Miami (Fla.)	0-1	Washington State	0-2
Montana	4-1	Weber State	4-2
Montana State	1-0	West Texas State	0-1
Nevada-Reno	8-4	Western Illinois	1-1
New Mexico	3-2	Wichita State	0-1
North Dakota	1-1-1	Wyoming	3-1

Other Opponents

Adams State	1-0	Nebraska-Omaha	2-0
Arkansas College	1-0	New Mexico Highlands	2-0
Azusa Pacific	2-0	Northern Colorado	1-0
Cal Lutheran	0-2	Oregon Tech	1-0
Cal Poly-San Luis Obispo	1-1	St. Mary's (Ca.)	1-0
California-Riverside	1-2	San Francisco	1-0
California-San Diego	1-0	Santa Clara	4-2
California Tech	1-0	South Dakota State	2-0
Hiram Scott	1-0	Southern Colorado State	1-0
LaVerne	1-0	Southern Utah	3-0
Los Angeles State	2-1	Troy State	1-0
Mexico	1-0	Westminster (Ut.)	1-0
Missouri Southern	1-1	Wisconsin-Milwaukee	1-0

Total Overall Record   109-77-3   .585
Total Conference Record   5-14-0   .263
Overall Bowl Game Record   0-1-0   .000

NEW MEXICO STATE

Nickname: Aggies
Colors: Crimson and white
Location: Las Cruces, New
   Mexico
Stadium: Aggie Memorial
   (30,500)

First year of football: 1893
Year entered conference: 1984
Conference championships: 0

Pacific Coast Conference Competition

Cal State-Fullerton	0-1	Pacific	4-1
Cal State-Long Beach	0-1	San Jose State	0-1
Fresno State	0-4	Utah State	4-6
Nevada-Las Vegas	1-0		

Division I Competition

Arizona	5-29-1	Louisiana Tech	2-1
Arizona State	6-20-1	Montana State	1-0
Arkansas	0-1	Nebraska	0-2
Arkansas State	1-1	New Mexico	24-46-5
Colorado State	1-6	North Texas State	8-14-2
Drake	8-5	Northern Arizona	17-7-1
Florida State	0-1	Northern Illinois	1-0
Hawaii	0-1	Oklahoma State	0-1
Idaho	0-3	San Diego State	1-6-1
Illinois State	2-0	Southern Illinois	3-4
Indiana State	1-4	Southern Methodist	0-3
Lamar	6-4	Southwestern Louisiana	0-2

Texas-Arlington	12-6	Western Illinois	1-0
Texas-El Paso	27-35-2	Wichita State	16-7-1
Texas Tech	0-4	Wisconsin	0-1
Tulsa	2-13	Wyoming	0-1
West Texas State	11-20-2		

Other Opponents

Adams State	2-0	Howard Payne	3-4
Albuquerque Athletics	1-1	Kirtland Field	1-0
Albuquerque Guards	2-0	Las Cruces	1-0-1
Albuquerque Indians	3-4-2	Las Cruces H.S.	2-0
Bradley	0-3	McMurry	4-7
Cal Poly-San Luis Obispo	0-2	Mexico	3-0
California-Santa Barbara	1-1	Midwestern	0-1
Colorado College	1-0	Montezuma	3-0-1
Colorado Mines	0-2	Nebraska-Omaha	1-1
Corpus Christi	2-0	Nebraska Wesleyan	1-0
Detroit	1-0	New Mexico Highlands	9-3
Eastern Arizona J.C.	3-0	New Mexico Military	15-12-3
Eastern New Mexico	5-0	New Mexico Tech	14-0
El Paso	4-1	New Mexico Western	12-0-1
El Paso All-Stars	1-0	Northern Colorado	1-0
El Paso Athletics	6-1-1	Organ	1-0
El Paso Catholic	1-0	Panhandle State	1-0
El Paso Grocers	1-0	San Diego Marines	0-2
El Paso Guards	2-0	Santa Fe Indians	0-0-1
El Paso H.S.	15-5-3	Southwest Oklahoma	0-2
El Paso J.C.	3-0	Stephen F. Austin	0-1
El Paso Military	4-0-1	Sul Ross State	4-7
El Paso Y.	3-0	Texas Athletics	1-0
Fort Bliss	20-2-1	Trinity (Tex.)	5-2
Fort Hays State	2-0	Wayland Baptist	3-7
Garden Grocers	1-0	Western State	3-1
Hardin-Simmons	5-9-1		

Total Overall Record	342-344-32	.499
Total Conference Record	2-5-0	.286
Overall Bowl Game Record	2-0-1	.833

PACIFIC

Nickname: Tigers
Colors: Orange and black
Location: Stockton, California
Stadium: Pacific Memorial
(30,000)

First year of football: 1919
Year entered conference: 1969
Conference championships: 0

Pacific Coast Conference Competition

Cal State-Fullerton	6-4	New Mexico State	1-4
Cal State-Long Beach	9-11	San Jose State	21-32-4
Fresno State	25-33-2	Utah State	5-12
Nevada-Las Vegas	4-0		

Division I Competition

Air Force	0-3	Northern Arizona	2-0
Arizona	0-6	Northwestern	0-1
Arizona State	1-5	Notre Dame	0-1
Boise State	0-1	Oregon	3-3
Boston College	0-1	Oregon State	1-1
Boston University	1-1	Purdue	0-1
Brigham Young	3-2	San Diego State	7-14
California	3-9	South Carolina	1-2
Central Michigan	1-0	South Dakota	2-0
Cincinnati	3-5	Southern California	0-6
Clemson	1-0	Southern Methodist	0-1
Colorado State	3-7	Southern Mississippi	1-0
Hawaii	15-7	Southwestern Louisiana	2-1
Idaho	12-9-1	Stanford	1-4
Indiana	0-1	Texas-Arlington	1-0
Iowa State	1-2	Texas-El Paso	6-3
Kansas	0-0-1	Texas Tech	2-3
Kansas State	0-1-1	Tulsa	1-2
Louisiana State	0-3	UCLA	1-4
Miami (Fla.)	0-2	Utah	1-0
Miami (of Ohio)	1-1	Washington	0-4
Montana	4-2	Washington State	5-7
Montana State	1-0	West Texas State	0-4
Nevada-Reno	10-10-1	West Virginia	0-1
New Mexico	0-1	Western Michigan	1-1
North Texas State	1-1	Wichita State	1-0
Northeast Louisiana	1-0-1	Wyoming	1-1

Other Opponents

Alameda C.G.	1-2	Hardin-Simmons	1-1-1
Albany Navy	0-1	Healanis Club	0-1
Cal Poly-San Luis Obispo	5-0	Humbolt State	1-0
California-Davis	17-6-2	Invincibles	1-0
California Frosh	0-2	Los Angeles State	5-1
California Ramblers	7-1-1	Loyola (Ca.)	4-6-2
California-Santa Barbara	6-3	March Field	0-1
Camp Beale	0-2	Mare Island	2-0
Chicago	1-0	Marquette	4-3-2
Chico State	19-1	Modesto J.C.	11-0
Del Monte Pre-Flight	1-0	Monmouth	0-1
Denver	1-1	9th Army Corps	1-0
Fairfield A.F.B.	1-0	Olympic Club	0-1
Fleet City	0-1	Pacific Lutheran	0-1

Portland	2-0	Santa Barbara A.B.	0-0-1
Quantico Marines	1-0	Santa Clara	8-6
S.F. Veteran Post #49	0-1	Stanford (B)	0-1
Sacramento J.C.	6-3	Stanford Frosh	0-2
Sacramento State	2-0	Stockton A.F.B.	0-2
St. Mary's (Ca.)	2-6-1	Stockton Legion	0-2
St. Mary's Pre-Flight	2-2	USS Camden	1-0
San Benito J.C.	1-0	Villanova	1-0
San Diego	1-0	Wanderers Club	1-0
San Diego Marines	5-4-2	Whitman	1-1
San Diego Navy	0-2	Whittier	0-1
San Francisco	4-1	Willamette	1-0
San Francisco C.G.	0-1	Williams Field	1-0
San Jose Alumni	1-0	Yuma A.B.	1-0
San Mateo J.C.	1-0		

Total Overall Record	306-312-23	.495
Total Conference Record	29-48-1	.378
Overall Bowl Game Record	3-1-1	.700

SAN JOSE STATE

Nickname: Spartans
Colors: Gold and white
Location: San Jose,
    California
Stadium: Spartan (30,000)

First year of football: 1898
Year entered conference: 1969
Conference championships: 4

Pacific Coast Conference Competition

Cal State-Fullerton	9-2	New Mexico State	1-0
Cal State-Long Beach	12-3	Pacific	32-21-4
Fresno State	29-20-3	Utah State	9-8-1
Nevada-Las Vegas	3-1		

Division I Competition

Arizona	1-2	Iowa State	0-3
Arizona State	11-16	Kansas State	1-0
Baylor	1-0	Memphis State	0-1
Boise State	0-1	Montana	2-0
Brigham Young	9-4	Montana State	5-0
California	4-19	Nevada-Reno	4-4-2
Central Michigan	0-1	New Mexico	9-4-1
Colorado	0-2	North Texas State	2-1-1
Colorado State	1-1	Northern Arizona	2-0
Drake	2-0	Oregon	6-9
Hawaii	11-6	Oregon State	1-1
Houston	0-1	San Diego State	16-10-2
Idaho	8-6-1	South Dakota	1-0

Southwestern Louisiana	1-2	Washington	0-2
Stanford	7-33-1	Washington State	3-6-1
Texas-El Paso	1-0	Weber State	1-0
Texas Tech	1-0	West Texas State	0-2
Toledo	0-1	Wyoming	0-3
Utah	1-3		

Other Opponents

Alameda C.G.	1-0	Moililli (Hi.)	1-0
Alameda H.S.	1-0	Oakland H.S.	1-0
Antioch A.L.	0-1	Occidental	1-0
Bakersfield J.C.	2-0	Olympic Club	0-1
Cal Poly-Pomona	1-0	Pacific (Ore.)	1-0
Cal Poly-San Luis Obispo	8-4	Palo Alto H.S.	1-0
California-Davis	2-3-2	Pepperdine	3-0
California Ramblers	2-1	Portland	1-0
California-Santa Barbara	12-1	Puget Sound	2-0
California Seconds	1-0	Redlands	4-1
Chico State	5-8-1	Sacramento J.C.	1-4-1
Denver	3-1	St. Mary's (Ca.)	2-1
Fireman's A.C.	0-1	St. Matthew's	1-0
Fort Ord	0-0-1	San Diego Marines	1-1-1
Hardin-Simmons	1-1-1	San Diego Navy	0-1
Hollister J.C.	2-1	San Francisco	2-8
Honolulu	1-0	San Francisco State	2-0
Honolulu All-Stars	1-0-1	San Jose H.S.	0-1-2
Humboldt State	3-1	San Mateo J.C.	2-6-2
Idaho College	1-0	Santa Barbara J.C.	1-1
Kamehameha (Hi.)	2-0	Santa Clara	12-4-2
Leiluhua (Hi.)	1-0	Santa Clara H.S.	1-1
Lowell H.S.	1-0	Santa Clara Prep	1-0
Loyola (Ca.)	2-2	Santa Rosa J.C.	3-2
McClellan Field	1-0	Stanford Frosh	0-1
McKinley (Hi.)	1-0	Stanford Grays	0-1
Marin J.C.	2-0	Stockton H.S.	1-0
Marquette	0-1	Texas A&I	2-1
Mexico	2-0	Whittier	1-1-1
Modesto J.C.	1-7-1	Willamette	4-2
Moffet Field	0-1		

Total Overall Record	324-270-35	.543
Total Conference Record	52-22-3	.695
Overall Bowl Game Record	2-2-0	.500

UTAH STATE

Nickname: Aggies	First year of football: 1892
Colors: Blue and white	Year entered conference: 1978
Location: Logan, Utah	Conference championships: 2
Stadium: Romney (30,250)	

Pacific Coast Conference Competition

Cal State-Fullerton	4-2	New Mexico State	6-4
Cal State-Long Beach	2-6	Pacific	12-5
Fresno State	7-4	San Jose State	8-9-1
Nevada-Las Vegas	3-1		

Division I Competition

Air Force	0-1	Montana State	21-4-5
Arizona	2-3	Nebraska	0-3
Arizona State	3-7	Nevada-Reno	2-4
Arkansas	0-2	New Mexico	6-8
Army	1-0	Oklahoma	0-2
Baylor	0-1	Oregon	0-1
Boise State	2-1	Oregon State	0-1
Bowling Green	2-0	Penn State	0-1
Brigham Young	32-25-3	San Diego State	1-9
Colorado	6-10-1	Southern California	0-3
Colorado State	30-32-2	Southern Mississippi	1-2
Drake	1-0	Stanford	0-1
Florida State	0-1	Texas	0-3
Hawaii	4-1	Texas Christian	0-2-1
Houston	0-1	Texas-El Paso	2-0
Idaho	11-11-2	UCLA	0-1
Idaho State	8-1	Utah	26-52-4
Iowa	0-1	Washington	0-1
Kansas State	2-1	Washington State	1-2
Kent State	1-1	Weber State	9-1
Kentucky	1-1	West Texas State	5-0
Memphis State	3-4	Western Michigan	1-0
Miami (Fla.)	0-1	Wichita State	6-6-2
Missouri	0-1	Wisconsin	1-0
Montana	26-8	Wyoming	34-20-4

Other Opponents

All Hallows	1-0	Logan All-Stars	3-1
Alumni	2-0	Montana Mines	11-0
Brigham Young Acad.	2-2	Montana Wesleyan	1-0
Colorado College	3-0	Ogden A.C.	2-0
Colorado Mines	5-4	Ogden H.S.	2-0
Denver	13-19-3	Pacific Fleet	1-0
Fort Douglas	2-0	Regis	1-0
Gonzaga	0-1	St. Vincent's	0-1
Granite H.S.	1-0	Salt Lake City H.S.	2-0
Idaho Acad.	2-0	Utah Field Artil.	1-0
Idaho College	3-0	West H.S.	1-0
Idaho Marines	5-0	Western State	7-0

Total Overall Record	364-301-28	.545
Total Conference Record	23-15-1	.603
Overall Bowl Game Record	0-4-0	.000

Pacific Ten Conference

Formed: 1916
Charter Members: California, Oregon, Oregon State, Washington.
Former Members: Idaho, Montana.

Overall Records

	Years	W	L	T	Pct.
Southern California	95	565	213	49	.713
Stanford	91	524	298	48	.630
Washington	95	490	278	47	.630
Arizona State	71	380	220	21	.629
UCLA	66	368	246	34	.594
Arizona	81	391	272	28	.586
California	102	379	304	31	.553
Oregon	88	381	356	47	.516
Washington State	88	356	344	43	.508
Oregon State	87	370	366	47	.503

Conference Records

	Years	W	L	T	Pct.
Southern California	62	256	92	25	.720
UCLA	57	205	124	17	.617
Arizona State	7	28	21	1	.570
Washington	69	234	184	22	.557
Arizona	7	27	23	2	.538
Stanford	64	194	168	20	.534
California	69	195	189	17	.507
Washington State	62	166	206	24	.449
Oregon	62	147	215	20	.411
Oregon State	62	148	226	22	.402
Idaho	35	30	123	5	.206
Montana	24	9	79	3	.115
Combined bowl game record:		54	47	5	.533

Total Championships

1. Southern California	26	6. Oregon State	4
2. California	13	Oregon	4
3. UCLA	12	8. Washington State	2
4. Stanford	10	9. Arizona State	0
Washington	10	Arizona	0

Past Champions

1984	Southern California	1948	Oregon	
1983	UCLA		California	
1982	UCLA	1947	Southern California	
1981	Washington	1946	UCLA	
1980	Washington	1945	Southern California	
1979	Southern California	1944	Southern California	
1978	Southern California*	1943	Southern California	
1977	Washington	1942	UCLA	
1976	Southern California	1941	Oregon State	
1975	UCLA	1940	Stanford	
	California	1939	Southern California	
1974	Southern California	1938	California	
1973	Southern California		Southern California	
1972	Southern California	1937	California	
1971	Stanford	1936	Washington	
1970	Stanford	1935	California	
1969	Southern California		Stanford	
1968	Southern California**		UCLA	
1967	Southern California	1934	Stanford	
1966	Southern California	1933	Oregon	
1965	UCLA		Stanford	
1964	Oregon State	1932	Southern California	
	Southern California	1931	Southern California	
1963	Washington	1930	Washington State	
1962	Southern California	1929	Southern California	
1961	UCLA	1928	Southern California	
1960	Washington	1927	Southern California	
1959	Washington***		Stanford	
	Southern California	1926	Stanford	
	UCLA	1925	Washington	
1958	California	1924	Stanford	
1957	Oregon State	1923	California	
	Oregon	1922	California	
1956	Oregon State	1921	California	
1955	UCLA	1920	California	
1954	UCLA	1919	Washington	
1953	UCLA		Oregon	
1952	Southern California	1918	California	
1951	Stanford	1917	Washington State	
1950	California	1916	Washington****	
1949	California			

*Pacific Ten Conference
**Pacific Eight Conference
***Athletic Association of Western Universities
****Pacific Coast Conference

ARIZONA

Nickname: Wildcats
Colors: Cardinal and navy
Location: Tucson, Arizona
Stadium: Arizona (51,950)

First year of football: 1899
Year entered conference: 1978
Conference championships: 0

Pacific Ten Conference Competition

Arizona State	32-26	Stanford	3-2
California	2-3-1	UCLA	3-5-2
Oregon	6-7	Washington	0-5
Oregon State	8-1	Washington State	8-5
Southern California	1-11		

Division I Competition

Air Force	3-6	Nevada-Reno	1-1-1
Auburn	1-2	New Mexico	40-18-3
Brigham Young	10-8-1	New Mexico State	29-5-1
Cal State-Fullerton	2-0	Northern Arizona	5-1
Cal State-Long Beach	1-0	Northwestern	2-0
Colorado	0-11	Notre Dame	1-2
Colorado State	12-2-1	Ohio State	1-0
Drake	1-1	Oklahoma State	3-3
Fresno State	0-2	Pacific	6-0
Hawaii	3-0	Pittsburgh	0-1
Houston	0-1	Rice	0-4
Idaho	8-2	San Diego State	6-5
Indiana	2-2	San Jose State	2-1
Iowa	5-3	Southern Methodist	0-1
Iowa State	4-1-1	Syracuse	0-1
Kansas	2-3-1	Texas	0-1
Kansas State	5-1-1	Texas A&M	0-1
Louisiana State	0-1	Texas-El Paso	34-11-2
Michigan	0-2	Texas Tech	3-25-2
Michigan State	0-3	Tulsa	0-2
Minnesota	0-1	Utah	13-16-2
Missouri	0-3	Utah State	3-2
Montana	4-1	West Texas State	9-2-1
Nebraska	0-0-1	Wyoming	12-10

Other Opponents

Arizona Indians	2-0	Centenary	3-2-1
Bisbie Legion	1-0	Centre	0-1
California-Davis	1-1	Denver	1-1
California Tech	2-0	DePaul	1-0
Camp Jones	1-0	Douglas Y.	3-0

Eastern Arizona J.C.	1-0	Pomona	6-4
El Paso Military	2-0	Redlands	1-0
Fort G. Wright	0-1	St. Mary's (Ca.)	1-1
Fort Grant	1-0	Santa Clara	1-2-1
Fort Huachua	2-0	Silver City	0-1
Hardin-Simmons	4-6	Soldiers	1-0
Loyola (Ca.)	4-5	South Dakota State	1-0
Marquette	4-6	Tombstone	1-0-1
New Mexico Militia	1-0	Tucson A.C.	1-0
Occidental	5-3-1	Tucson H.S.	5-0
Officers	0-1	Tucson Indians	16-0-1
Oklahoma City	2-0	Tucson Town	2-0-1
Phoenix H.S.	0-1	22nd Infantry	2-0
Phoenix Indians	10-2	U.S. Infantry	1-0
Phoenix J.C.	2-0	Whittier	9-3
Prescott H.S.	1-0	Williams Field	1-0

Total Overall Record	391-272-28	.586
Total Conference Record	27-23-2	.538
Overall Bowl Game Record	0-4-0	.000

ARIZONA STATE

Nickname: Sun Devils
Colors: Maroon and gold
Location: Tempe, Arizona
Stadium: Sun Devil (70,021)

First year of football: 1897
Year entered conference: 1978
Conference championships: 0

Pacific Ten Conference Competition

Arizona	26-32	Stanford	4-2
California	4-4	UCLA	0-5-1
Oregon	6-0	Washington	2-4
Oregon State	9-6	Washington State	7-5-1
Southern California	3-2		

Division I Competition

Air Force	2-2	Minnesota	1-0
Arkansas	0-1	Missouri	1-2
Brigham Young	18-5	Montana State	2-0
Cincinnati	0-2	Nebraska	1-0
Colorado State	17-1	Nevada-Reno	0-2
Florida State	1-3	New Mexico	22-5-1
Fresno State	3-0	New Mexico State	20-6-1
Hawaii	5-1	North Carolina	1-0
Houston	5-2	North Carolina State	1-1
Idaho	5-0	North Dakota	1-0
Kansas State	4-0	North Texas State	2-1
Miami (of Ohio)	0-1	Northern Arizona	16-14-4

Northwestern	2-0	Texas Christian	2-0
Ohio State	0-1	Texas-El Paso	30-13-3
Oklahoma	1-0	Toledo	0-1
Oklahoma State	0-1	Utah	12-6
Pacific	5-1	Utah State	7-3
Penn State	0-1	West Texas State	13-7
Pittsburgh	1-0	West Virginia	1-0
Rutgers	1-0	Wichita State	8-2-1
San Diego State	6-0-1	Wisconsin	2-0
San Jose State	16-11	Wyoming	9-6

Other Opponents

Abilene Christian	0-1	Phoenix Indians	11-6-1
Albuquerque A.F.B.	0-1	Phoenix Indians Alumni	1-1
Arizona All-Stars	1-0	Phoenix Indians 2nd Team	1-0
Arizona Frosh	4-1	Phoenix J.C.	5-3
California-Davis	4-0	Phoenix Union H.S.	9-5-1
California-Santa Barbara	1-1	Portland	0-1
California Tech	2-0	Prescott H.S.	1-1
Case Western Reserve	0-1	Sacaton Indians	3-0
Catholic	0-0-1	Sacramento J.C.	0-1
Detroit	2-0	San Diego Marines	0-3
Eastern Arizona J.C.	4-0	San Diego Navy	1-2
Fullerton J.C.	1-0	San Francisco	0-1
Glendale H.S.	1-0	Santa Ana A.F.B.	0-1
Gonzaga	1-0-1	Sherman Indians	0-0-1
Hardin-Simmons	8-13	Tempe H.S.	1-2
Loyola Marymount	0-6	Texas A&I	0-1
Marquette	1-0	Wayne State	1-0
Mesa H.S.	1-1	Western State	1-0
Midwestern State	1-1-1	Whittier	3-2-1
Northern Colorado	2-0	Williams A.F.B.	0-0-1
Pepperdine	3-1	Xavier	0-1

Total Overall Record	380-220-21	.629
Total Conference Record	28-21-1	.570
Overall Bowl Game Record	7-4-1	.625

CALIFORNIA

Nickname: Golden Bears	First year of football: 1886
Colors: Blue and gold	Year entered conference: 1916
Location: Berkeley, California	Conference championships: 13
Stadium: Memorial (75,660)	

Pacific Ten Conference Competition

Arizona	3-2-1	Oregon	31-18-2
Arizona State	4-4	Oregon State	25-16

Southern California	23-45-4	Washington	32-31-4
Stanford	36-41-10	Washington State	32-14-4
UCLA	19-35-1		

Division I Competition

Air Force	4-1	Nebraska	0-1
Alabama	1-1	Nevada-Reno	21-1-1
Arkansas	0-1	Northwestern	0-1
Army	2-4	Notre Dame	0-4
Baylor	0-2	Ohio State	1-5
Colorado	2-2	Oklahoma	0-2
Duke	0-1-1	Pacific	9-3
Florida	0-2	Penn State	1-3
Georgia	0-2	Pennsylvania	7-0
Georgia Tech	4-3	Pittsburgh	2-3
Hawaii	1-1	Rice	1-1
Idaho	4-0	San Diego State	1-1
Illinois	1-5	San Jose State	19-4
Indiana	2-0	Southern Methodist	0-1
Iowa	0-3	Syracuse	1-1
Iowa State	1-0	Temple	0-1
Kansas	1-2	Tennessee	1-0
Miami (Fla.)	1-0	Texas	0-4
Michigan	2-6	Texas A&M	1-1
Michigan State	0-2	Tulane	0-1
Minnesota	2-1	Utah	3-1
Missouri	3-2-1	West Virginia	2-1
Montana	5-0	Wisconsin	3-1
Navy	3-1		

Other Opponents

Alameda C.G.	0-1	League of the Cross	1-0
Alumni	1-0	Los Angeles A.C.	1-0
Alumni Club	4-0	Lowell H.S.	2-0
Berkeley Gym	1-0	Mare Island	3-2
Cal Poly-Pomona	3-0	Mather Field	0-1
California-Davis	8-0	Multnomah Club	3-0
Carlisle	0-1	Occidental	2-1
Chemawa Indians	1-0	Olympic Club	31-6-5
Coast Guard	0-1	Originals	3-0
Coast Naval Academy	1-0	Orions	1-1
Commercial Club	0-1	Pacific Fleet	1-0
Del Monte Pre-Flight	0-1	Perris Indians	2-0
Fleet City	0-1	Posens	5-0
Fort MacDowell	0-1	Redlands H.S.	1-0
Fort Scott	1-0	Reliance Club	15-6-9
Honolulu	0-1	St. Mary's (Ca.)	28-8-2
Hopkins A.C.	1-0	St. Mary's Pre-Flight	2-1
Hospital Corp.	1-0	St. Vincent	1-0
Iowa Volunteers	0-0-1	San Diego H.S.	1-0
Kansas Volunteers	1-0	San Francisco	2-0

San Francisco All-Stars	1-0	Volunteers	1-1
San Francisco Club	4-1	Washington and Jefferson	0-0-1
San Francisco Parsido	1-0	Washington Volunteers	2-0
San Pedro Navy	1-0	Wasps	4-0
Santa Clara	17-5	West Coast Navy	1-0
Sherman Indians	3-0	Whittier	2-0
Southern California A.C.	1-0	Willamette	0-0-1

Total Overall Record	379-304-31	.553
Total Conference Record	195-189-17	.507
Overall Bowl Game Record	2-6-1	.278

OREGON

Nickname: Ducks	First year of football: 1894
Colors: Green and yellow	Year entered conference: 1916
Location: Eugene, Oregon	Conference championships: 4
Stadium: Autzen (41,010)	

Pacific Ten Conference Competition

Arizona	7-6	Stanford	16-33-1
Arizona State	0-6	UCLA	14-29
California	18-31-2	Washington	26-47-5
Oregon State	41-37-10	Washington State	27-29-7
Southern California	9-26-2		

Division I Competition

Air Force	6-4-1	Michigan	0-3
Army	0-0-2	Michigan State	1-1
Boston	0-1	Minnesota	0-2
Brigham Young	2-1	Missouri	0-1
Cal State-Long Beach	1-0	Montana	5-0-1
Colorado	4-5	Montana State	1-0
Colorado State	1-0	Nebraska	1-3
Drake	1-0	Nevada-Las Vegas	1-0
Florida	0-1	Nevada-Reno	0-1
Fresno State	0-2	North Dakota	0-0-1
Georgia	0-1	Northwestern	0-1
Harvard	0-1	Notre Dame	0-1-1
Hawaii	4-0	Ohio State	0-6
Houston	1-0	Oklahoma	0-4
Idaho	48-3-4	Pacific	3-3
Illinois	0-1	Penn State	1-2
Indiana	2-0	Pennsylvania	1-0
Iowa	0-1	Pittsburgh	3-1
Kansas	0-1-1	Purdue	0-1
Louisiana State	1-2	Rice	1-0
Miami (Fla.)	0-1	San Jose State	9-6

Southern Methodist	1-1	Utah State	1-0
Texas	0-4	West Virginia	2-0
Texas Christian	1-1	Wisconsin	0-2
Utah	14-5		

Other Opponents

Albany	3-0-2	Oregon Normal	2-0
Alumni	6-0	Pacific (Ore.)	14-0-2
Bremerton Navy	1-0	Pearl Harbor	1-0
California-Santa Barbara	1-0	Pendleton H.S.	1-0
Camp Lewis	1-0	Portland	5-1
Capital A.C.	0-1	Puget Sound	1-0
Chemawa Indians	5-0	St. Mary's (Ca.)	3-7
Fordham	0-1	St. Mary's Pre-Flight	0-1
Foundation	1-0	San Diego Marines	2-0
Gonzaga	5-1	San Francisco	1-0
Honolulu	1-0	Santa Clara	2-0
Linfield	3-0	Southern Oregon	2-0
Mare Island	0-1	Vancouver Barracks	1-0
Multnomah A.C.	11-19-4	Whitman	7-2
New York	1-0	Whitworth	1-1
Oregon Medics	1-0	Willamette	22-1-1

Total Overall Record	381-356-47	.516
Total Conference Record	147-215-20	.411
Overall Bowl Game Record	2-4-0	.333

OREGON STATE

Nickname: Beavers
Colors: Orange and black
Location: Corvallis, Oregon
Stadium: Parker (40,600)

First year of football: 1893
Year entered conference: 1916
Conference championships: 4

Pacific Ten Conference Competition

Arizona	1-8	Stanford	15-35-2
Arizona State	6-9	UCLA	9-24-4
California	16-25	Washington	24-42-4
Oregon	37-41-10	Washington State	36-34-3
Southern California	7-41-4		

Division I Competition

Auburn	0-1	Colorado State	1-1
Baylor	2-0	Columbia	3-0
Brigham Young	4-3	Duke	1-0
Cal State-Long Beach	0-1	Fresno State	1-0
Colorado	3-1	Georgia	0-2

Grambling State	0-1	Nevada-Reno	1-0
Hawaii	3-1	New Mexico	0-1
Houston	1-2	Northwestern	1-3
Idaho	33-7	Ohio State	0-2
Illinois	1-0	Oklahoma	1-1
Indiana	2-1	Pacific	1-1
Iowa	5-7	Purdue	1-0
Iowa State	1-0	San Diego State	0-2
Kansas	2-2	San Jose State	0-2
Kansas State	0-1	Southern Methodist	0-2
Kentucky	0-2	Syracuse	3-5
Louisiana State	0-3	Tennessee	0-1-1
Michigan	0-3	Texas	0-1
Michigan State	2-6-1	Texas Tech	0-1
Minnesota	1-2	Utah	8-2-1
Missouri	1-0	Utah State	1-0
Montana	12-0-2	West Virginia	2-0
Nebraska	2-7	Wisconsin	0-1
Nevada-Las Vegas	0-1	Wyoming	1-2

Other Opponents

A.C. Jrs.	1-0	McMinnville	1-0
Albany A.C.	1-0	Marquette	1-0
Albany Col.	3-1	Monmouth	3-0
Ashland Normal	1-0	Multnomah A.C.	7-11-4
Astoria A.C.	1-0	New York	1-0
California-Davis	4-0	Occidental	1-0
Camp Beale	0-0-1	Oregon Normal	1-0
Camp Lewis	0-1	Pacific (Ore.)	12-0-2
Carnegie Tech	0-1-1	Portland	7-2
Catholic Y.	1-0	Portland Meds	1-0
Chemawa Indians	4-1	Portland State	1-0
Columbia A.C.	2-0	Puget Sound	1-0
Detroit	1-1	St. Vincent	1-0
Field Hospital Corps	2-0	San Francisco	1-1
Fordham	2-0	Santa Clara	0-1
Forest Grove	0-0-1	Standifer Ship.	1-0
Fort Vancouver	1-0	Villanova	1-0
Gonzaga	6-0-1	West Coast Army	1-0
Hawaiian All-Stars	1-1	Whitman	12-0
Linfield	2-0	Willamette	21-2

Total Overall Record	370-366-47	.503
Total Conference Record	148-226-22	.402
Overall Bowl Game Record	2-2-0	.500

SOUTHERN CALIFORNIA

Nickname: Trojans
Colors: Cardinal and gold

First year of football: 1888
Year entered conference: 1923

Location: Los Angeles,   Conference championships: 26
           California
Stadium: L.A. Coliseum
         (92,000)

Pacific Ten Conference Competition

Arizona	11-1	Stanford	42-18-3
Arizona State	2-3	UCLA	30-18-6
California	45-23-4	Washington	35-19-3
Oregon	26-9-2	Washington State	38-4-4
Oregon State	41-7-4		

Division I Competition

Alabama	2-4	Nevada-Reno	5-0
Arkansas	2-1	North Carolina	0-1
Army	2-0	Northwestern	4-0
Baylor	1-1	Notre Dame	23-29-4
Clemson	1-0	Ohio State	9-9-1
Colorado	3-0	Oklahoma	3-2-1
Duke	3-0	Pacific	6-0
Florida	0-1-1	Penn State	1-1
Georgia	3-0	Pittsburgh	6-4
Georgia Tech	2-1	Purdue	2-1
Hawaii	3-0	Rice	2-0-1
Idaho	7-0	South Carolina	1-1
Illinois	7-1	Southern Methodist	2-0
Indiana	4-0	Syracuse	1-0
Iowa	6-2	Tennessee	4-0
Kansas	0-1	Texas	4-0
Louisiana State	1-1	Texas A&M	3-0
Miami (Fla.)	1-1	Texas Christian	2-2
Michigan	3-3	Texas Tech	2-0
Michigan State	4-1	Tulane	2-1
Minnesota	4-1-1	Utah	5-2
Missouri	2-1	Utah State	3-0
Montana	5-0	West Virginia	1-0
Navy	2-1	Wisconsin	6-0
Nebraska	1-0-1	Wyoming	1-0

Other Opponents

Alliance A.C.	2-0	Fort MacArthur	1-0
Alumni	2-0	Kamehameha	1-0
Arrowhead A.C.	1-0	Long Beach Poly H.S.	1-0
Cal Poly-San Luis Obispo	1-0	Los Angeles A.C.	3-1
California Tech	12-1-1	Los Angeles H.S.	4-3-3
Carnegie Tech	1-0	Los Angeles Poly H.S.	1-0
Chaffey	1-1	Loyola (Ca.)	6-3-1
Chaffey H.S.	1-0	March Field	0-1
Chow-Sir Club	1-0	Mare Island	0-1
Denver	1-0	National Guard	1-0

Normal School	1-0	Santa Ana H.S.	1-0
Occidental	16-5-2	Santa Barbara A.C.	0-1
Olive Club	0-1	Santa Clara	3-0
Orange A.C.	2-0	Santa Fe A.C.	1-0
Pasadena	1-0	7th Regiment	1-0
Pasadena A.C.	1-0	Sherman Indians	1-3-1
Perris Indians	0-1	Southern California Acad.	1-0
Phoenix Indians	1-0	Southern California Prep	1-0
Pomona	13-4-4	Sub Base	1-0
Redlands	4-0	21st Infantry	1-0
St. Mary's (Ca.)	5-4	USS Arizona	1-0
St. Mary's Pre-Flight	4-0	USS Colorado	1-0
San Diego H.S.	1-0	USS Mississippi	1-0
San Diego Navy	3-2	USS New York	1-0
San Diego Y.	0-1	Venture	1-0
San Francisco	1-0	Whittier	11-1
Santa Ana	1-2	Whittier Reform	3-1-1

Total Overall Record	565-213-49	.713
Total Conference Record	256-92-25	.720
Overall Bowl Game Record	21-7-0	.750

STANFORD

Nickname: Cardinals
Colors: Cardinal and white
Location: Stanford, California
Stadium: Stanford (84,800)

First year of football: 1891
Year entered conference: 1918
Conference championships: 10

Pacific Ten Conference Competition

Arizona	2-3	Southern California	21-42-3
Arizona State	2-4	UCLA	23-29-3
California	41-36-10	Washington	31-25-4
Oregon	33-16-1	Washington State	20-17-1
Oregon State	35-15-2		

Division I Competition

Air Force	4-3	Harvard	1-0
Alabama	0-1-1	Hawaii	3-0
Arkansas	1-0	Idaho	6-1
Army	5-5	Illinois	6-4
Boston College	1-1	Kansas	1-0
Colorado	1-1	Louisiana State	1-0
Columbia	0-2-1	Michigan	3-6-1
Dartmouth	4-0	Michigan State	1-3
Duke	1-1	Minnesota	1-1-1
Fresno State	3-0	Missouri	1-0
Georgia	1-0	Montana	3-0

Navy	0-1-1	Purdue	1-3
Nebraska	1-0	Rice	1-3
Nevada-Reno	16-1-2	San Jose State	33-7-1
Northwestern	2-1-1	Southern Methodist	1-0
Notre Dame	1-3	Tulane	7-1
Ohio State	3-2	Utah	2-0
Oklahoma	1-3	Utah State	1-0
Pacific	4-1	West Virginia	1-0
Penn State	0-4	Wisconsin	0-2
Pittsburgh	1-2		

Other Opponents

All-Seattle	1-0	Pacific Fleet	0-1
Alumni	3-1	Pensacola	3-0
Berkeley Gym	1-0	Port Townsend	1-0
California-Davis	1-0	Reliance Club	18-3-2
California Tech	3-0	Sacramento Club	1-0
Chemawa Indians	1-0	St. Mary's (Ca.)	2-1
Chicago	1-1	St. Mary's Pre-Flight	1-0
15th Infantry	1-0	St. Vincent	1-0
Fort Baker	1-0	San Francisco	6-0
Hopkins Acad.	1-0	Santa Clara	22-11-2
Iowa Volunteers	0-1	Santa Cruz	1-0
Kansas Volunteers	2-0	Sherman Indians	2-1
League of the Cross	1-0	Tacoma	1-0
Los Angeles A.C.	1-0	U.S. Marines	1-0
Mare Island	1-1	USS Boston	1-0
Mather Field	0-1	Washington Volunteers	1-0
Multnomah A.C.	2-1-2	West Coast Army	5-0
Occidental	4-0	Willamette	1-0
Olympic Club	31-12-8	Y.M.I.	0-1

Total Overall Record	524-298-48	.630
Total Conference Record	194-168-20	.534
Overall Bowl Game Record	7-5-1	.577

UCLA

Nickname: Bruins	First year of football: 1919
Colors: Blue and gold	Year entered conference: 1928
Location: Los Angeles,	Conference championships: 12
California	
Stadium: Rose Bowl (104,090)	

Pacific Ten Conference Competition

Arizona	5-3-2	Oregon	29-14
Arizona State	5-0-1	Oregon State	24-9-4
California	35-19-1	Southern California	18-30-6

Stanford	29-23-3	Washington State	26-8-1
Washington	22-23-1		

Division I Competition

Air Force	6-4-1	Missouri	2-0-1
Alabama	0-1	Montana	7-0
Arkansas	0-0-1	Nebraska	3-3
Brigham Young	0-1	North Carolina State	2-0
Cal State-Long Beach	2-0	Northwestern	2-3
Colorado	4-0	Notre Dame	0-2
Colorado State	4-0	Ohio State	3-3-1
Drake	0-1	Pacific	4-1
Duke	1-0	Penn State	4-2
Florida	2-2	Pittsburgh	9-5
Fresno State	2-0	Purdue	3-0-2
Georgia	0-2	Rice	2-0
Hawaii	2-0	San Diego State	7-0-1
Houston	0-2	Southern Methodist	0-4
Idaho	6-1	Syracuse	2-6
Illinois	2-5	Tennessee	3-3-1
Iowa	6-2	Texas	0-2
Iowa State	1-1	Texas A&M	1-2
Kansas	4-1	Texas Christian	3-1
Maryland	1-1	Utah	7-0
Miami (Fla.)	1-0	Utah State	1-0
Michigan	2-5	Vanderbilt	1-0
Michigan State	3-3	Wisconsin	7-1
Minnesota	1-2		

Other Opponents

Alameda C.G.	1-0	March Field	0-2
Bakersfield H.S.	0-1	Occidental	4-6
California-Davis	2-0	Occidental Frosh	1-1
California-Santa Barbara	3-0	Pomona	8-5-1
California Tech	5-6-1	Redlands	4-3-1
Camp Haan	1-0	St. Mary's (Ca.)	7-5
Del Monte Pre-Flight	0-1	St. Mary's Pre-Flight	0-3
Hollywood H.S.	0-1	San Diego Marines	1-0
Honolulu	1-0	San Diego N.T.C.	1-0
LaVerne	2-1	San Diego Navy	1-2
Los Angeles J.C.	2-1	Santa Clara	3-3-1
Loyola (Ca.)	4-0-1	USS Idaho	0-1
Manual Arts H.S.	0-1	Whittier	1-6-1

Total Overall Record	368-246-34	.594
Total Conference Record	205-124-17	.617
Overall Bowl Game Record	5-7-1	.423

WASHINGTON

Nickname: Huskies
Colors: Purple and gold
Location: Seattle, Washington
Stadium: Husky (59,800)

First year of football: 1889
Year entered conference: 1916
Conference championships: 10

Pacific Ten Conference Competition

Arizona	5-0	Southern California	19-35-3
Arizona State	4-2	Stanford	25-31-4
California	31-32-4	UCLA	23-22-1
Oregon	47-26-5	Washington State	49-22-6
Oregon State	42-24-4		

Division I Competition

Air Force	2-3	Nebraska	1-1-1
Alabama	0-3	Nevada-Reno	1-0
Baylor	1-3	Northwestern	3-0
Cincinnati	1-0	Notre Dame	0-2
Colorado	2-2-1	Ohio State	1-4
Dartmouth	0-1	Oklahoma	1-0
Duke	1-1	Oklahoma State	1-0
Fresno State	1-0	Pacific	4-0
Hawaii	1-1	Penn State	0-2
Houston	1-0	Pittsburgh	1-4
Idaho	30-2-2	Purdue	2-1-1
Illinois	5-4	Rice	0-0-1
Indiana	0-2	San Diego State	1-0
Iowa	2-2	San Jose State	2-0
Iowa State	1-0	Syracuse	1-1
Kansas	1-0	Texas	1-2
Kansas State	3-0	Texas A&M	0-1
Louisiana State	0-1	Texas Christian	1-0
Maryland	1-0	Texas-El Paso	1-0
Miami (of Ohio)	1-0	Texas Tech	2-0
Michigan	3-5	Utah	6-0
Michigan State	1-1	Utah State	1-0
Minnesota	7-10	Virginia	1-0
Mississippi State	1-0	Wisconsin	3-0
Montana	16-1-1	Wyoming	1-0
Navy	3-2-1		

Other Opponents

Aberdeen H.S.	1-0	Ballard Meteors	2-0
All-Navy	1-0	Bremerton Navy	1-0
All-Seattle	1-0-1	Bremerton Sailors	1-0
Alumni	1-0	Bremerton Sub.	1-0

California-Santa Barbara	1-0	Seattle Y.	2-0
Chemawa Indians	2-0	Second Air Force	0-1
Chicago	0-1	Sherman Indians	1-0
Everett A.C.	1-0	Spokane Air Command	2-0
Everett H.S.	1-0	Tacoma A.C.	1-1
Fort Worden	1-0	Vashon	3-0
Gonzaga	3-0	Viciendas	1-0
Honolulu	1-0	Washington College	0-0-1
Lincoln H.S.	4-0	Washington H.S.	1-0
March Field	1-1	Washington Park A.C.	2-0
Multnomah A.C.	1-5	West Seattle A.C.	3-0
Navy Pre-Flight	0-0-1	Whitman	29-2-3
9th Army Corps	1-0	Whitworth	5-0
Pacific (Ore.)	1-0	Willamette	9-0-1
Pacific Fleet	1-0	Willson Bus. Col.	1-0
Pt. Townsend A.C.	1-2-2	USS Chicago	1-0
Pt. Townsend H.S.	1-0	USS Idaho	3-0
Puget Sound	13-0	USS Maryland	1-0
Puyallup Indians	1-1	USS Milwaukee	1-0
Queen Anne H.S.	1-0	USS Mississippi	1-0
Rainier Valley A.C.	1-0	USS Nebraska	0-1
St. Mary's (Ca.)	1-1	USS New York	2-0
Santa Clara	1-0	USS Oklahoma	1-0
Seattle A.C.	3-4-2	USS Philadelphia	1-0
Seattle H.S.	2-0-1	USS Tennessee	1-0

Total Overall Record	490-278-47	.630
Total Conference Record	234-184-22	.557
Overall Bowl Game Record	7-6-1	.536

WASHINGTON STATE

Nickname: Cougars	First year of football: 1893
Colors: Crimson and gray	Year entered conference: 1917
Location: Pullman, Washington	Conference championships: 2
Stadium: Martin (40,000)	

Pacific Ten Conference Competition

Arizona	5-8	Southern California	4-38-4
Arizona State	5-7-1	Stanford	17-20-1
California	14-32-4	UCLA	8-26-1
Oregon	31-25-7	Washington	22-49-6
Oregon State	34-36-3		

Division I Competition

Alabama	0-1	Baylor	0-3
Army	1-1-1	Brigham Young	0-1
Ball State	1-0	Brown	1-0

Colorado	1-1	Ohio State	0-5
Hawaii	1-1	Oklahoma	0-2
Houston	1-1	Oklahoma State	2-0
Idaho	61-14-3	Pacific	7-5
Illinois	1-2	Penn State	0-2
Indiana	2-1	San Jose State	6-3-1
Iowa	1-3-1	Syracuse	0-1
Kansas	2-7	Tennessee	0-3
Michigan	0-1	Texas	0-2
Michigan State	2-5	Texas A&M	0-2
Minnesota	2-2	Texas Christian	0-1
Missouri	0-1	Texas Tech	0-2
Montana	30-2	Tulane	0-1
Montana State	3-0	Utah	3-3
Nebraska	3-0	Utah State	2-1
Nevada-Las Vegas	2-0	Wisconsin	0-1
Northwestern	0-1	Wyoming	1-1

Other Opponents

Blair Bus. Col.	2-0	Puget Sound	3-0-1
Bremerton Navy	2-0	St. Louis	1-0
Company C-NWG	1-0	St. Mary's (Ca.)	0-1-1
Denver	0-2	Santa Clara	1-0
Detroit	0-1	Second Air Force	0-0-1
Eastern Washington	2-0	Spokane A.C.	7-0
Gonzaga	18-5-3	Spokane H.S.	2-1
Honolulu	1-0	Spokane Y.	1-0
Honolulu All-Stars	1-0	362nd Infantry	0-0-1
Idaho College	7-0	Villanova	2-0
Lewiston	4-1-1	Walla Walla A.C.	1-0
Mount St. Charles	1-0-1	Whitman	18-3-1
Multnomah A.C.	2-1	Whitworth	1-0
Pacific (Ore.)	2-1	Willamette	2-1
Portland	1-0		

Total Overall Record	356-344-43	.508
Total Conference Record	166-206-24	.449
Overall Bowl Game Record	1-2-0	.333

Southeastern Conference

Formed: 1933
Charter Members: Alabama, Auburn, Florida, Georgia, Georgia
Tech, Kentucky, Louisiana State, Mississippi, Mississippi State,
Sewanee, Tennessee, Tulane, Vanderbilt.

Overall Records

	Years	W	L	T	Pct.
Alabama	90	606	213	42	.728
Tennessee	88	558	251	47	.679
Louisiana State	91	517	281	44	.640
Georgia	91	521	294	49	.631
Auburn	92	482	310	42	.603
Florida	79	407	300	37	.572
Vanderbilt	95	476	356	49	.568
Mississippi	90	456	334	33	.562
Kentucky	94	442	389	43	.530
Mississippi State	85	358	373	37	.490

Conference Records

	Years	W	L	T	Pct.
Alabama	51	239	89	19	.719
Tennessee	51	181	108	17	.619
Georgia	52	177	116	11	.600
Louisiana State	52	171	123	20	.576
Mississippi	51	157	126	14	.552
Auburn	51	159	145	14	.522
Florida	51	132	152	15	.467
Kentucky	51	100	192	9	.347
Mississippi State	51	99	194	12	.344
Vanderbilt	50	87	205	17	.309
Georgia Tech	31	110	68	9	.612
Tulane	33	67	105	15	.398
Sewanee	8	0	37	0	.000
Combined bowl game record:		91	82	8	.525

Total Championships

1.	Alabama	18	3. Tennessee	8
2.	Georgia	10	4. Louisiana State	6

101

Mississippi	6	9.	Kentucky	1
6. Georgia Tech	5		Mississippi State	1
7. Tulane	4	11.	Florida	0
8. Auburn	2		Vanderbilt	0

Past Champions

1984	Louisiana State*	1956	Tennessee
1983	Auburn	1955	Mississippi
1982	Georgia	1954	Mississippi
1981	Alabama	1953	Alabama
	Georgia	1952	Georgia Tech
1980	Georgia	1951	Georgia Tech
1979	Alabama		Tennessee
1978	Alabama	1950	Kentucky
1977	Alabama	1949	Tulane
1976	Georgia	1948	Georgia
1975	Alabama	1947	Mississippi
1974	Alabama	1946	Georgia
1973	Alabama		Tennessee
1972	Alabama	1945	Alabama
1971	Alabama	1944	Georgia Tech
1970	Louisiana State	1943	Georgia Tech
1969	Tennessee	1942	Georgia
1968	Georgia	1941	Mississippi State
1967	Tennessee	1940	Tennessee
1966	Alabama	1939	Georgia Tech
	Georgia		Tennessee
1965	Alabama		Tulane
1964	Alabama	1938	Tennessee
1963	Mississippi	1937	Alabama
1962	Mississippi	1936	Louisiana State
1961	Alabama	1935	Louisiana State
	Louisiana State		Tulane
1960	Mississippi	1934	Alabama
1959	Georgia		Tulane
1958	Louisiana State	1933	Alabama
1957	Auburn		

*Regular season champion Florida was declared ineligible by special SEC ruling.

ALABAMA

Nickname: Crimson Tide
Colors: Crimson and white
Location: Tuscaloosa, Alabama
Stadium: Bryant-Denny
      (58,000)
      Legion Field (68,000)

First year of football: 1892
First year in conference: 1933
Conference championships: 18

Southeastern Conference Competition

Auburn	29-19-1	Mississippi	30-5-2
Florida	15-5	Mississippi State	55-11-3
Georgia	31-21-4	Tennessee	34-26-7
Kentucky	28-1-1	Vanderbilt	40-18-4
Louisiana State	32-12-4		

Division I Competition

Arkansas	2-0	Oklahoma	1-0-1
Arkansas State	1-0	Penn State	5-2
Baylor	2-0	Pennsylvania	1-0
Boston College	1-3	Rice	0-3
California	1-1	Richmond	1-0
Cincinnati	3-0	Rutgers	2-0
Clemson	11-3	South Carolina	7-0
Colorado	0-1	Southern California	4-2
Davidson	1-0	Southern Methodist	2-0
Duke	1-1	Southern Mississippi	18-3-2
Florida State	3-0-1	Southwest Louisiana	4-0
Furman	5-0	Stanford	1-0-1
Georgia Tech	28-21-3	Syracuse	1-1
Illinois	1-0	Tennessee-Chattanooga	8-0
Louisiana Tech	1-0	Texas	0-7-1
Louisville	2-0	Texas A&M	1-1
Maryland	2-1	Texas Christian	2-3
Memphis State	3-0	Tulane	23-10-3
Miami (Fla.)	13-2	Tulsa	3-0
Missouri	1-2	UCLA	1-0
Nebraska	3-2	Virginia Tech	10-0
North Carolina State	3-0	Washington	3-0
Notre Dame	0-4	Washington State	1-0
Ohio State	1-0	Wisconsin	0-1

Other Opponents

Birmingham A.C.	2-3	Haskell	1-0
Birmingham College	2-0	Howard	20-0-1
Birmingham H.S.	2-0	Keesler A.A.F.	1-0
Birmingham Southern	3-0	Loyola (La.)	1-0
Bryson	1-0	Marion	9-0
Camp Gordon	0-1	Maryville	3-0
Carlisle	0-1	Mercer	2-0
Case Tech	1-0	Millsaps	3-0
Central Kentucky	2-0	Mississippi College	7-0
Centre	0-1	Montgomery A.C.	1-0
Cumberland	0-1	Nashville	1-0
Delta State	1-0	New Orleans A.C.	0-1
Duquesne	3-0	Oglethorpe	2-0
Fordham	1-1	Ohio Am. Corp.	1-0
George Washington	3-0	Owenton	5-0
Georgia Pre-Flight	0-1	Pensacola A.C.	1-0

Pensacola N.A.S.	2-0	Tampa	1-0
St. Mary's (Ca.)	1-0	Taylor School	1-0
Sewanee	17-10-3	Tuscaloosa A.C.	2-0
Southern	1-0	Union	4-0
Southern Military Inst.	1-0	Villanova	0-1
Southern Presb.	1-0	Washington and Lee	1-0
Southwestern (Tx.)	1-0	Wetumpka	1-0
Spring Hill	3-0		

Total Overall Record	606-213-42	.728
Total Conference Record	239-89-19	.719
Overall Bowl Game Record	20-14-3	.581

AUBURN

Nickname: Tigers
Colors: Orange and blue
Location: Auburn, Alabama
Stadium: Jordan-Hare
　　　　(72,170)

First year of football: 1892
Year entered conference: 1933
Conference championships: 2

Southeastern Conference Competition

Alabama	19-29-1	Mississippi	8-5
Florida	34-25-2	Mississippi State	40-16-2
Georgia	40-41-7	Tennessee	20-15-1
Kentucky	18-5-1	Vanderbilt	8-19-1
Louisiana State	9-14-1		

Division I Competition

Arizona	2-1	Miami (Fla.)	7-4
Arkansas	1-0	Michigan	1-0
Army	0-2	Michigan State	1-0
Baylor	1-2-1	Missouri	0-1
Boston College	1-2	Nebraska	0-3
Cincinnati	1-0	North Carolina	0-3
Clemson	31-11-2	North Carolina State	1-1
Colorado	1-0	North Texas State	1-0
Davidson	0-2	Ohio State	0-0-1
Duke	3-3	Oklahoma	0-1
Florida State	11-1-1	Oregon State	1-0
Furman	3-0	Rice	0-2
Georgia Tech	44-39-4	Richmond	1-0
Houston	5-1	Rutgers	1-0
Kansas State	2-0	South Carolina	2-1-1
Louisiana Tech	3-0-1	Southeastern Louisiana	0-1
Louisville	1-0	Southern Methodist	0-3
Maryland	2-1	Southern Mississippi	11-3
Memphis State	0-2	Southwestern Louisiana	1-0

Tennessee-Chattanooga	18-0	Tulane	14-17-6
Texas	1-5	Virginia Tech	2-1-1
Texas A&M	0-1	Wake Forest	6-2
Texas Christian	3-0	Wisconsin	0-0-1
Texas Tech	0-1		

Other Opponents

Birmingham-Southern	13-3	Marion	6-0
Camp Gordon	1-1	Marquette	0-1
Camp Greenleaf	0-1	Maryville	1-0-1
Camp Sheridan	0-1	Maxwell Field	0-1
Camp Sherman	1-0	Mercer	11-0
Carlisle	1-0	Montgomery	2-0
Centre	1-2	Nashville	3-1
Detroit	1-0	North Alabama A.C.	1-0
Erskine	1-0	Oglethorpe	4-0
Fort Benning	5-0	Presbyterian	1-0
George Washington	0-1	St. Louis	1-0
Georgetown	0-0-1	Santa Clara	0-1
Georgia Pre-Flight	0-1	Sewanee	4-6-2
Gordon	4-0	Spring Hill	5-0
Hardin-Simmons	1-0	Stetson	1-1
Howard	23-0-1	Villanova	4-1-2
Louisiana College	1-0	Washington and Lee	1-0
Loyola (La.)	1-0	Wofford	3-1
Manhattan	0-1		

Total Overall Record	482-310-42	.603
Total Conference Record	159-145-14	.522
Overall Bowl Game Record	9-7-1	.559

FLORIDA

Nickname: Gators	First year of football: 1906
Colors: Orange and blue	Year entered conference: 1933
Location: Gainesville, Florida	Conference championships: 0
Stadium: Florida Field	
(72,800)	

Southeastern Conference Competition

Alabama	5-15	Mississippi	6-8-1
Auburn	25-34-2	Mississippi State	23-13-2
Georgia	21-39-2	Tennessee	5-13
Kentucky	19-16	Vanderbilt	13-8-2
Louisiana State	13-15-3		

Division I Competition

Air Force	1-0	Miami (of Ohio)	0-1
Arkansas	0-1	Missouri	0-1
Arkansas State	1-0	Nebraska	0-1
Army	1-2	North Carolina	2-7-1
Baylor	1-0	North Carolina State	8-4-1
Boston College	1-1	North Texas State	0-1
California	2-0	Northwestern	2-0
Cincinnati	1-0	Oregon	1-0
Citadel	12-0	Penn State	1-0
Clemson	9-3-1	Pittsburgh	0-0-1
Davidson	0-1	Rice	3-4-1
Drake	1-0	Richmond	2-0
Duke	3-2	South Carolina	6-3-3
East Carolina	1-0	Southern California	1-0-1
Florida State	20-6-1	Southern Methodist	2-2
Furman	5-2	Southwestern Louisiana	1-0
Georgia Tech	9-23-6	Syracuse	1-1
Harvard	0-2	Temple	0-2
Houston	2-1	Texas	0-2-1
Illinois	1-0	Texas A&M	1-1
Indiana	0-1	Tulane	13-6-2
Indiana State	1-0	Tulsa	3-1
Iowa	1-0	UCLA	2-2
Kansas State	2-0	Utah	1-0
Louisville	1-0	Virginia	1-0
Maryland	11-6	West Texas State	1-0
Miami (Fla.)	24-22		

Other Opponents

American Legion	1-0	Mercer	10-6-1
Athens A.C.	1-0	Mississippi College	1-0-1
Camp Johnson	0-1	Newberry	1-0
Carlstrom Flyers	0-1	Oglethorpe	3-1
Charleston College	3-0	Olympics	2-0
Chicago	1-1	Presbyterian	1-0
Columbia College	3-0	Randolph-Macon	2-0
Duquesne	1-0	Rollins	13-2-1
Gainesville A.C.	3-0	Savannah A.C.	1-1
Gainesville Guards	1-0	Sewanee	7-2
George Washington	2-0	Southern	13-1
Georgia A&M	2-0	Stetson	15-2-2
Hampden-Sydney	1-0-1	Tallahassee A.C.	1-0
Howard	2-0	Tampa	5-0
Jacksonville A.C.	6-0	Tampa A.C.	1-0
Jacksonville N.A.S.	1-1	U.S. Amphib. Navy	0-1
Kings College	1-0	U.S. Infantry	2-0
Loyola (Ca.)	1-0	Vadada Club	1-0
Maryville	1-0	Villanova	0-4
Mayport N.A.S.	1-0		

Total Overall Record   407-300-37   .572
Total Conference Record   132-152-15   .467
Overall Bowl Game Record   7-8-0   .467

GEORGIA

Nickname: Bulldogs   First year of football: 1892
Colors: Red and black   Year entered conference: 1933
Location: Athens, Georgia   Conference championships: 10
Stadium: Sanford (80,078)

Southeastern Conference Competition

Alabama	21-31-4	Mississippi	15-7-1
Auburn	41-40-7	Mississippi State	10-5
Florida	40-21-2	Tennessee	9-8-2
Kentucky	29-7-2	Vanderbilt	29-15-1
Louisiana State	6-9-1		

Division I Competition

Arkansas	0-2	Oklahoma State	2-0
Baylor	2-0	Oregon	1-0
Boston College	2-0	Oregon State	2-0
Brigham Young	1-0	Penn State	0-1
California	2-0	Pennsylvania	1-0
Cincinnati	2-0	Pittsburgh	0-3-1
Citadel	9-0-1	Rice	0-1
Clemson	35-14-4	Richmond	2-0
Columbia	1-1	South Carolina	30-7-2
Dartmouth	1-1	South Carolina State	1-0
Davidson	2-2-1	Southern California	0-3
Florida State	5-4-1	Southern Methodist	1-0
Furman	21-2	Southern Mississippi	1-1
Georgia Tech	42-30-5	Stanford	0-1
Harvard	0-1	Temple	3-0
Holy Cross	0-3	Tennessee-Chattanooga	8-0-1
Houston	0-2-1	Tennessee Tech	1-0
Maryland	2-3	Texas	1-3
Memphis State	2-0	Texas A&M	1-3
Miami (Fla.)	7-4-1	Texas Christian	2-0
Miami (of Ohio)	0-1	Texas Tech	1-0
Michigan	1-1	Tulane	13-10-1
Missouri	1-0	Tulsa	1-0
Murray State	1-0	UCLA	2-0
Navy	0-2	Virginia	6-6-3
Nebraska	0-1	Virginia Military	4-0
North Carolina	15-11-2	Virginia Tech	1-1
North Carolina State	6-1-1	Wake Forest	1-2
Notre Dame	1-0	Yale	6-5

Other Opponents

Ala. Presbyterian	2-0	Jacksonville N.A.S.	1-0
Atlanta A.C.	1-0	Locust Grove	1-0
Augusta A.C.	2-0	Mercer	22-0
Centre	1-1-1	New York	3-3
Chicago	0-1	Newberry	2-0
Cumberland	0-1	Oglethorpe	7-1
Dahlonega	6-0	Presbyterian	3-0
Daniel Field	1-1	St. Mary's (Ca.)	0-0-1
Duquesne	1-0	Savannah A.C.	1-2-1
Fordham	0-1	Sewanee	5-7-1
George Washington	1-0	Stetson	1-0
Gordon	1-0	Villanova	1-0
Hardin-Simmons	1-0	Wofford	3-0
Howard	1-0		

Total Overall Record	521-294-49	.631
Total Conference Record	177-116-11	.600
Overall Bowl Game Record	11-11-2	.500

KENTUCKY

Nickname: Wildcats	First year of football: 1881
Colors: Blue and white	Year entered conference: 1933
Location: Lexington, Kentucky	Conference championships: 1
Stadium: Commonwealth (56,700)	

Southeastern Conference Competition

Alabama	1-28-1	Mississippi	10-19-1
Auburn	5-18-1	Mississippi State	11-5
Florida	16-19	Tennessee	23-48-9
Georgia	7-29-2	Vanderbilt	25-28-4
Louisiana State	9-25-1		

Division I Competition

Baylor	2-2	Illinois	1-1
Boston College	0-1	Indiana	5-11-1
Bowling Green	2-0	Kansas	0-3-1
Central Michigan	1-0	Kansas State	3-1
Cincinnati	16-7-3	Kent State	1-0
Citadel	1-0	Louisville	6-0
Clemson	6-3	Marshall	6-0
Duke	0-4	Maryland	2-3-2
Florida State	3-1-1	Memphis State	4-0
Georgia Tech	7-11-1	Miami (Fla.)	5-3
Hawaii	1-0	Miami (of Ohio)	5-4-1
Houston	0-2	Michigan	0-1

Michigan State	2-2	South Carolina	1-1-1
Missouri	2-1	Southern Methodist	0-1
North Carolina	4-4	Southern Mississippi	1-0
North Carolina State	1-1	Tennessee Tech	1-0
North Dakota	1-0	Texas	0-1
North Texas State	3-0	Texas A&M	1-1
Northwestern	0-1	Texas Christian	1-0
Ohio	1-1	Tulane	8-6
Ohio State	0-3	Utah State	1-1
Oklahoma	1-2	Virginia	1-0
Oregon State	2-0	Virginia Military	12-4
Penn State	2-2	Virginia Tech	10-5-2
Purdue	1-2	West Virginia	11-8-1
Rice	2-0	Wisconsin	1-0
Rutgers	1-0		

Other Opponents

All-Kentucky	0-1	Lexington H.S.	1-0
Alumni	1-0	Louisville A.C.	2-0
Avondale A.C.	0-2	Louisville Y.	2-2
Baldwin-Wallace	1-0	Manhattan	1-1
Berea	5-0	Manual H.S.	1-0
Bethany (W.V.)	1-0	Marietta	1-1
Butler	4-0	Marquette	2-1
Carson-Newman	2-0	Maryville	19-0-1
Cattlesburg A.C.	1-1	Mooney School	0-1
Central	4-10-1	Morris Harvey	2-0
Centre	11-18-1	Nashville	0-1
Chicago	0-1	Newcastle A.C.	1-0
Co. H 8th Mass	1-0	Oglethorpe	2-0
Cumberland	1-0	Ohio Northern	1-0
Cynthiana	2-0	Paris A.C.	1-0
Dayton	1-0	Q and C R.R.	1-0
DePaul	0-1	Rose Poly	2-0
Detroit	4-0	St. Louis	0-2
Earlham	3-0	St. Mary's (Ca.)	1-0
Emiance A.C.	1-0	Santa Clara	0-1
Evansville	1-0	Sewanee	7-3-3
Frankfort A.C.	1-0	Southwestern (Tenn.)	2-0
George Washington	3-0	Transylvania	15-5-1
Georgetown (Ky.)	22-1	Villanova	7-1-1
Hanover	2-0	Washington and Lee	11-7-2
Jeffersonville A.C.	1-0	West Virginia Wesleyan	1-0
Kentucky Mil. Inst.	4-0	Wilmington	2-0
Kentucky Wesleyan	4-1	Winchester A.C.	1-0
Lexington A.C.	1-2	Xavier	18-2

Total Overall Record	442-389-43	.530
Total Conference Record	100-192-9	.347
Overall Bowl Game Record	5-2-0	.714

LOUISIANA STATE

Nickname: Tigers
Colors: Purple and gold
Location: Baton Rouge,
         Louisiana
Stadium: Tiger (75,670)

First year of football: 1893
Year entered conference: 1933
Conference championships: 6

Southeastern Conference Competition

Alabama	12-32-4	Mississippi	40-29-4
Auburn	14-9-1	Mississippi State	45-30-3
Florida	16-12-3	Tennessee	2-16-3
Georgia	9-6-1	Vanderbilt	14-6-1
Kentucky	25-9-1		

Division I Competition

Arizona	1-0	Oregon State	3-0
Arkansas	23-12-2	Pacific	3-0
Army	0-1	Penn State	0-1
Baylor	8-2	Rice	35-13-5
Boston College	2-0	Rutgers	0-1
Cincinnati	1-0	South Carolina	11-1
Clemson	1-0	Southeastern Louisiana	1-0
Colorado	5-1	Southern California	1-1
Duke	1-1	Southern Methodist	0-1-1
Florida State	2-4	Southern Mississippi	1-0
Georgia Tech	5-12	Southwestern Louisiana	19-0
Holy Cross	2-1	Stanford	0-1
Indiana	2-1	Syracuse	1-0
Iowa State	1-0	Tennessee-Chattanooga	1-0
Louisiana Tech	15-1	Texas	7-8-1
Maryland	0-3	Texas A&M	22-14-3
Miami (Fla.)	8-2	Texas Christian	5-2-1
Missouri	0-1	Texas Tech	2-0
Nebraska	0-4-1	Tulane	53-22-7
North Carolina	3-1	Utah	2-0
Northwestern Louisiana	10-0	Wake Forest	3-0
Notre Dame	1-3	Washington	1-0
Oklahoma	0-1	Wichita State	1-0
Oklahoma State	1-0	Wisconsin	2-0
Oregon	2-1	Wyoming	3-0

Other Opponents

Alumni	2-0	Fordham	2-0
Centenary	3-1-1	George Washington	1-0
Cumberland	0-1	Georgia Navy	1-0
Eagles Club	1-0	Hardin-Simmons	1-0

Haskell	1-1	Montgomery A.C.	1-0
Havana	1-0	Nashville Med.	1-0
Howard	1-0	Natchez A.C.	1-0
Jackson Barracks	2-0	New Orleans Y.	1-0
Jefferson College	6-0	S.D. Wesleyan	1-0
Louisiana College	2-0	Santa Clara	0-2
Loyola (La.)	4-1	Sewanee	3-6
Manhattan	1-0	Shreveport A.C.	1-1
Mercer	1-0	Southern A.C.	1-0
Meteor A.C.	1-0	Southwestern (Tenn.)	1-0
Millsaps	2-1	Southwestern (Tx.)	1-0
Mississippi College	9-0-1	Spring Hill	8-0
Monroe A.C.	1-0	Transylvania	1-0

Total Overall Record	517-281-44	.640
Total Conference Record	171-123-20	.576
Overall Bowl Game Record	10-13-1	.438

MISSISSIPPI

Nickname: Rebels	First year of football: 1893
Colors: Red and blue	Year entered conference: 1933
Location: University, Miss.	Conference championships: 6
Stadium: Vaught-Hemingway	
(42,500)	
Mississippi Memorial	
(62,500)	

Southeastern Conference Competition

Alabama	5-30-2	Louisiana State	29-40-4
Auburn	5-8	Mississippi State	46-29-6
Florida	8-6-1	Tennessee	18-32-1
Georgia	7-15-1	Vanderbilt	28-29-2
Kentucky	19-10-1		

Division I Competition

Arkansas	16-14-1	Maryland	1-1
Arkansas State	7-1-1	Memphis State	32-5-1
Baylor	0-1	Miami (Fla.)	2-1
Boston College	3-0-1	Minnesota	0-1
Cal State-Long Beach	1-0	Missouri	1-3
Clemson	2-0	Navy	0-1
Drake	0-1	North Texas State	4-0
Florida State	1-0	Notre Dame	1-0
Furman	0-1	Purdue	0-1
Georgia Tech	1-2	Rice	1-0
Holy Cross	2-0	South Carolina	4-5
Houston	15-3	Southern Methodist	0-1
Louisiana Tech	6-1	Southern Mississippi	18-6

Temple	0-1-1	Tulane	29-27
Tennessee-Chattanooga	13-1	Tulsa	0-3
Texas	1-5	Virginia Military	0-1
Texas A&M	0-4	Virginia Tech	1-1
Texas Christian	5-1	Western Kentucky	2-0
Texas-El Paso	0-1		

Other Opponents

Bethel	1-0	Memphis H.S.	3-0
Birmingham Southern	3-1	Memphis Med. Sch.	6-0
Camp Benning	1-1	Memphis U.S.	4-0
Castle Heights	1-0	Mercer	1-0
Catholic	1-1	Millsaps	5-0
Centenary	4-3	Mississippi College	8-4-1
Central	1-0	Missouri Normal	1-1
Centre	1-1	Nashville	1-1
Chicago Cags.	0-0-1	Ouachita	1-1-1
Cumberland	2-1	Ozarks College	1-0
Duquesne	1-0	Payne Field	0-1
George Washington	2-0-1	St. Louis	4-1
Georgetown	0-2	St. Thomas Hall	4-0
Hardin-Simmons	2-0	Sewanee	6-8-1
Havana	0-1	Southern A.C.	1-1
Henderson-Brown	1-0-1	Southern Presb.	20-1-2
Hendrix	3-1-1	Southwestern (Tenn.)	0-1
Howard	1-1	Tampa	3-0
Jackson A.B.	0-1	Tennessee Med.	0-2
Loyola (Chi.)	1-1	Transylvania	0-1
Loyola (La.)	2-1	Trinity (Tx.)	2-0
Marquette	2-3	Union	14-0-1
Maryville	1-0	Villanova	2-0
Memphis A.C.	3-0	Virginia Meds.	1-0

Total Overall Record	456-334-33	.562
Total Conference Record	157-126-14	.552
Overall Bowl Game Record	11-10-0	.524

MISSISSIPPI STATE

Nickname: Bulldogs
Colors: Maroon and white
Location: State College, Miss.
Stadium: Scott Field (43,000)
         Mississippi Memorial
         (62,500)

First year of football: 1895
Year entered conference: 1933
Conference championships: 1

Southeastern Conference Competition

Alabama	11-55-3	Florida	13-23-2
Auburn	16-40-2	Georgia	5-10

Kentucky	5-11	Tennessee	13-19-1
Louisiana State	30-45-3	Vanderbilt	6-5-2
Mississippi	29-46-6		

Division I Competition

Arkansas	2-0	Missouri	0-2
Arkansas State	12-0	Murray State	1-0
Army	1-0	Navy	1-0
Baylor	0-2-1	Nebraska	0-1
Cincinnati	1-1	North Carolina	1-0
Clemson	0-1-1	North Carolina State	2-2
Colorado State	2-0	North Texas State	6-2
Drake	0-1	Northeast Louisiana	1-0-1
Florida State	2-7	Northwest Louisiana	2-0
Georgia Tech	0-2	Oklahoma State	1-1
Houston	6-6	Rice	1-0
Illinois	1-1	Richmond	2-0
Indiana	0-3	Southern Mississippi	8-11-1
Kansas	1-0	Southwest Louisiana	4-0
Kansas State	1-1	Tennessee-Chattanooga	4-0
Lamar	1-0	Texas	0-1
Louisiana Tech	3-1	Texas A&M	2-2
Louisville	2-2	Texas Christian	0-0-1
Marshall	1-0	Texas Tech	4-2-1
Maryland	0-1	Tulane	20-22-2
Memphis State	15-8	Washington	0-1
Miami (Fla.)	2-3	West Texas State	1-0
Michigan State	1-2-1	William and Mary	1-0

Other Opponents

Birmingham Southern	8-0	Memphis A.C.	0-1
Cal Poly-Pomona	0-1	Mercer	3-0
Camp Shelby	1-0	Meridian A.C.	2-0
Centenary	0-1-2	Millsaps	14-2-1
Centre	2-0	Mississippi College	16-3
Christian Brothers	0-0-1	New Orleans A.C.	0-1
Cumberland	2-3	Ouachita	3-1-2
Delta State	1-0	Park Field	0-1
Detroit	1-0	Payne Field	0-1
Drury	1-0	San Francisco	4-0
Duquesne	3-3	Sewanee	4-1
Georgetown	1-0	Southern Mil. Acad.	1-0
Hardin-Simmons	1-0	Southwestern (Tenn.)	9-4
Haskell	1-0	Spring Field	1-0
Havana A.C.	1-0	Tampa	1-1
Henderson-Brown	0-2	Tennessee Med.	1-0
Howard	16-1-1	Transylvania	1-0-1
Jackson A.B.	1-0	Trinity (Tx.)	1-0
Loyola (La.)	3-0	Union	4-2
Marion	4-0	Washington (Mo.)	0-1
Maryville	0-0-1	Xavier	1-0
Maxwell Field	1-0		

Total Overall Record   358-373-37   .490
Total Conference Record   99-194-12   .344
Overall Bowl Game Record   4-2-0   .667

TENNESSEE

Nickname: Volunteers   First year of football: 1891
Colors: Orange and white   Year entered conference: 1933
Location, Knoxville, Tennessee   Conference championships: 8
Stadium: Neyland (91,250)

Southeastern Conference Competition

Alabama	26-34-7	Louisiana State	15-2-3
Auburn	15-20-1	Mississippi	32-18-1
Florida	13-5	Mississippi State	19-13-1
Georgia	8-9-2	Vanderbilt	47-26-5
Kentucky	48-23-9		

Division I Competition

Air Force	1-0	Oklahoma	1-1
Arkansas	2-0	Oregon State	1-0-1
Army	5-1-1	Penn State	2-0
Baylor	0-1	Pittsburgh	0-2
Boston College	6-1	Purdue	0-1
California	0-1	Rice	2-1
Cincinnati	3-1	Richmond	1-0
Citadel	3-0	Rutgers	1-1
Clemson	11-5-2	South Carolina	7-1-2
Colorado State	2-0	Southern California	0-4
Dartmouth	0-1	Southern Methodist	1-0
Davidson	1-0	Southern Mississippi	1-0
Duke	11-12-2	Syracuse	1-0
Florida State	0-1	Temple	1-0
Furman	2-0	Tennessee-Chattanooga	36-2-2
Georgia Tech	23-16-1	Tennessee Tech	5-0
Hawaii	2-0	Texas	1-2
Houston	1-1	Texas A&M	1-0
Iowa	0-1	Texas Christian	2-0
Iowa State	1-0	Texas Tech	0-1
Kansas	2-0	Tulane	4-1
Louisville	2-0	Tulsa	5-0
Maryland	5-2	UCLA	3-3-1
Memphis State	9-0	Utah	3-0
New Mexico	1-0	Virginia	2-1
North Carolina	20-10-1	Virginia Military	0-1
North Carolina State	1-1	Virginia Tech	4-2
North Texas State	0-1	Wake Forest	5-3
Notre Dame	1-1	Washington State	3-0

Wichita State	1-0	Wisconsin	1-0
William and Mary	1-0		

Other Opponents

American	2-0	Maryville	25-1-1
Asheville A.C.	1-0	Mercer	2-1
Athens	1-0	Mooney School	2-0
Bristol A.C.	1-0	Nashville	2-1-1
California–Santa Barbara	1-0	New York	1-0
Camp Benning	1-0	Sewanee	12-10
Carson-Newman	12-0	Southwestern (Tenn.)	3-0
Central	1-0	Tampa	2-0
Centre	10-2-2	Tennessee Med.	1-0-1
Chattanooga A.C.	2-0	Tennessee Military Inst.	1-0
Cumberland	1-0	Tenn. School for Deaf	1-0
Dayton	4-0	Transylvania	4-1
Emory and Henry	5-0	Tusculum	3-0
Fordham	1-1	Villanova	1-0
George Washington	1-0	Washington and Lee	5-0
Georgetown	3-0	Williamsburg	2-0
Howard	2-0	Wofford	1-0
King	7-0		

Total Overall Record	558-251-47	.679
Total Conference Record	181-108-17	.619
Overall Bowl Game Record	13-14-0	.481

VANDERBILT

Nickname: Commodores	First year of football: 1890
Colors: Gold and black	Year entered conference: 1933
Location: Nashville, Tennessee	Conference championships: 0
Stadium: Vanderbilt (41,000)	

Southeastern Conference Competition

Alabama	18-40-4	Louisiana State	6-14-1
Auburn	19-9-1	Mississippi	29-28-2
Florida	8-13-2	Mississippi State	5-6-2
Georgia	15-29-1	Tennessee	26-47-5
Kentucky	28-25-4		

Division I Competition

Air Force	2-3	Cincinnati	2-3
Arkansas	1-2	Citadel	3-2
Army	3-1	Clemson	3-1
Baylor	0-2	Colgate	1-0
Boston College	0-2	Davidson	2-0

Furman	1-1	Penn State	1-0
Georgia Tech	15-16-3	Pennsylvania	0-1
Harvard	0-1	Princeton	1-1
Indiana	0-2	Purdue	2-0
Iowa State	1-0	Rice	2-1
Kansas	1-0	South Carolina	0-1
Kansas State	1-0	Southern Methodist	1-1
Louisville	2-0-1	Temple	0-1
Marshall	2-0	Tennessee-Chattanooga	16-1
Maryland	7-3	Tennessee Tech	10-0-1
Memphis State	6-2	Texas	8-3-1
Miami (Fla.)	4-4	Texas Tech	0-0-1
Miami (of Ohio)	1-0	Tulane	16-25-3
Michigan	0-9-1	UCLA	0-1
Middle Tennessee	12-0	Virginia	12-7-2
Minnesota	2-2	Virginia Military	3-2
Missouri	1-2-1	Virginia Tech	3-3
Navy	0-1-2	Wake Forest	3-1
North Carolina	5-8	West Virginia	1-1
North Carolina State	1-0	Western Kentucky	3-0
Northwestern	1-0-1	William and Mary	4-0
Ohio State	1-3	Yale	1-0-1
Oklahoma	0-2-1		

Other Opponents

Alumni	0-1	Marquette	1-0
Bethel	3-0	Maryville	6-0
Birmingham-Southern	3-0	Memphis A.C.	2-0
Bryson	1-0	Mercer	4-0
Camp Campbell	1-0	Milligan	1-0
Camp Greenleaf	0-1	Missouri Mines	1-0
Camp Hancock	0-1	Mooney School	1-0
Carlisle	1-0	Nashville	7-0-1
Carson-Newman	1-0	Nashville A.C.	1-0
Castle Heights	1-0	Ouachita	2-0
Central	13-1-1	Quantico Marines	0-0-1
Centre	4-2-1	Rose Poly	8-0
Chicago	2-1	Sewanee	40-8-4
Cumberland	6-1	Southwestern (Tenn.)	7-1
Florence State	1-0	Spring Hill	1-0
Fordham	0-1	Tampa	3-1
George Washington	3-0	Transylvania	2-0
Georgetown (Ky.)	2-0	Union	3-0
Henderson-Brown	6-0	Villanova	1-0
Howard	2-0	Washington (Mo.)	6-3
Kentucky State	2-0	Washington and Lee	2-0
Louisville A.C.	1-1		

Total Overall Record	476-356-49	.568
Total Conference Record	87-205-17	.309
Overall Bowl Game Record	1-1-1	.500

Southwest Conference

Formed: 1915
Charter Members: Arkansas, Baylor, Oklahoma, Oklahoma State, Rice, Southwestern, Texas, Texas A&M.
Former Members: Phillips.

Overall Records

	Years	W	L	T	Pct.
Texas	91	622	227	31	.717
Arkansas	90	483	319	37	.599
Houston	38	235	165	13	.585
Texas A&M	89	463	344	47	.570
Texas Tech	59	338	270	31	.553
Southern Methodist	69	368	302	51	.546
Baylor	82	407	357	44	.531
Texas Christian	87	401	385	55	.510
Rice	72	319	377	30	.460

Conference Record

	Years	W	L	T	Pct.
Texas	69	291	122	14	.698
Houston	9	48	22	2	.681
Arkansas	69	208	179	16	.536
Southern Methodist	66	199	188	31	.513
Baylor	67	197	228	35	.466
Texas A&M	69	182	217	30	.459
Texas Christian	60	167	201	22	.456
Texas Tech	24	81	98	5	.454
Rice	67	155	249	12	.387
Oklahoma	5	10	3	1	.750
Oklahoma State	10	6	23	0	.207
Southwestern	2	0	5	0	.000
Phillips	1	0	3	0	.000
Combined bowl game record:		59	71	9	.457

Total Championships

1.	Texas	22	6. Rice	6
2.	Arkansas	11	7. Baylor	5
	Southern Methodist	11	8. Houston	4
	Texas A&M	11	9. Texas Tech	1
5.	Texas Christian	8	Oklahoma	1

Past Champions

1984	Houston	1952	Texas
	Southern Methodist	1951	Texas Christian
1983	Texas	1950	Texas
1982	Southern Methodist	1949	Rice
1981	Southern Methodist	1948	Southern Methodist
1980	Baylor	1947	Southern Methodist
1979	Houston	1946	Arkansas
	Arkansas		Rice
1978	Houston	1945	Texas
1977	Texas	1944	Texas Christian
1976	Houston	1943	Texas
	Texas Tech	1942	Texas
1975	Arkansas	1941	Texas A&M
	Texas	1940	Texas A&M
	Texas A&M		Southern Methodist
1974	Baylor	1939	Texas A&M
1973	Texas	1938	Texas Christian
1972	Texas	1937	Rice
1971	Texas	1936	Arkansas
1970	Texas	1935	Southern Methodist
1969	Texas	1934	Rice
1968	Texas	1933	(No Champion)
	Arkansas	1932	Texas Christian
1967	Texas A&M	1931	Southern Methodist
1966	Southern Methodist	1930	Texas
1965	Arkansas	1929	Texas Christian
1964	Arkansas	1928	Texas
1963	Texas	1927	Texas A&M
1962	Texas	1926	Southern Methodist
1961	Texas	1925	Texas A&M
	Arkansas	1924	Baylor
1960	Arkansas	1923	Southern Methodist
1959	Texas	1922	Baylor
	Texas Christian	1921	Texas A&M
	Arkansas	1920	Texas
1958	Texas Christian	1919	Texas A&M
1957	Rice	1918	Texas
1956	Texas A&M	1917	Texas A&M
1955	Texas Christian	1916	Texas
1954	Arkansas	1915	Baylor
1953	Texas		Oklahoma
	Rice		

ARKANSAS

Nickname: Razorbacks   First year of football: 1894
Colors: Cardinal and white   Year entered conference: 1915

Location: Fayetteville,   Conference championships: 11
           Arkansas
Stadium: Razorback (52,055)
          War Memorial (53,250)

Southwest Conference Competition

Baylor	31-30-2	Texas	16-50
Houston	6-5	Texas A&M	35-20-3
Rice	29-28-3	Texas Christian	37-22-2
Southern Methodist	28-27-5	Texas Tech	24-4

Division I Competition

Air Force	1-0	Nebraska	1-0
Alabama	0-2	New Mexico	1-0
Arizona State	1-0	New Mexico State	1-0
Auburn	0-1	North Carolina	0-1
California	1-0	North Texas State	7-0
Colorado State	2-0	Northwestern	1-0
Duke	0-1	Northwestern Louisiana	3-0
Florida	1-0	Oklahoma	4-8-1
Georgia	2-0	Oklahoma State	30-15-1
Georgia Tech	1-1	Southern California	1-2
Iowa	0-1	Southwest Missouri State	3-2
Iowa State	1-0	Stanford	0-1
Kansas	0-2	Tennessee	0-2
Kansas State	1-3	Tulane	3-0
Kentucky	0-1	Tulsa	44-15-3
Louisiana State	12-23-2	UCLA	0-0-1
Louisiana Tech	1-0	Utah State	2-0
Mississippi	15-15-1	Vanderbilt	2-1
Mississippi State	0-2	Wichita State	7-0
Missouri	1-2	William and Mary	1-2
Navy	2-0	Wisconsin	0-1

Other Opponents

Abilene Christian	1-0	East Texas State	1-0
Arkansas A&M	1-0	Fordham	0-1
Arkansas Teachers	2-0	Ft. Scott H.S.	2-2
Austin College	2-0	Ft. Smith H.S.	8-0
Barksdale Field.	1-0	George Washington	0-1-1
Camp Pike	0-1	Hardin-Simmons	3-0
Centenary	3-1-2	Haskell	1-0-1
Central Missouri State	1-0	Henderson State	5-0
Chicago	0-0-1	Hendrix	15-0-2
Chiloco	1-1	Joplin H.S.	1-0-1
College of the Ozarks	8-0	Kansas City Medics	1-1
Dallas Medics	0-1	Kingfisher	1-0
Detroit	2-0	Little Rock H.S.	0-1
Drury	12-5-2	Missouri Mines	15-4
East Central Oklahoma	5-0	Monticello Navy	0-1

Neosho H.S.	1-0	St. Louis	1-2-1
Norman Navy	0-1	Santa Clara	0-2
Northeast Oklahoma	1-0	Southeast Missouri	1-0
Oklahoma Baptist	2-1	Southwestern (Tx.)	3-0-1
Oklahoma Mines	1-0	Tehlequah Sem.	1-0
Ouachita	5-2-1	Villanova	0-1
Phillips	4-0-1	Washington (Mo.)	4-1
Pierce C.C.	1-2	Webb City H.S.	1-0
Pittsburg State	4-0		

Total Overall Record	483-319-37	.599
Total Conference Record	208-179-16	.536
Overall Bowl Game Record	8-9-3	.475

BAYLOR

Nickname: Bears
Colors: Green and gold
Location: Waco, Texas
Stadium: Baylor (48,500)

First year of football: 1899
Year entered conference: 1915
Conference championships: 5

Southwest Conference Competition

Arkansas	30-31-2	Texas	16-53-5
Houston	7-9-1	Texas A&M	28-42-8
Rice	36-27-2	Texas Christian	40-44-7
Southern Methodist	25-35-7	Texas Tech	24-17-1

Division I Competition

Air Force	3-0	Lamar	2-1
Alabama	0-2	Louisiana State	2-8
Army	2-0	Louisiana Tech	1-0
Auburn	2-1-1	Maryland	1-1
Boston College	0-2	Miami (Fla.)	3-4
Bowling Green	1-0	Michigan	0-0-1
Brigham Young	1-1	Michigan State	0-1
California	2-0	Mississippi	1-0
Clemson	1-0	Mississippi State	2-0-1
Colorado	2-3	Missouri	1-2
Duke	0-1	Nebraska	1-2
Florida	0-1	New Mexico	1-0
Florida State	2-1-1	North Texas State	9-0
Georgia	0-2	Notre Dame	0-1
Georgia Tech	0-2	Ohio State	0-2
Illinois	1-0	Oklahoma	0-4
Indiana	1-1	Oklahoma State	10-3
Kansas	0-1	Oregon State	0-2
Kansas State	0-1	Penn State	0-1
Kentucky	2-2	Pittsburgh	2-2

Purdue	0-1	Tulsa	3-4
San Jose State	0-1	Utah State	1-0
South Carolina	2-1	Vanderbilt	2-0
Southern California	1-1	Wake Forest	4-0
Southwest Texas State	3-0	Washington	3-1
Syracuse	1-1	Washington State	3-0
Tennessee	1-0	West Texas State	2-0
Texas-El Paso	1-0	Wyoming	1-1
Tulane	3-3		

Other Opponents

Austin College	6-3-1	Ouachita	1-0
Blackland A.F.B.	2-0	Phillips	1-1
Centenary	5-7	Polytechnic	2-0-2
Central Oklahoma	0-1	Rusk	1-0
Daniel Baker	3-0-1	St. Edward's	11-1
Deaf Mutes	2-0-1	Sewanee	1-1
Denver	2-0	Southwestern (Tex.)	13-6-1
Fort Worth	2-0	Stephen F. Austin	3-0
Hardin-Simmons	13-1	Tarleton State	1-0
Haskell	2-1	Texas A&I	1-0
Howard Payne	9-0	Toby's	2-0
Loyola (Ca.)	2-0	Trinity (Tex.)	15-6-1
Loyola (La.)	1-1	Villanova	3-1
Mississippi College	2-0	Weatherford	1-0
Oklahoma Baptist	1-0	Winchester	1-0
Oklahoma City	3-0		

Total Overall Record	407-357-44	.531
Total Conference Record	197-228-35	.466
Overall Bowl Game Record	5-7-0	.417

HOUSTON

Nickname: Cougars
Colors: Red and white
Location: Houston, Texas
Stadium: Astrodome (50,155)

First year of football: 1946
Year entered conference: 1976
Conference championships: 4

Southwest Conference Competition

Arkansas	5-6	Texas	3-6-2
Baylor	9-7-1	Texas A&M	11-9-3
Rice	11-3	Texas Christian	8-1
Southern Methodist	5-5	Texas Tech	13-4

Division I Competition

Alabama	0-6	Arizona State	2-5
Arizona	1-0	Auburn	1-5

Boston College	1-2	Oklahoma State	7-7-1
Cincinnati	11-2	Oregon	0-1
Colorado	0-1	Oregon State	2-1
Colorado State	2-0	Penn State	0-2
Florida	1-2	San Diego State	2-0
Florida State	12-2-2	San Jose State	1-0
Georgia	2-0-1	South Carolina	2-0
Idaho	2-0	Southern Mississippi	1-0
Kentucky	2-0	Southwest Louisiana	1-2
Lamar	3-0	Southwest Texas State	0-3
Louisiana Tech	2-0	Syracuse	1-0
Louisville	3-2	Tennessee	1-1
Maryland	1-0	Tennessee-Chattanooga	1-0
Memphis State	5-4	Texas-El Paso	0-2
Miami (Fla.)	7-8	Tulane	2-0
Miami (of Ohio)	2-0	Tulsa	14-11
Michigan State	1-0	UCLA	2-0
Mississippi	3-15	Utah	3-0
Mississippi State	6-6	Utah State	1-0
Montana	1-0	Virginia Tech	3-1-1
Navy	1-0	Wake Forest	2-0
Nebraska	1-0	Washington	0-1
New Mexico	2-0	Washington State	1-1
North Carolina State	1-1-1	West Texas State	4-1
North Texas State	4-7	Wichita State	6-3
Notre Dame	0-1	William and Mary	1-1
Oklahoma	0-1	Wyoming	5-0

Other Opponents

Camp Hood	1-0	St. Bonaventure	0-2
Centenary	1-0	St. Louis	1-0
Daniel Baker	1-0	Sam Houston State	1-2
Dayton	1-0	Stephen F. Austin	1-2
Detroit	6-0	Tampa	1-0
East Texas State	1-2	Texas A&I	2-1
Hardin-Simmons	1-2-1	Trinity (Tex.)	2-3
McMurry	1-0	Villanova	5-1
Midwestern	1-1		

Total Overall Record	235-165-13	.585
Total Conference Record	48-22-2	.681
Overall Bowl Game Record	7-3-1	.682

RICE

Nickname: Owls
Colors: Blue and gray
Location: Houston, Texas
Stadium: Rice (70,000)

First year of football: 1912
Year entered conference: 1915
Conference championships: 6

Southwest Conference Competition

Arkansas	28-29-3	Texas	20-50-1
Baylor	27-36-2	Texas A&M	27-39-3
Houston	3-11	Texas Christian	27-33-3
Southern Methodist	24-39-1	Texas Tech	16-18-1

Division I Competition

Alabama	3-0	Navy	2-1
Arizona	4-0	New Mexico	1-0
Army	0-1	North Carolina	1-0
Auburn	2-0	Northwestern	1-0
California	1-1	Notre Dame	0-3
Cincinnati	0-1	Oklahoma	0-6
Clemson	3-4	Oklahoma State	0-2-1
Colorado	1-0	Oregon	0-1
Cornell	2-0	Penn State	0-2
Duke	0-3	Pittsburgh	2-0
Florida	4-3-1	Purdue	1-1
Georgia	1-0	Southern California	0-2-1
Georgia Tech	0-2-1	Southwest Texas State	1-1
Idaho	1-0	Southwestern Louisiana	2-1
Iowa State	1-1	Stanford	3-1
Kansas	0-1	Tennessee	1-2
Lamar	1-0	Tulane	10-8-1
Louisiana State	13-35-5	Tulsa	0-0-1
Louisiana Tech	1-0	UCLA	0-2
Miami (Fla.)	0-1	Utah	2-0
Minnesota	0-2	Vanderbilt	1-2
Mississippi	0-1	Virginia Military	2-0
Mississippi State	0-1	Washington	0-0-1
Missouri	0-1	West Virginia	1-0
Montana	1-0	Wisconsin	0-2

Other Opponents

Austin College	3-2-1	Illinois Medics	1-0
Camp Logan	0-1-1	Kelly Field	0-1
Centenary	3-1	Loyola (La.)	3-2
Co. B. Signal Corps	1-0	Orange H.S.	1-0
Corpus Christi Navy	2-1	Park Place Flyers	0-2
Creighton	3-1	Randolph Field	0-2
Daniel Baker	2-0	St. Edward's	2-2-1
Duquesne	1-1	St. Mary's (Tex.)	1-0
Fordham	0-1	Sam Houston State	14-1
Galveston A.A.F.	1-0	Santa Clara	1-1
George Washington	2-0	Sewanee	2-0
Hardin-Simmons	1-0	Southwestern (Tex.)	16-5
Haskell	1-0	Stephen F. Austin	2-0
Houston H.S.	2-0	Texas A&I	6-0
Howard Payne	1-0	Trinity (Tex.)	5-1-1

Total Overall Record   319-377-30 .460
Total Conference Record   155-249-12 .387
Overall Bowl Game Record   4-3-0 .571

SOUTHERN METHODIST

Nickname: Mustangs   First year of football: 1915
Colors: Red and blue   Year entered conference: 1918
Location: Dallas, Texas   Conference championships: 11
Stadium: Texas (65,100)

Southwest Conference Competition

Arkansas	27-28-5	Texas	21-39-4
Baylor	35-25-7	Texas A&M	29-32-6
Houston	5-5	Texas Christian	32-28-7
Rice	39-24-1	Texas Tech	14-18

Division I Competition

Air Force	2-3	New Mexico State	3-0
Alabama	0-2	North Carolina State	1-0
Arizona	1-0	North Texas State	24-2-1
Army	0-2	Northwestern	1-0
Auburn	3-0	Notre Dame	3-8
Brigham Young	0-1	Ohio State	1-7-1
California	1-0	Oklahoma	1-3-1
Drake	1-0	Oklahoma State	5-1-2
Duke	0-2	Oregon	1-1
Florida	2-2	Oregon State	2-0
Georgia	0-1	Pacific	1-0
Georgia Tech	2-8-1	Penn State	0-1-1
Grambling State	2-0	Pittsburgh	2-2-1
Illinois	1-1	Purdue	0-1-1
Indiana	1-0	Southern California	0-2
Kansas	3-1	Stanford	0-1
Kentucky	1-0	Syracuse	1-0
Louisiana State	1-0-1	Temple	0-0-2
Louisville	2-0	Tennessee	0-1
Maryland	0-2	Texas-Arlington	5-1
Memphis State	0-1	Texas-El Paso	1-0
Miami (Fla.)	1-0	Tulane	3-4
Michigan	0-1	Tulsa	1-1
Michigan State	0-1	UCLA	4-0
Minnesota	0-1	Vanderbilt	1-1
Mississippi	1-0	Virginia Tech	2-1
Missouri	13-7-1	Wake Forest	3-0
Navy	5-1	West Virginia	0-1
Nebraska	0-1-1	Wichita State	1-0
Nevada-Las Vegas	1-0		

Other Opponents

Abilene Christian	1-0	Marquette	1-1
Austin College	9-4-1	Meridian	1-0
Blackland A.F.B.	1-0	Missouri Mines	1-0
Burleson	1-0	Randolph Field	0-1
Centenary	2-4	S.M.U. Frosh	1-0
Corpus Christi Navy	1-1	St. Mary's (Tex.)	0-2
Dallas	1-1-1	Santa Clara	3-0
Daniel Baker	2-2	Southwestern (Tex.)	2-2-3
Fordham	1-2	Texas A&I	1-0
Hardin-Simmons	3-1-1	Trinity (Tex.)	6-2
Henderson-Brown	1-0	Washington (Mo.)	4-0
Hendrix	1-0	Wesley	1-0
Howard Payne	5-2-1	West Virginia Wesleyan	0-1
Love Field	1-0		

Total Overall Record	368-302-51	.546
Total Conference Record	199-188-31	.513
Overall Bowl Game Record	4-5-1	.450

TEXAS

Nickname: Longhorns
Colors: Orange and white
Location: Austin, Texas
Stadium: Memorial (80,000)

First year of football: 1893
Year entered conference: 1915
Conference championships: 22

Southwest Conference Competition

Arkansas	50-16	Southern Methodist	39-21-4
Baylor	54-16-4	Texas A&M	63-23-5
Houston	6-3-2	Texas Christian	50-19-1
Rice	50-20-1	Texas Tech	28-6

Division I Competition

Alabama	7-0-1	Indiana	3-0
Arizona	1-0	Iowa	0-1
Army	1-0	Iowa State	1-0
Auburn	5-1	Kansas	0-2
Boston College	2-1	Kansas State	3-1
California	4-0	Kentucky	1-0
Colorado	4-0	Louisiana State	8-7-1
Colorado State	1-0	Maryland	3-0
Florida	2-0-1	Miami (Fla.)	2-1
Georgia	3-1	Minnesota	0-1
Georgia Tech	1-0	Mississippi	5-1
Harvard	0-1	Mississippi State	1-0
Idaho	1-0	Missouri	8-4

Navy	2-0	Syracuse	0-1
Nebraska	1-3	Temple	1-0
New Mexico	1-0	Tennessee	2-1
North Carolina	3-3	Tulane	15-1-1
North Texas State	4-0	UCLA	2-0
Northwestern	0-1	Utah	1-0
Notre Dame	2-6	Utah State	3-0
Oklahoma	47-28-4	Vanderbilt	3-8-1
Oklahoma State	9-1	Virginia	1-0
Oregon	4-0	Wake Forest	1-0
Oregon State	1-0	Washington	2-1
Penn State	1-1	Washington State	2-0
Purdue	2-0	West Virginia	0-1
South Carolina	0-1	Wisconsin	1-0
Southern California	0-4	Wyoming	2-0

Other Opponents

Austin College	6-0	Missouri Mines	2-0
Austin Y.	3-0	Nashville	1-0-1
Bergstrom Field	1-0	Phillips	5-1
Blackland A.A.F.	1-0	Polytechnic	1-0
Centenary	3-2-2	Radio School	2-0
Chicago	0-1	Randolph Field	0-1-1
Colorado College	0-1	St. Edward's	3-0
Corpus Christi Navy	1-0	San Antonio	8-0
Dallas	7-1-1	Sewanee	4-3
Daniel Baker	3-0	Southwestern (Tex.)	20-2
Fort Worth	1-1	Texas A&I	1-0
Galveston	3-0	Transylvania	1-1
Hardin-Simmons	2-0	Trinity (Tex.)	6-0
Haskell	6-5	26th Infantry	1-0
Houston H.S.	2-0	Villanova	1-0
Howard Payne	5-0	Wabash	1-0
Kansas City Medics	1-0	Washington (Mo.)	2-0
Kirksville	0-1		

Total Overall Record	622-227-31	.717
Total Conference Record	291-122-14	.698
Overall Bowl Game Record	15-14-2	.516

TEXAS A&M

Nickname: Aggies
Colors: Maroon and white
Location: College Station,
      Texas
Stadium: Kyle Field (72,387)

First year of football: 1894
Year entered conference: 1915
Conference championships: 11

Southwest Conference Competition

Arkansas	20-35-3	Southern Methodist	32-29-6
Baylor	42-28-8	Texas	23-63-5
Houston	9-11-3	Texas Christian	44-29-7
Rice	39-27-3	Texas Tech	23-18-1

Division I Competition

Alabama	1-1	Mississippi	4-0
Arizona	1-0	Mississippi State	2-2
Arkansas State	3-0	Missouri	2-0
Army	1-1	Nebraska	1-4
Auburn	1-0	Nevada-Reno	1-0
Boston College	1-3	New Mexico	1-0
Brigham Young	0-1	North Texas State	2-0
California	1-1	Ohio State	0-2
Cincinnati	0-1	Oklahoma	5-7
Clemson	2-0	Oklahoma State	7-3
Florida	1-1	Penn State	1-1
Florida State	0-2	Purdue	0-1
Georgia	3-1	Southern California	0-3
Georgia Tech	1-1	Southern Mississippi	1-0
Illinois	2-0	Southwest Texas State	1-0
Iowa	1-0	Temple	0-2
Iowa State	2-0	Tennessee	0-1
Kansas	2-1	Texas-Arlington	1-0
Kansas State	2-2	Texas-El Paso	1-0
Kentucky	1-1	Tulane	10-5
Louisiana State	14-22-3	Tulsa	2-1
Louisiana Tech	2-0	UCLA	2-1
Maryland	2-0	Utah	1-0
Memphis State	2-0	Virginia Military	1-0
Miami (Fla.)	1-0	Virginia Tech	2-0
Michigan	0-2	Washington	1-0
Michigan State	1-2	Washington State	2-0

Other Opponents

Austin College	12-0	Hardin-Simmons	1-0
Ball H.S.	1-0-1	Haskell	5-3
Bryan A.F.	2-0	Henry	1-0
Camp Mabry	1-0	Houston H.S.	3-2
Camp Travis	2-0	Houston Y.	1-0
Centenary	3-6	Howard Payne	3-1
Centre	1-0	Kansas City Medics	0-0-1
Corpus Christi Navy	0-1	Manhattan	2-0
Dallas	3-0	Missouri Mines	2-0
Daniel Baker	3-0	New York	1-0
Deaf & Dumb Inst.	1-0	North Texas Aggies	1-0-1
Ellington Field	1-0	Ouachita	1-0
Fordham	1-0	Phillips	1-0
Fort Worth	2-0	Polytechnic	1-0

Ream Field	1-0	Stephen F. Austin	2-0
St. Edward's	1-0	Tarlenton State	2-0
Sam Houston State	9-0	Texas A&I	5-0-1
San Francisco	2-0	Transylvania	1-1
Santa Clara	1-1	Trinity (Tex.)	18-1-2
Sewanee	5-2-1	Villanova	2-2
Southwestern (Tex.)	18-0	Waxahachie A.C.	1-0

Total Overall Record	463-344-47	.570
Total Conference Record	182-217-30	.459
Overall Bowl Game Record	8-5-0	.615

TEXAS CHRISTIAN

Nickname: Horned Frogs
Colors: Purple and white
Location: Fort Worth, Texas
Stadium: Amon G. Carter
          (46,000)

First year of football: 1896
Year entered conference: 1923
Conference championships: 8

Southwest Conference Competition

Arkansas	22-37-2	Southern Methodist	28-32-7
Baylor	44-40-7	Texas	19-50-1
Houston	1-8	Texas A&M	29-44-7
Rice	33-27-3	Texas Tech	20-18-3

Division I Competition

Air Force	0-0-1	North Carolina	0-1
Alabama	3-2	North Dakota	1-0
Arizona State	0-2	North Texas State	12-0
Auburn	0-3	Notre Dame	0-1
Clemson	1-2	Ohio State	1-4-1
Florida State	2-1	Oklahoma	2-4
Georgia	0-2	Oklahoma State	6-10-2
Georgia Tech	0-2	Oregon	1-1
Idaho	1-0	Penn State	1-3
Indiana	4-0	Pittsburgh	1-0-1
Iowa	1-2	Purdue	0-2
Kansas	15-5-4	Southern California	2-2
Kansas State	1-2	Syracuse	1-0
Kentucky	0-1	Temple	1-1
Louisiana State	2-5-1	Tennessee	0-2
Miami (Fla.)	3-5	Texas-Arlington	6-2
Michigan State	0-1	Texas-El Paso	0-1
Minnesota	0-1	Tulane	1-1
Mississippi	1-5	Tulsa	10-4
Mississippi State	0-0-1	UCLA	1-3
Nebraska	1-5	Utah State	2-0-1

Wake Forest	1-0	West Texas State	1-0
Washington	0-1	West Virginia	0-1
Washington State	1-0	Wisconsin	0-0-1

Other Opponents

Abilene Christian	2-0	Hardin-Simmons	9-1-2
Austin College	18-5	Haskell	0-1
Britten Training	1-0	Houston Heavyweights	0-1-1
Burleson	1-0	Howard Payne	6-2
Carnegie Tech	1-0	Loyola (La.)	2-0
Carruthers Field	0-1	Marquette	4-0
Centenary	8-4-1	Meridian	2-0
Centre	0-1	Missouri Osteopaths	2-0
Chatham Field	1-0	Pensacola Navy	1-0
Dallas	2-1-1	Phillips	1-0-1
Daniel Baker	11-4	Polytechnic	3-1-1
Deaf & Dumb Inst.	2-0	Santa Clara	3-0
Decatur Baptist	0-1	Second Texas 132nd	0-1
Detroit	0-1	South Plains A.A.F.	1-0
East Texas State	4-0	Southeast Oklahoma	1-0
11th Ambulance	1-0	Southwest Oklahoma	2-0-1
Epworth	0-1	Southwestern (Tex.)	7-5
First Texas Artillery	1-0	Texas Military	1-0
Fordham	0-2	Toby's Bus. Col.	2-0
Fort Worth	2-2-2	Trinity (Tex.)	15-4-2
Fort Worth Central	1-0		

Total Overall Record	401-385-55	.510
Total Conference Record	167-201-22	.456
Overall Bowl Game Record	4-8-1	.346

TEXAS TECH

Nickname: Red Raiders
Colors: Scarlet and black
Location: Lubbock, Texas
Stadium: Jones (47,000)

First year of football: 1925
Year entered conference: 1960
Conference championships: 1

Southwest Conference Competition

Arkansas	4-24	Southern Methodist	18-14
Baylor	17-24-1	Texas	6-28
Houston	4-13	Texas A&M	18-23-1
Rice	18-16-1	Texas Christian	18-20-3

Division I Competition

Air Force	1-1	Auburn	1-0
Arizona	25-3-2	Boston College	2-1

Brigham Young	1-0	North Texas State	0-1
Cincinnati	0-0-1	Northern Arizona	2-0
Colorado	2-1	Oklahoma State	11-7-3
Colorado State	1-0	Oregon State	1-0
Florida State	1-3	Pacific	3-2
Georgia	0-1	San Jose State	0-1
Georgia Tech	0-2	Southern California	0-2
Iowa State	2-0	Tennessee	1-0
Kansas	4-0	Texas-Arlington	1-0
Kansas State	2-0	Texas-El Paso	11-6-1
Louisiana State	0-2	Tulane	2-3
Louisiana Tech	1-0	Tulsa	9-11
Miami (Fla.)	1-2	Utah	2-0
Miami (of Ohio)	0-1	Vanderbilt	0-0-1
Mississippi State	2-4-1	Wake Forest	2-0
Montana	2-1	Washington	0-2
Montana State	2-0	Washington State	2-0
Nebraska	0-1	West Texas State	21-7
New Mexico	23-5-2	West Virginia	0-1
New Mexico State	4-0	Wichita State	1-1
North Carolina	1-2	Wyoming	1-2
North Carolina State	1-0		

Other Opponents

Abilene Christian	6-3	Marquette	2-1
Austin College	1-0-1	Montezuma	1-0
California-Santa Barbara	1-0	New Mexico Highlands	1-0
Centenary	4-0-1	North Dakota State	0-0-1
Clareton	2-0	North Texas Aggies	0-1
Colorado Mines	2-0	Notre Dame (B)	1-0
Creighton	2-1	Oklahoma City	3-0-1
Daniel Baker	2-1-2	Panhandle State	2-0
Denver	2-0	St. Edward's	3-0
DePaul	1-1-1	St. Louis	2-0
Detroit	0-2	St. Mary's (Ca.)	0-1
Dixie	1-0	St. Mary's (Tex.)	1-0
Duquesne	2-1	San Francisco	1-0
Gonzaga	1-1	Schreiner	1-0-1
Hardin-Simmons	14-7-3	South Plains A.A.F.	2-0
Haskell	1-1	Southwestern (Tex.)	1-1
Howard Payne	1-3	Sul Ross State	2-0-1
Loyola (Ca.)	2-3	Texas Wesleyan	2-0
Loyola (La.)	3-1	Trinity (Tex.)	1-0
Lubbock A.A.F.	1-2	Wayland Baptist	2-1
McMurry	4-0-2		

Total Overall Record	338-270-31	.553
Total Conference Record	81-98-5	.454
Overall Bowl Game Record	3-12-1	.219

Western Athletic Conference

Formed: 1962
Charter Members: Arizona, Arizona State, Brigham Young, New Mexico, Utah, Wyoming.

Overall Records

	Years	W	L	T	Pct.
San Diego State	64	348	222	27	.606
Utah	91	418	299	31	.580
Brigham Young	60	288	272	24	.514
New Mexico	82	336	340	31	.497
Hawaii	70	181	183	2	.497
Wyoming	87	331	356	27	.482
Air Force	29	143	154	12	.482
Colorado State	87	318	364	32	.468
Texas-El Paso	67	258	330	28	.442

Conference Records

	Years	W	L	T	Pct.
Brigham Young	23	98	48	1	.670
Hawaii	6	25	17	1	.593
Utah	23	70	63	4	.526
Wyoming	23	78	73	0	.517
San Diego State	7	23	27	2	.462
Air Force	5	16	19	0	.457
New Mexico	23	61	80	2	.434
Colorado State	17	39	65	2	.377
Texas-El Paso	17	19	99	0	.161
Arizona State	16	71	18	0	.798
Arizona	16	50	43	0	.538
Combined bowl game record:		22	18	2	.548

Total Championships

1.	Brigham Young	11	7.	Air Force	0
2.	Arizona State	7		Colorado State	0
3.	Wyoming	4		Hawaii	0
4.	New Mexico	3		San Diego State	0
5.	Arizona	2		Texas-El Paso	0
6.	Utah	1			

131

Past Champions

1984	Brigham Young		Arizona
1983	Brigham Young	1972	Arizona State
1982	Brigham Young	1971	Arizona State
1981	Brigham Young	1970	Arizona State
1980	Brigham Young	1969	Arizona State
1979	Brigham Young	1968	Wyoming
1978	Brigham Young	1967	Wyoming
1977	Arizona State	1966	Wyoming
	Brigham Young	1965	Brigham Young
1976	Wyoming	1964	Arizona
	Brigham Young		New Mexico
1975	Arizona State		Utah
1974	Brigham Young	1963	New Mexico
1973	Arizona State	1962	New Mexico

AIR FORCE ACADEMY

Nickname: Falcons
Colors: Silver and blue
Location: Colorado Springs,
　　　　　Colorado
Stadium: Falcon (46,668)

First year of football: 1956
Year entered conference: 1980
Conference championships: 0

Western Athletic Conference Competition

Brigham Young	1-6	San Diego State	4-1
Colorado State	14-8-1	Texas-El Paso	4-0
Hawaii	2-2	Utah	2-2
New Mexico	5-4	Wyoming	10-10-3

Division I Competition

Arizona	6-3	Illinois	0-1-1
Arizona State	2-2	Iowa	0-0-1
Arkansas	0-1	Iowa State	0-2
Army	9-9-1	Kansas State	0-3
Baylor	0-3	Kent State	1-1
Boston College	4-3	Maryland	0-2
California	1-4	Miami (Fla.)	0-2
Cincinnati	1-0	Michigan	0-1
Citadel	0-1	Mississippi	1-0
Colorado	4-12	Missouri	2-4
Davidson	2-0	Navy	9-8
Florida	0-1	Nebraska	1-1
Georgia Tech	0-3	Nevada-Las Vegas	0-1
Holy Cross	0-1	North Carolina	4-1
Idaho	3-0	Notre Dame	3-11
Idaho State	0-1	Oklahoma State	1-0-1

Oregon	4-6-1	Tulane	3-3
Pacific	3-0	Tulsa	2-3
Penn State	0-3	UCLA	4-6-1
Pittsburgh	2-0	Utah State	1-0
Rutgers	1-1	Vanderbilt	3-2
Southern Methodist	3-2	Virginia Tech	1-0
Stanford	3-4	Washington	3-2
Tennessee	0-1	Wisconsin	0-1
Texas Christian	0-0-1	Yale	0-1
Texas Tech	1-1		

Other Opponents

Colorado College	1-0	Northern Colorado	2-0
Colorado Mines	1-0	Occidental	1-0
Denver	2-1	San Diego	1-0
Detroit	2-0	Trinity (Tex.)	1-0
Eastern New Mexico	1-0	Western State	1-0
George Washington	0-2	Whittier	0-0-1

Total Overall Record	143-154-12	.482
Overall Conference Record	16-19-0	.457
Overall Bowl Game Record	3-2-1	.583

BRIGHAM YOUNG

Nickname: Cougars
Colors: Blue and white
Location: Provo, Utah
Stadium: BYU (65,000)

First year of football: 1922
Year entered conference: 1962
Conference championships: 11

Western Athletic Conference Competition

Air Force	6-1	San Diego State	9-2
Colorado State	22-22-3	Texas-El Paso	17-5-1
Hawaii	7-4	Utah	17-38-4
New Mexico	22-11-1	Wyoming	26-26-3

Division I Competition

Arizona	8-10-1	Indiana	0-1
Arizona State	5-17	Iowa	0-4
Baylor	1-1	Kansas State	3-4
Bowling Green	1-1	Michigan	1-0
Cal State-Long Beach	5-0	Missouri	1-0
Colorado	2-8-1	Montana	10-4
Fresno State	1-3	Montana State	10-7
Georgia	0-1	Navy	0-1
Idaho	1-2	Nevada-Las Vegas	3-1
Idaho State	3-0	Nevada-Reno	3-0-2

North Texas State	3-2	Texas A&M	1-0
Northern Arizona	0-2	Texas Tech	0-1
Ohio State	0-1	Tulsa	2-0
Oklahoma State	0-2	UCLA	1-0
Oregon	1-2	Utah State	25-32-3
Oregon State	3-4	Washington State	1-0
Pacific	2-3	Weber State	2-0
San Jose State	4-9	West Texas State	0-1
South Dakota	1-0	Western Michigan	3-2
Southern Methodist	1-0	Wichita State	0-1
Southern Mississippi	1-1	Wisconsin	1-0

Other Opponents

Cal Poly-San Luis Obispo	1-0	Mt. St. Charles	0-0-1
California-Davis	2-2-1	Occidental	2-0
Colorado College	4-3	Pacific Fleet	0-2
Colorado Mines	1-1-1	Pepperdine	3-1
Colorado State College	6-3-1	Portland	0-2
Denver	7-15	Regis	1-0
Fort Douglas	0-1	San Diego Marines	0-1
Fort Hood	1-0	San Diego N.A.S.	1-0
George Washington	0-2	San Francisco	0-2
Idaho College	1-0-1	UAY All-Stars	1-0
Los Angeles State	1-0	Western State	20-0

Total Overall Record	288-272-24	.514
Total Conference Record	98-48-1	.670
Overall Bowl Game Record	5-5-0	.500

COLORADO STATE

Nickname: Rams
Colors: Green and gold
Location: Ft. Collins, Colorado
Stadium: Hughes (30,000)

First year of football: 1892
Year entered conference: 1968
Conference championships: 0

Western Athletic Conference Competition

Air Force	8-14-1	San Diego State	3-4
Brigham Young	22-22-3	Texas-El Paso	15-6
Hawaii	4-5	Utah	13-40-2
New Mexico	18-16	Wyoming	40-31-5

Division I Competition

Arizona	2-12-1	Cal State-Fullerton	0-1
Arizona State	1-16	Colorado	15-44-2
Arkansas	0-2	Drake	3-2
Army	0-1	Florida State	1-1

Houston	0-2	Oklahoma State	1-1
Idaho	3-1	Oregon	0-1
Iowa State	1-4	Oregon State	1-1
Kansas	0-3	Pacific	7-3
Kansas State	1-4	San Jose State	1-1
Memphis State	0-1	Tennessee	0-1
Mississippi State	0-2	Texas Tech	0-1
Montana	10-6	Toledo	1-1
Montana State	0-0-1	Tulsa	0-2
Nebraska	0-3	UCLA	0-1
Nevada-Las Vegas	0-3-1	Utah State	32-30-2
Nevada-Reno	1-0	West Texas State	3-4-1
New Mexico State	6-1	West Virginia	1-2
North Texas State	0-2	Wichita State	4-2

Other Opponents

Bradley	0-1	Northern Colorado	15-0-1
Chicago	0-1	Occidental	0-1
Colorado College	20-16-5	Regis	3-1
Colorado Mines	27-16-2	South Dakota State	2-0
Denver	28-26-5	Western State	2-0
Kansas St. Teachers	1-0	Xavier	0-1
Longmont Acad.	1-1		

Total Overall Record	318-364-32	.468
Total Conference Record	39-65-2	.377
Overall Bowl Game Record	0-1-0	.000

HAWAII

Nickname: Rainbow Warriors   First year of football: 1909
Colors: Green and white   Year entered conference: 1979
Location: Honolulu, Hawaii   Conference championships: 0
Stadium: Aloha (50,000)

Western Athletic Conference Competition

Air Force	2-2	San Diego State	5-4-1
Brigham Young	4-7	Texas-El Paso	8-5
Colorado State	5-4	Utah	5-11
New Mexico	7-3	Wyoming	3-4

Division I Competition

Arizona	0-3	California	1-1
Arizona State	1-5	Cincinnati	0-1
Bowling Green	1-0	Colorado	1-0
Cal State-Fullerton	7-1	Fresno State	9-13
Cal State-Long Beach	2-4	Iowa	0-2

Kent State	0-1	South Carolina	2-0
Kentucky	0-1	Southern California	0-3
Michigan State	0-2	Southern Mississippi	0-1
Nebraska	1-5	Southwestern Louisiana	1-0
Nevada-Las Vegas	7-3	Stanford	0-3
New Mexico State	1-0	Temple	0-1
Oklahoma	0-2	Tennessee	0-2
Oregon	0-4	UCLA	0-2
Oregon State	1-3	Utah State	1-4
Pacific	5-14	Washington	1-1
Rutgers	1-1	Washington State	1-1
San Jose State	6-11	West Virginia	1-0

Other Opponents

(Because the University of Hawaii has played numerous informal contests against obscure opponents, no series records are listed.)

Record against other opponents in recorded games: 98-52-1

Total Overall Record	181-183-2	.497
Total Conference Record	25-17-1	.593
Overall Bowl Game Record	0-0-0	

NEW MEXICO

Nickname: Lobos
Colors: Cherry and silver
Location: Albuquerque, New Mexico
Stadium: University (30,650)

First year of football: 1892
Year entered conference: 1962
Conference championships: 3

Western Athletic Conference Competition

Air Force	4-5	San Diego State	5-6
Brigham Young	11-22-1	Texas-El Paso	32-21-3
Colorado State	16-18	Utah	8-16-2
Hawaii	3-7	Wyoming	20-21

Division I Competition

Arizona	18-39-3	Idaho State	1-0
Arizona State	5-22-1	Iowa State	1-5
Arkansas	0-1	Kansas	1-2
Army	0-2	Kansas State	4-0
Baylor	0-1	Louisiana Tech	1-0
Colorado	3-6	Missouri	0-1
Drake	1-1	Montana	10-4
Fresno State	2-1	Montana State	0-1-1
Houston	0-2	Nevada-Las Vegas	2-3

Nevada–Reno	1-0-1	Tennessee	0-1
New Mexico State	47-23-5	Texas	0-1
North Texas State	1-1	Texas A&M	0-1
Northern Arizona	19-3	Texas Tech	5-23-2
Oklahoma	0-2	Utah State	8-6
Oregon State	1-0	West Texas State	6-8
Pacific	1-0	Western Michigan	1-0
Rice	0-1	Wichita State	2-0
San Jose State	4-9-1		

Other Opponents

Albuquerque H.S.	4-5-1	Loyola (Ca.)	0-3-1
Albuquerque Indians	14-4-1	Lubbock A.F.B.	1-0
Amarillo A.F.B.	0-1	Marquette	0-1
Bradley	0-1	Menaul H.S.	4-0-1
Colorado College	5-5-1	Mexico	1-0
Colorado Mines	1-1-1	Montezuma	7-0
Colorado State College	0-2	New Mexico Highlands	6-1
Denver	9-9	New Mexico Military	11-7-3
Eastern New Mexico	1-0	New Mexico Mines	8-1
El Paso Military	1-2	New Mexico Western	6-1
Fort Bliss	2-0	Occidental	1-1
Hardin-Simmons	0-4	Santa Fe Indians	2-0-1
Hawaiian All-Stars	0-1	Second Army A.F.	0-1
Kirtland A.F.B.	2-0	Southwestern (Tex.)	0-1
Lombard	0-0-1	Western Colorado State	3-1

Total Overall Record	336-340-31	.497
Total Conference Record	61-80-2	.434
Overall Bowl Game Record	2-2-1	.500

SAN DIEGO STATE

Nickname: Aztecs	First year of football: 1921
Colors: Scarlet and black	Year entered conference: 1978
Location: San Diego, California	Conference championships: 0
Stadium: Jack Murphy (60,400)	

Western Athletic Conference Competition

Air Force	1-4	New Mexico	6-5
Brigham Young	2-9	Texas-El Paso	9-1
Colorado State	4-3	Utah	3-3-1
Hawaii	4-5-1	Wyoming	3-4

Division I Competition

Akron	1-0	Arizona State	0-6-1
Arizona	5-6	Arkansas State	1-0

Boston	1-0	Northern Arizona	2-0
Bowling Green	2-0-1	Northern Illinois	4-0
Cal State-Fullerton	3-0	Oklahoma State	2-2
Cal State-Long Beach	13-10	Oregon State	2-0
California	1-1	Pacific	14-7
Florida State	2-0	San Jose State	10-16-2
Fresno State	22-16-4	Southern Mississippi	2-1
Houston	0-2	Tennessee State	1-0-1
Iowa State	3-3	Texas-Arlington	2-0
Kent State	2-0	Texas Southern	1-0
Miami (Fla.)	1-1	Tulsa	1-1
Missouri	0-2	UCLA	0-7-1
Montana State	3-0	Utah State	9-1
Nevada-Las Vegas	4-2	Washington	0-1
Nevada-Reno	0-2	Weber State	2-0
New Mexico State	6-1-1	West Texas State	2-0
North Texas State	6-1	Wisconsin	1-1

Other Opponents

Army-Navy Academy	2-0	North Dakota State	1-0
Cal Poly-Pomona	3-1	Northridge State	6-0
Cal Poly-San Luis Obispo	13-9	Occidental	11-7-1
California Christian	8-0	Pepperdine	11-2-1
California-Santa Barbara	26-8-1	Pomona	10-7-1
California Tech	4-6	Redlands	17-7-2
California Western	3-0	Reserve Destroyers	0-1
Chaffey J.C.	2-0	Riverside J.C.	3-1
Coronado H.S.	1-0	San Diego	1-0
El Centro J.C.	1-0	San Diego Marines	5-4-1
Fullerton J.C.	1-1	San Francisco State	7-1
Hardin-Simmons	0-1	Santa Ana J.C.	3-1
LaVerne	10-2-3	Submarines Pacific	0-1
Loyola (Ca.)	3-4	Tampa	1-0
Mexico Poly	1-0	Whittier	11-10-2
Naval Air	0-2		

Total Overall Record	348-222-27	.606
Total Conference Record	23-27-2	.462
Overall Bowl Game Record	1-1-0	.500

TEXAS-EL PASO

Nickname: Miners
Colors: Orange, white, and
    blue
Location: El Paso, Texas
Stadium: Sun Bowl (52,000)

First year of football: 1914
Year entered conference: 1968
Conference championships: 0

Western Athletic Conference Competition

Air Force	0–4	New Mexico	21–32–3
Brigham Young	5–17–1	San Diego State	1–9
Colorado State	6–15	Utah	4–14
Hawaii	5–8	Wyoming	6–17

Division I Competition

Arizona	11–36–2	North Dakota	1–0
Arizona State	13–30–3	North Texas State	5–13–3
Baylor	0–1	Northern Arizona	5–0–1
Bowling Green	0–1	Oklahoma State	0–3
Cal State–Long Beach	1–1	Pacific	2–7
Cincinnati	0–2	San Jose State	1–0
Drake	1–1	Southern Methodist	0–3
East Tennessee State	1–0	Southern Mississippi	1–0
Florida State	1–0	Texas	0–2
Fresno State	0–1–1	Texas A&M	0–1
Houston	2–0	Texas-Arlington	3–0
Idaho	1–1	Texas Christian	1–0
Idaho State	1–1	Texas Tech	6–11–1
Kansas State	1–0	Utah State	0–2
Lamar	0–2	Washington	0–1
Louisiana Tech	1–2–1	Weber State	1–0
Mississippi	1–0	West Texas State	15–9–1
Nevada–Las Vegas	1–4	West Virginia	1–1–1
New Mexico State	35–27–2	Wichita State	2–0

Other Opponents

Abilene Christian	2–3	Lower Valley	1–0
Army All-Stars	1–0	Loyola (Ca.)	0–1
Base Hospital	1–0	McMurry	4–0
Calamus Club	0–1	Midwestern	1–0
California–Santa Barbara	1–0–2	Motor Transport	1–0
Commercial Club	0–1	New Mexico Military	12–5–1
Daniel Baker	2–0	New Mexico Mines	2–0
8th Cavalry	2–0	New Mexico Teachers	1–0
El Paso H.S.	1–3–2	New Mexico Western	4–0
El Paso J.C.	2–0	St. Edward's	2–1–2
El Paso Y.	1–0	St. Mary's (Tex.)	0–0–2
Fort Bliss All-Stars	0–1	Southwestern (Tex.)	0–1
George Washington	0–1	Sul Ross State	10–4–1
Georgetown	1–0	Texas A&I	0–1
Gila J.C.	2–0	Trinity (Tex.)	6–4
Greeley State	2–0	20th Infantry	1–0
Hardin-Simmons	10–19–1	Wayland Baptist	4–0
Howard Payne	1–1	Xavier	2–1
John Carroll	1–0		

Total Overall Record	258–330–28	.442
Total Conference Record	19–99–0	.161
Overall Bowl Game Record	5–3–0	.625

UTAH

Nickname: Utes
Colors: Crimson and white
Location: Salt Lake City, Utah
Stadium: Rice (35,000)

First year of football: 1892
Year entered conference: 1962
Conference championships: 1

Western Athletic Conference Competition

Air Force	2-2	New Mexico	16-7-2
Brigham Young	38-17-4	San Diego State	3-3-1
Colorado State	39-13-2	Texas-El Paso	14-4
Hawaii	11-5	Wyoming	36-21-1

Division I Competition

Arizona	16-13-2	Nevada-Reno	0-4-1
Arizona State	6-12	Northwestern	1-1
Army	0-3	Oklahoma State	0-1
Boise State	0-1	Oregon	5-14
Cal State-Fullerton	1-0	Oregon State	2-8-1
Cal State-Long Beach	1-0	Pacific	0-1
California	1-3	Rice	0-2
Colorado	24-30-3	San Jose State	3-1
Drake	1-0	South Dakota	1-0
Florida	0-1	Southern California	2-5
Fresno State	1-0	Stanford	0-2
Houston	0-3	Tennessee	0-3
Idaho	14-11-2	Texas	0-1
Indiana	0-1	Texas A&M	0-1
Iowa State	0-4	Texas Tech	0-2
Kansas	0-2	Tulsa	0-1
Louisiana State	0-2	UCLA	0-7
Minnesota	0-1	Utah State	52-26-4
Missouri	1-1	Washington	0-6
Montana	10-0	Washington State	3-3
Montana State	9-0	Weber State	2-0
Nebraska	0-2	West Virginia	1-0
Nevada-Las Vegas	3-1	Wisconsin	0-1

Other Opponents

All Hallows	2-0	Colorado State College	5-0
All-Stars	1-0	Creighton	0-1-1
Alumni	1-0	Crescents	0-1
Brigham Young Acad.	3-2	Denver	28-9-5
Carlisle	0-1	Diamond Butchers	1-0
Collegiates	0-1	Fort Douglas	6-0
Colorado College	14-11	Fort Team	2-0
Colorado Mines	7-3	Fort Warren	0-1

Greeley State	2–0	Pomona	0–0–1
Honolulu All-Stars	1–0	Portland State	1–0
Idaho College	3–0	St. Mary's (Ca.)	0–1
Idaho Navy	2–0	St. Vincent's	0–1
Idaho Southern	1–0	Salt Lake City H.S.	3–4
L.D.S.	1–0	Salt Lake City Y.	1–6
National Guard	0–1	San Francisco	1–0
Occidental	1–1	Santa Clara	1–2–1
Ogden H.S.	6–0	Western State	1–0
Old Timers	1–0	Whitman	2–0
Pocatello A.C.	1–0		

Total Overall Record	418–299–31	.580
Total Conference Record	70–63–4	.526
Overall Bowl Game Record	2–1–0	.667

WYOMING

Nickname: Cowboys	First year of football: 1893
Colors: Brown and yellow	Year entered conference: 1962
Location: Laramie, Wyoming	Conference championships: 4
Stadium: War Memorial	
(33,500)	

Western Athletic Conference Competition

Air Force	10–10–3	New Mexico	22–19
Brigham Young	26–26–3	San Diego State	4–3
Colorado State	31–40–5	Texas-El Paso	17–6
Hawaii	4–3	Utah	22–36–1

Division I Competition

Arizona	10–12	Louisiana State	0–3
Arizona State	6–9	Michigan State	0–2
Arkansas State	1–0	Minnesota	0–1
Army	0–1	Montana	12–0
Baylor	1–1	Montana State	11–6
Cal State-Fullerton	1–1	Nebraska	0–4
Cal State-Long Beach	1–0	Nevada-Las Vegas	1–3
Colgate	1–0	Nevada-Reno	0–1
Colorado	2–21–1	New Mexico State	1–0
Florida	0–1	North Carolina State	2–0
Florida State	1–0	Northwestern	0–1
Houston	0–5	Oklahoma	0–2
Idaho	2–1	Oklahoma State	0–3
Idaho State	3–1	Oregon State	2–1
Iowa	0–1	Pacific	1–1
Kansas	1–2–1	Richmond	2–0
Kansas State	4–3	San Jose State	3–0

South Dakota	5-0	Utah State	20-34-4
Southern California	0-1	Washington	0-1
Texas	0-2	Washington State	1-1
Texas Tech	2-1	Wichita State	3-1
Tulsa	2-0	Wisconsin	0-1

Other Opponents

Alumni	1-0	Laramie A.C.	3-0
Black Hills	3-0	Laramie All-Stars	1-0
Chadron State	4-2	Laramie H.S.	5-1
Cheyenne H.S.	9-0	Laramie Town Team	2-0
Chicago	0-1	Montezuma	1-0
Colorado College	1-16-1	Nebraska Wesleyan	2-3
Colorado Mines	9-16-2	#5 Hose Company	1-0
Colorado State College	17-5-3	Ogden A.C.	1-0
Creighton	0-4	Regis	1-1
Denver	11-32-2	St. Louis	0-2
Denver A.C.	0-1	San Francisco	0-1
Denver Manual	1-0	Santa Clara	0-1
Faculty	1-1	South Dakota Mines	1-0-1
Fort Warren	12-1	South Dakota State	1-0
Gonzaga	0-1	Washington & Lee	1-0
Grand Island	1-0	Western State	4-0
Hardin-Simmons	1-0	Wilson Beauties	1-0
Kearney State	3-1		

Total Overall Record	331-356-27	.482
Total Conference Record	78-73-0	.517
Overall Bowl Game Record	4-2-0	.667

Independent Schools

Overall Records

	Years	W	L	T	Pct.
Notre Dame	96	641	186	40	.762
Penn State	98	593	266	40	.682
Army	95	532	282	50	.645
Pittsburgh	95	520	333	38	.605
Southern Mississippi	49	364	241	25	.598
Boston College	86	449	297	34	.597
Navy	104	520	351	58	.591
West Virginia	92	486	337	40	.586
Syracuse	95	509	354	45	.585
Virginia Tech	91	459	324	43	.582
Florida State	38	222	160	16	.578
Miami (Fla.)	58	313	249	19	.555
East Carolina	49	235	207	11	.532
Rutgers	115	466	411	35	.530
Memphis State	69	317	290	28	.521
Southwestern Louisiana	77	360	335	30	.517
Temple	86	338	321	52	.512
Cincinnati	94	405	389	46	.510
South Carolina	90	396	388	38	.505
Tulane	91	388	384	38	.502
Louisville	66	275	299	15	.480
Combined bowl game record:		66	75	6	.469

BOSTON COLLEGE

Nickname: Eagles
Colors: Maroon and gold
Location: Chestnut Hill, Massachusetts

Stadium: Alumni (32,000)
Sullivan (61,000)
First year of football: 1893

Division I Competition

Air Force	3-4	Auburn	2-1
Alabama	3-1	Baylor	2-0
Army	10-10	Boston	27-4-1

Brown	0-5	Northeastern	3-0
Cincinnati	2-1	Northern Illinois	1-0
Clemson	5-7-2	Northwestern	0-1
Connecticut	6-0-2	Notre Dame	0-2
Dartmouth	1-2	Ohio	0-1
Drake	1-0	Oklahoma	0-2
Duke	2-1	Pacific	1-0
Florida	1-1	Penn State	1-12
Florida State	1-2	Pittsburgh	2-9
Georgia	0-2	Rhode Island	4-2
Georgia Tech	0-1	Richmond	4-1
Harvard	0-3-1	Rutgers	5-1
Holy Cross	46-31-3	Stanford	1-1
Houston	2-1	Syracuse	11-14
Idaho	1-0	Temple	12-3-2
Indiana	1-0	Tennessee	1-6
Iowa State	1-0	Texas	1-2
Kansas State	3-0	Texas A&M	3-1
Kentucky	1-0	Texas Tech	1-2
Lafayette	0-1	Tulane	5-7
Louisiana State	0-2	Vanderbilt	2-0
Maine	2-3	Virginia	1-0
Massachusetts	16-5	Virginia Military	7-1-1
Miami (Fla.)	3-8	Wake Forest	5-3-2
Michigan State	2-0-1	West Virginia	5-8
Mississippi	0-3-1	Western Carolina	1-0
Navy	10-9	Wichita State	1-0
New Hampshire	6-5	William and Mary	3-0-1
North Carolina	1-1	Yale	4-0
North Carolina State	1-1		

Other Opponents

Allegheny	2-0	Loyola (Md.)	2-0
Bates	0-2-1	M.I.T.	1-1
Bowdoin	0-2	Manhatten	3-0
Brandeis	2-0	Marietta	2-0
Brooklyn College	2-0	Marquette	6-6-1
Buffalo	5-3	Melville P.T.	0-1
Canisius	5-0	Merchant Marine	1-1
Catholic	7-0	Middlebury	2-0
Centenary	1-1	Morgan State	1-0
Centre	5-0	New York	3-0
Colby	0-2	New York C.C.	1-0
Dayton	4-0	Norwich	4-0
Detroit	12-7	Providence	6-1
Fordham	14-11-2	Quantico Marines	2-1
Geneva	0-1	St. Anselm's	11-3-3
Georgetown	11-5-1	St. Bonaventure	0-0-1
Gettysburg	1-0	St. Joseph's	1-0
Haskell	2-0-1	St. Louis	1-0
Lebanon Valley	1-0	St. Mary's (Ca.)	2-0
Loyola (Chi.)	1-0	Scranton	2-0

Springfield	4-1	Villanova	29-15-1
Squantum N.A.S.	1-0	West Virginia Wesleyan	2-1
Trinity (Ct.)	1-0	Western Maryland	4-2-1
Tufts	3-9	Worcester Tech	2-0
Vermont	1-0-1	Xavier	1-3

Total Overall Record   449-297-34   .597
Overall Bowl Game Record   2-4-0   .333

CINCINNATI

Nickname: Bearcats
Colors: Red and black
Location: Cincinnati, Ohio

Stadium: Riverfront (59,750)
Nippert (26,590)
First year of football: 1888

Division I Competition

Air Force	0-1	Morehead State	0-1
Akron	1-0	Navy	0-2
Alabama	0-3	Nebraska	0-1
Arizona State	2-0	Nevada-Reno	0-1
Arkansas State	0-1	North Carolina	0-1
Army	0-1	North Texas State	7-8-1
Auburn	0-1	Northeast Louisiana	3-0
Boston College	1-2	Northwest Louisiana	1-0
Boston University	1-3	Northwestern	0-2
Cal State-Long Beach	1-0	Notre Dame	0-1
Colorado	0-1	Ohio	23-23-4
Cornell	1-0	Ohio State	2-9
Dartmouth	1-0	Oklahoma State	1-2
Drake	1-0	Pacific	5-3
Florida	0-1	Penn State	1-1
Florida State	0-5	Pittsburgh	0-4
Georgia	0-2	Rice	1-0
Hawaii	1-0	Richmond	3-3
Houston	2-11	Rutgers	2-2
Indiana	3-6-2	South Carolina	0-2
Indiana State	1-0	South Dakota	4-0
Kansas State	4-0	Southern Mississippi	3-1
Kent State	1-0	Southwestern Louisiana	4-0
Kentucky	7-16-3	Temple	2-8-1
Louisiana State	1-0	Tennessee	1-3
Louisville	19-7-1	Tennessee-Chattanooga	1-0
Marshall	5-2-1	Texas A&M	1-0
Maryland	0-2	Texas-El Paso	2-0
Memphis State	5-11	Texas Tech	0-0-1
Miami (Fla.)	1-4	Toledo	3-0
Miami (of Ohio)	34-49-6	Tulane	2-5
Michigan State	1-1	Tulsa	9-16-2
Mississippi State	1-1	Vanderbilt	3-2

Virginia Military	2-0	Western Michigan	2-0
Virginia Tech	1-0	Wichita State	13-7-2
Washington	0-1	William and Mary	3-1
West Texas State	0-1	Wisconsin	0-1
West Virginia	0-6	Youngstown State	1-2

Other Opponents

Alumni	2-1	Kenyon	9-4
Antioch	1-1	Lebanon Valley	1-0
Ashland	1-0	Marietta	4-6-1
Avondale	1-3	Marquette	6-2
Baldwin-Wallace	1-0	Morgan State	1-0
Baltimore C.C.	1-0	Muskingum	0-1
Butler	6-2-1	Nashville Guards	0-0-1
Carlisle	0-4	Oberlin	1-2
Carnegie Tech	2-1	Ohio Medics	1-0
Case Tech	2-1	Ohio National Guards	1-0
Cedarville	2-0	Ohio Northern	2-2
Centre	6-5-3	Ohio Wesleyan	9-9-1
Chicago	0-1	Oklahoma City	1-0
Cincinnati Gym	1-0-1	Otterbein	6-3
Cincinnati Y.	0-1	Rio Grande	2-0
Covington Y.	1-0	St. Bonaventure	1-0
Dayton	15-17-1	South Dakota State	1-0
Dayton Y.	1-1	Southern A.C.	1-0
Denison	7-14-2	Stumps	0-2
DePauw	2-1	Tampa	3-0
Detroit	5-4-1	Transylvania	6-2
Duquesne A.C.	0-1	Villanova	2-2
Earlham	5-4	Wabash	2-0
Fort Thomas	1-0	Walnut Hills Gym	1-0
Franklin	1-0-1	Washington (Mo.)	0-1
George Washington	1-1	Washington and Jefferson	0-1
Georgetown	0-2	Washington and Lee	1-0
Georgetown (Ky.)	8-3	Wayne State	2-0
Hanover	10-1	Western Reserve	10-3-2
Hardin-Simmons	5-1-1	Wilmington	1-0
Haskell	0-1	Wittenberg	10-11-5
Heidelberg	1-0	Woodward	1-1
Hughes	1-0	Wooster	0-3
Illinois Wesleyan	1-0	Wyoming Sem.	2-0
Indianapolis	1-0	Xavier	18-12
Kentucky Wesleyan	5-2-1		

Total Overall Record   405-389-46   .510
Overall Bowl Game Record   2-1-0   .667

EAST CAROLINA

Nickname: Pirates
Colors: Purple and gold
Location: Greenville, North
        Carolina

Stadium: Ficklen (35,000)
First year of football: 1932

Division I Competition

Appalachian State	10-19	North Carolina State	4-11
Bowling Green	1-1	North Texas State	1-0
Central Michigan	1-1	Northeast Louisiana	1-1
Citadel	14-4	Northeastern	1-0
Davidson	5-2	Pittsburgh	0-1
Duke	2-2	Richmond	13-11
East Tennessee State	5-4-1	South Carolina	0-2
Eastern Kentucky	1-1	Southern Illinois	8-2
Florida	0-1	Southern Mississippi	3-7
Florida State	0-4	Southwestern Louisiana	3-3
Furman	11-3	Temple	2-1
Georgia Southern	1-0	Tennessee-Chattanooga	1-0
Illinois State	1-0	Texas-Arlington	2-0
Indiana State	1-0	Toledo	2-2
Louisiana Tech	1-2	Tulsa	0-1
Louisville	2-1	Virginia	1-0
Maine	1-0	Virginia Military	7-1
Marshall	4-1	Virginia Tech	0-1
Massachusetts	1-0	Wake Forest	1-1
Miami (Fla.)	0-3	West Texas State	0-2
Missouri	1-1	West Virginia	0-4
Murray State	1-0	Western Carolina	17-13
North Carolina	1-6-1	William and Mary	11-4-1

Other Opponents

Albright	1-0	Howard	2-0
Atlantic Christian	3-1-1	Kutztown State	1-1
Belmont Abbey	1-2	Lenoir-Rhyne	6-15
Bergen	1-0	Little Creek (Va.)	0-1
Campbell	1-3	Louisburg	3-1
Catawba	8-3-1	Morris-Harvey	0-2
Cherry Point Marines	3-1	Newberry	3-3
Chowan	1-0	Newport News Apprent.	10-1
Clarion State	0-1	Norfolk Navy	4-3
Dayton	2-0	No. Carolina St. Frosh	0-4
Duke (B)	0-1	Oak Ridge	0-1
Edenton Flyers	1-0	Parsons	2-0
Elon	9-9	Presbyterian	6-5
Emory and Henry	1-0	Randolph-Macon	1-0
Erskine	2-1	Stetson	2-0-2
Fort Bragg	1-0	Tampa	1-5
George Washington	1-1	Tusculum	1-0
Guilford	9-5-1	Wake Forest Frosh	0-2
Hampden-Sydney	0-2	West Chester State	2-2
High Point	2-4-1	West Virginia Tech	1-0

| William and Mary (Norf.) | 3-3-1 | Wingate | 0-2 |
| Wilson Teachers | 1-0 | Wofford | 3-1-1 |

Total Overall Record	235-207-11	.532
Overall Bowl Game Record	3-0-0	1.000

FLORIDA STATE

Nickname: Seminoles
Colors: Garnet and gold
Location: Tallahassee, Florida

Stadium: Doak Campbell
(55,250)
First year of football: 1947

Division I Competition

Alabama	0-2-1	Ohio State	2-0
Arizona State	3-1	Oklahoma	1-3
Auburn	1-11-1	Oklahoma State	2-1
Baylor	1-2-1	Penn State	0-0-1
Boston College	2-1	Pittsburgh	3-5
Cincinnati	5-0	Richmond	3-0
Citadel	4-0-1	San Diego State	0-2
Clemson	2-1	South Carolina	9-3
Colorado State	1-1	Southern Illinois	1-0
East Carolina	4-0	Southern Mississippi	9-7-1
Florida	6-20-1	Syracuse	1-1
Furman	7-2	Temple	1-0
Georgia	4-5-1	Tennessee	1-0
Georgia Tech	0-7-1	Tennessee-Chattanooga	1-0
Houston	2-12-2	Tennessee Tech	1-1
Iowa State	0-1	Texas A&M	2-0
Kansas	3-2	Texas Christian	1-2
Kansas State	3-0	Texas-El Paso	0-1
Kentucky	1-3-1	Texas Tech	3-1
Louisiana State	4-2	Tulane	1-1
Louisiana Tech	0-2	Tulsa	4-0
Louisville	8-1	Utah State	1-0
Maryland	2-0	Virginia Military	2-1
Memphis State	6-7-1	Virginia Tech	14-10-1
Miami (Fla.)	13-15	Wake Forest	7-2-1
Mississippi	0-1	West Virginia	1-0
Mississippi State	7-2	Western Carolina	1-0
Navy	1-0	Wichita State	1-0
Nebraska	1-1	William and Mary	1-1
New Mexico State	1-0	Wyoming	0-1

Other Opponents

| Abilene Christian | 1-2 | Delta State | 1-0 |
| Cumberland | 1-1 | Erskine | 1-1 |

George Washington	1-0	Sewanee	2-0
Howard	1-0	Stetson	6-1-1
Jacksonville N.A.S.	1-0	Sul Ross State	1-0
Jacksonville State	0-1	Tampa	9-2
Livingston State	1-1	Troy State	4-1
Millsaps	2-0	Villanova	3-1
Mississippi College	3-0	Whiting Field	1-0
Newberry	1-0	Wofford	3-0
Randolph-Macon	1-0		

Total Overall Record   222-160-16   .578
Overall Bowl Game Record   4-7-2   .385

LOUISVILLE

Nickname: Cardinals
Colors: Red, white, and black
Location: Louisville, Kentucky

Stadium: Cardinal (37,000)
First year of football: 1912

Division I Competition

Akron	2-0	North Carolina State	1-0
Alabama	0-2	North Texas State	6-10
Army	1-0	Northeast Louisiana	1-2
Auburn	0-1	Northern Illinois	1-0
Boston	2-1	Northwest Louisiana	1-0
Cal State-Long Beach	1-0-1	Ohio	2-2
Central Michigan	2-0	Oklahoma State	1-1
Cincinnati	8-19-1	Pittsburgh	0-4
Drake	10-5-1	Richmond	1-0
East Carolina	1-2	Rutgers	0-3
Eastern Kentucky	15-7-1	Southeastern Louisiana	1-0
Florida	0-1	Southern Illinois	7-3
Florida State	1-8	Southern Methodist	0-2
Furman	1-0	Southern Mississippi	3-7-1
Houston	2-3	Temple	0-3
Indiana State	5-3-1	Tennessee	0-2
Kansas	1-0	Tennessee-Chattanooga	3-4
Kent State	8-9	Tennessee State	0-2
Kentucky	0-6	Tennessee Tech	1-1
Louisiana Tech	0-1	Toledo	5-3
Marshall	16-8	Tulsa	7-11
Maryland	0-2	Vanderbilt	0-2-1
Memphis State	7-15	Virginia Tech	0-2
Miami (Fla.)	0-7-1	West Texas State	2-1
Mississippi State	2-2	West Virginia	0-1
Missouri	0-1	Western Kentucky	13-12
Morehead State	5-3	Wichita State	13-4
Murray State	8-6	William and Mary	1-1

Other Opponents

Alfred Holbrook	3-0	Long Island	0-1
Baldwin-Wallace	0-1	Moore Hill	1-0
Bethel	1-1-1	Morris Harvey	1-0
Bradley	4-0	Oakland City	0-1
Buffalo	1-1	Ogden	1-0
Butler	2-2	Rio Grande	2-0
Catawba	2-0	Rose Poly	6-1
Centenary	0-2	St. Bonaventure	0-1
Centre	3-10-3	St. Francis	1-0
Cumberland	1-1	St. Joseph's (Ind.)	5-2-1
Davis and Elkins	0-1	St. Louis	0-1
Dayton	13-12	South Dakota State	1-0
DePaul	0-2	Tampa	2-0
DePauw	1-2	Transylvania	7-12
Detroit	0-1	Union	2-2
Duquesne	0-1	Union (Ky.)	1-4
Earlham	2-0	Wabash	0-2
Evansville	12-2	Washington (Mo.)	3-1
Florida Southern	1-0	Washington (Tenn.)	1-0
Franklin	0-4	Washington and Lee	1-1
Georgetown (Ky.)	7-10	Wayne State	4-2
Hanover	8-4	Wittenberg	2-0
Kentucky Wesleyan	4-0-1	Xavier	0-13
King	0-1		

Total Overall Record	275-299-15	.480
Overall Bowl Game Record	1-1-1	.500

MEMPHIS STATE

Nickname: Tigers

Colors: Blue and gray

Location: Memphis, Tennessee

Stadium: Liberty Bowl Memorial (50,180)

First year of football: 1912

Division I Competition

Alabama	0-3	Kansas State	1-2
Arkansas State	16-18-3	Kentucky	0-4
Auburn	2-0	Louisiana Tech	5-5
Austin Peay	6-0	Louisville	15-7
Cincinnati	11-5	McNeese State	2-0
Citadel	2-1	Miami (Fla.)	1-0
Colorado State	1-0	Middle Tennessee State	7-12-1
Drake	0-1	Mississippi	5-32-1
East Tennessee State	2-0	Mississippi State	7-16
Florida State	7-6-1	Murray State	9-9-2
Furman	0-1	North Carolina	0-2
Georgia	0-2	North Texas State	15-4
Georgia Tech	1-2	Northeastern Louisiana	0-1
Houston	4-5	San Jose State	1-0

South Carolina	2-2	Tulane	3-5-1
Southeastern Louisiana	1-2	Tulsa	8-4
Southern Methodist	1-0	Utah State	4-3
Southern Mississippi	14-19-1	Vanderbilt	2-6
Southwestern Louisiana	5-0	Virginia Military	1-0
Tennessee	0-9	Virginia Tech	3-2
Tennessee-Chattanooga	8-5	Wake Forest	2-2
Tennessee Tech	9-7-4	West Texas State	6-0
Texas A&M	0-2	Western Kentucky	2-2-1
Texas-Arlington	2-0	Wichita State	10-0

Other Opponents

Abilene Christian	3-0-1	McKenzie-McTyiere	0-1
Arkansas College	2-2	Mayfield	2-0
Arkansas Monticello	1-0	Memphis U. School	1-6-1
Arkansas Teachers	1-3	Millsaps	2-2
Arkansas Tech	2-0	Mississippi Heights	1-1
Athens	1-0	Mississippi Reserves	0-1
Bethel	7-4-2	Mississippi Teachers	0-1
Blytheville H.S.	0-0-1	Missouri Mines	1-1
Bolton	2-0	Navy Millington NATTC	2-2
Caruthersville J.C.	2-0-1	Osceola A.C.	1-0
Castle Heights Mil. Inst.	0-1	Ouachita	0-1
Centenary	1-0	Paragould H.S.	0-1
Central H.S.	1-6	Pensacola Navy	2-0
Central-MUS All-Stars	0-1	Quantico Marines	1-1
Christian Brothers	3-2	Somerville H.S.	4-0
Cumberland	2-1	Southeast Missouri State	2-1-2
Delta State	9-4-1	Southwestern (Tenn.)	2-6
Detroit	1-0	Springfield State	1-1
East Central Oklahoma	1-0	Stephen F. Austin	1-0
1st Battalion Tenn.	1-0	Sunflower J.C.	2-0
Ford Kelvington	1-0	Tampa	3-0
Freed-Hardeman	1-0	Tech H.S.	1-0
Hall-Moody	0-2	Tennessee J.C.	3-0
Hardin-Simmons	2-0	Tennessee Med.	0-3
Haywood City H.S.	2-0-1	Tennessee Reserves	0-0-1
Hendrix	1-3	Trinity (Tex.)	0-2
Jackson H.S.	2-1	Troy State	4-1
Jacksonville State	1-0	Tupelo Mil. Inst.	1-0
Jonesboro	4-0-1	Union	9-13
Lambuth	3-1	Vocational H.S.	1-0
Little Rock College	1-3	Washington (Mo.)	2-0
Livingston State	1-0	Wilson H.S.	1-0
Louisiana College	5-3		

Total Overall Record	317-290-28	.521
Overall Bowl Game Record	1-0-0	1.000

MIAMI

Nickname: Hurricanes
Colors: Orange, green, and
　　white
Location: Coral Gables, Florida

Stadium: Orange Bowl (76,120)
First year of football: 1927

Division I Competition

Air Force	2-0	Nebraska	2-4
Alabama	2-13	Nevada-Las Vegas	1-0
Army	3-0	North Carolina	3-4
Auburn	4-7	North Carolina State	5-3-1
Baylor	4-3	North Texas State	1-0
Boston College	8-3	Northwestern	2-2
Boston University	2-1-1	Notre Dame	4-13-1
Bucknell	3-1-1	Ohio State	0-1
California	0-1	Oklahoma	0-2
Cincinnati	4-1	Oregon	1-0
Citadel	1-0	Pacific	2-0
Clemson	4-1	Penn State	3-5
Colorado	1-5	Pittsburgh	8-8-1
Drake	1-2	Purdue	5-1
Duke	0-1	Rice	1-0
East Carolina	3-0	Richmond	1-0
Florida	22-24	San Diego State	1-1
Florida A&M	1-1	South Carolina	6-5-2
Florida State	15-13	Southeastern Louisiana	2-0
Furman	2-1	Southern California	1-1
Georgia	4-7-1	Southern Methodist	0-1
Georgia Southern	1-2	Southwestern Louisiana	2-1
Georgia Tech	2-6	Syracuse	4-5
Holy Cross	2-0	Temple	0-1
Houston	8-7	Tennessee-Chattanooga	4-0
Indiana	1-1	Texas	1-2
Iowa	2-0	Texas A&M	0-1
Kansas	3-0	Texas Christian	5-3
Kentucky	3-5	Texas Tech	2-1
Louisiana State	2-8	Tulane	6-5-1
Louisiana Tech	1-0	Tulsa	0-1
Louisville	7-0-1	UCLA	0-1
Maryland	5-7	Utah State	1-0
Memphis State	0-1	Vanderbilt	4-4
Miami (of Ohio)	2-0	Virginia Military	2-0
Michigan	0-1	Virginia Tech	8-0
Michigan State	3-0	Wake Forest	3-3
Middle Tennessee State	0-2	West Virginia	4-1
Mississippi	1-2	Western Kentucky	0-2
Mississippi State	3-2	William and Mary	3-0
Missouri	1-0	Wisconsin	0-1
Navy	3-2		

Other Opponents

Alabama (B)	0-1	Louisiana College	2-0
Baltimore	1-0	Manhattan	1-0
Bowden	2-1	Marquette	1-0
Camp Gordon	1-0	Mercer	1-0
Catholic	1-3	Millsaps	0-1
Charleston C.G.	1-0	Murray Teachers	0-1-1
Detroit	4-0	Norman Park	0-1
Duquesne	1-1	Oglethorpe	3-1
Elon	2-1	Parris Island	1-0
Erskine	1-0	Piedmont	3-0
Fordham	1-1	Presbyterian	2-0
Fort Benning	1-0	Rollins	14-3-1
Fort Pierce Amph.	0-1	St. Louis	2-0
George Washington	1-0	South Florida	3-1-1
Georgetown	2-1	Spring Hill	2-1
Georgetown (Ky.)	0-0-1	Stetson	4-5-2
Georgia State	2-0	Tampa	6-5-2
Havana	1-0	Union	1-0
Howard	2-3	Villanova	3-1-1
Jacksonville A.B.	0-1	Washington and Lee	2-0
Jacksonville N.A.S.	1-1	West Virginia Wesleyan	1-0
Jacksonville State	1-0	Wofford	1-0

Total Overall Record	313-249-19	.555
Overall Bowl Game Record	5-6-0	.455

NOTRE DAME

Nickname: Fighting Irish   Stadium: Notre Dame (59,075)
Colors: Gold and blue   First year of football: 1887
Location: Notre Dame, Indiana

Division I Competition

Air Force	11-3	Florida State	0-1
Akron	1-0	Georgia	0-1
Alabama	4-0	Georgia Tech	25-4-1
Arizona	2-1	Houston	1-0
Army	33-8-4	Illinois	11-0-1
Baylor	1-0	Indiana	22-5-1
Boston College	2-0	Iowa	13-8-3
California	4-0	Kansas	3-1-1
Cincinnati	1-0	Louisiana State	3-1
Clemson	1-1	Miami (Fla.)	13-4-1
Colorado	2-0	Miami (of Ohio)	1-0
Dartmouth	2-0	Michigan	5-11
Drake	8-0	Michigan State	32-17-1
Duke	2-1	Minnesota	4-0-1

Mississippi	0-1	Rutgers	1-0
Missouri	2-2	South Carolina	3-1
Navy	48-9-1	South Dakota	5-0
Nebraska	7-6-1	Southern California	29-23-4
North Carolina	15-1	Southern Methodist	8-3
Northwestern	34-7-2	Stanford	3-1
Ohio State	2-0	Syracuse	2-1
Oklahoma	7-1	Tennessee	1-1
Oregon	1-0-1	Texas	6-2
Pacific	1-0	Texas Christian	1-0
Penn State	5-3-1	Tulane	8-0
Pennsylvania	5-0-1	UCLA	2-0
Pittsburgh	32-14-1	Washington	2-0
Princeton	2-0	Western Michigan	2-0
Purdue	34-20-2	Wisconsin	8-6-2
Rice	3-0	Yale	0-1

Other Opponents

Adrian	1-0	Knox	1-1
Albion	3-1-1	Lake Forest	4-0
Alma	4-0	Lombard	3-0
American Med. Col.	5-0	Loyola (Chi.)	1-0
Beloit	5-0-1	Loyola (La.)	1-0
Bennett Med. Col.	1-0	Marquette	3-0-3
Butler	3-0	Missouri Osteopaths	1-0
Carlisle	1-0	Morningside	2-0
Carnegie Tech	15-4	Morris Harvey	1-0
Case Tech	2-0	Mount Union	1-0
Chicago	0-4	North Division H.S.	1-0
Chicago Dental	1-0	Northwestern Law	1-0
Chicago P&S	7-2	Ohio Medical	4-0
Christian Brothers	1-0	Ohio Northern	4-0
Coe	1-0	Olivet	3-0
Creighton	1-0	Rose Poly	3-0
DeLaSalle	1-0	Rush Medical	3-0-1
DePauw	8-0	St. Bonaventure	1-0
Detroit	2-0	St. Louis	3-0
Englewood H.S.	2-0	St. Viator	4-0
Franklin	3-0	St. Vincent	1-0
Goshen	1-0	South Bend A.C.	1-0-1
Great Lakes	1-2-2	South Bend Comm. A.C.	1-0
Harvard Prep.	1-0	South Bend H.S.	1-0
Haskell	5-0	South Bend Howard Park	1-0
Highland Views	1-0	Toledo A.A.	1-0
Hillsdale	4-0-1	Valparaiso	1-0
Illinois Cycling Club	1-0	Wabash	10-1
Indianapolis Artillery	0-1	Washington (Mo.)	1-0
Iowa Pre-Flight	2-0	Washington and Jefferson	1-0
Kalamazoo	7-0	Western Reserve	1-0

Total Overall Record   641-186-40   .762
Overall Bowl Game Record   8-4-0   .667

PENN STATE

Nickname: Nittany Lions   Stadium: Beaver (83,770)
Colors: Blue and white   First year of football: 1887
Location: University Park,
          Pennsylvania

Division I Competition

Air Force	3-0	Navy	18-17-2
Alabama	2-5	Nebraska	6-5
Arizona State	1-0	North Carolina	0-1
Army	13-10-2	North Carolina State	17-2
Baylor	1-0	Notre Dame	3-5-1
Boston College	12-1	Ohio	5-0
Boston University	8-0	Ohio State	6-2
Brown	1-0	Oklahoma	0-1
Bucknell	28-10	Oregon	2-1
California	3-1	Pennsylvania	18-25-4
Cincinnati	1-1	Pittsburgh	41-39-4
Colgate	9-4-1	Princeton	0-5
Colorado	1-1	Purdue	0-1-1
Columbia	0-2	Rice	2-0
Cornell	4-8-2	Rutgers	12-1
Dartmouth	1-2	South Carolina	2-0
Florida	0-1	Southern California	1-1
Florida State	0-0-1	Southern Methodist	1-0-1
Furman	1-0	Stanford	4-0
Georgia	1-0	Syracuse	36-21-5
Georgia Tech	3-3	Temple	18-3-1
Harvard	0-3-2	Tennessee	0-2
Holy Cross	9-0	Texas	1-1
Houston	2-0	Texas A&M	1-1
Illinois	3-1	Texas Christian	3-1
Iowa	6-3	Tulane	1-0
Kansas	1-0	UCLA	2-4
Kansas State	2-0	Utah State	1-0
Kent State	2-0	Vanderbilt	0-1
Kentucky	2-2	Virginia	3-0
Lafayette	10-5-1	Virginia Military	1-0
Lehigh	16-6-1	Wake Forest	1-0
Louisiana State	1-0	Washington	2-0
Marshall	2-0	Washington State	2-0
Maryland	27-1	West Virginia	41-8-2
Miami (Fla.)	5-3	William and Mary	4-0
Michigan State	1-8-1	Wisconsin	0-2
Missouri	3-1	Yale	0-7

Other Opponents

Allegheny	3-0	Marietta	3-0
Altoona	1-0	Marquette	2-0
Altoona A.A.	1-0	Middlebury	1-0
Bellefonte	2-1	Muhlenberg	5-1
Bloomsburg State	1-0	New York	2-1-1
Buffalo	0-1	Niagara	2-0
Carlisle	1-4-1	Oberlin	1-0
Carnegie Tech	6-0	Pittsburgh A.C.	3-1
DC & AC	0-3	St. Bonaventure	4-0
Dickinson	11-5-1	Sewanee	1-0
Dickinson Sem.	2-0	Steelton Y.	0-1
Fordham	3-0	Sterling A.C.	1-0
Franklin and Marshall	2-1	Susquehanna	6-0
Geneva	7-0	Swarthmore	2-0
George Washington	3-0	USA Ambulance	1-0
Georgetown	1-0	Ursinus	2-0
Gettysburg	27-0-1	Villanova	5-3-1
Grove City	3-0	Washington & Jefferson	5-2-1
Harrisburg A.C.	1-0	Waynesburg	0-2
Haverford	1-0	West Virginia Wesleyan	3-0
Homestead A.C.	0-1	Western Maryland	1-0
Jersey Shore	1-0	Western Reserve	0-0-1
Johns Hopkins	1-0	Westminster (Pa.)	3-0
Lebanon Valley	20-0	Wissahickon	0-0-1
Mansfield State	1-0	Wyoming Sem.	1-0

Total Overall Record   593-266-40   .682
Overall Bowl Game Record   14-6-2   .682

PITTSBURGH

Nickname: Panthers   Stadium: Pitt (56,500)
Colors: Blue and gold   First year of football: 1890
Location: Pittsburgh,
                Pennsylvania

Division I Competition

Air Force	0-2	Cincinnati	4-0
Akron	1-0	Clemson	1-0
Arizona	1-0	Colgate	1-0
Arizona State	0-1	Cornell	2-4
Army	19-6-2	Drake	1-0
Baylor	2-2	Duke	9-8
Boston College	9-2	East Carolina	1-0
Brigham Young	0-1	Florida	0-0-1
Bucknell	7-2	Florida State	5-3
California	3-2	Georgia	3-0-1

Georgia Tech	5-2	Ohio State	4-14-1
Holy Cross	1-0	Oklahoma	1-8-1
Illinois	2-6	Oregon	1-3
Indiana	2-7	Penn State	39-41-4
Iowa	2-1	Pennsylvania	10-1-1
Kansas	3-0	Purdue	1-4
Kent State	1-0	Rice	0-2
Lafayette	1-5	Rutgers	2-0
Lehigh	2-0	South Carolina	2-1
Louisville	4-0	Southern California	3-5
Maryland	2-1	Southern Methodist	2-2-1
Miami (Fla.)	8-8-1	Stanford	2-1
Miami (of Ohio)	2-0	Syracuse	24-14-2
Michigan	0-2	Temple	12-2-1
Michigan State	0-4-1	Tennessee	2-0
Minnesota	1-9	Texas Christian	0-1-1
Missouri	1-0	Tulane	3-4
Navy	16-11-3	UCLA	5-9
Nebraska	15-4-3	Virginia	2-0
North Carolina	2-2	Washington	4-1
North Carolina State	2-1	West Virginia	52-24-1
Northwestern	3-3	William and Mary	5-0
Notre Dame	14-32-1	Wisconsin	3-0
Ohio	1-0		

Other Opponents

Allegheny	8-2	Great Lakes	0-2
Allegheny A.A.	1-2	Greensburg A.A.	1-2
Allegheny A.C.	1-0	Grove City	8-2-1
Bellevue Outing	0-1	Hiram	1-0
Bethany	8-0	Indiana Teachers	1-2-1
Butler Y.	1-0	J.F. Lalus A.C.	0-1
California N.	2-0	Johns Hopkins	2-0
California Teachers	2-0	Kiski	1-0
Carlisle	4-4	Latrobe	2-2
Carnegie A.C.	0-1	Manchester A.C.	0-1
Carnegie Tech	24-5-1	Marietta	3-1
Centre	1-0	Marquette	3-0
Chatham Field	1-0	Mount Union	5-0
Cleveland Nav. Rsv.	0-1	Muskingum	1-0
DC & AC	0-3	Natrona A.C.	1-0
Dickinson	2-0	New Castle Terrors	0-0-1
Duquesne	5-2	Ohio Medical	2-0
Duquesne A.C.	1-0	Ohio Northern	1-0
East End A.A.	0-1	Ohio Wesleyan	2-0
East End Gym	0-2	Pittsburgh A.C.	0-3
Emerald A.A.	1-0	Pittsburgh Academy	1-0
Fordham	2-2-3	Pittsburgh H.S.	1-0
Franklin and Marshall	1-0	St. Louis	1-0
Geneva	16-6	Sewickley A.A.	1-0
Georgetown	2-0-1	Sewickley A.C.	1-0
Gettysburg	2-0	Shady Side Academy	0-1

158   College Football Records

Susquehanna	1-0	West Penn Med.	1-0
Swissvale A.C.	1-0	Western Reserve	3-0
Thiel	4-0	Western Theological Sem.	1-0
Villanova	1-0	Westminster (Pa.)	15-0-2
Washington and Jefferson	18-13-2	Wheeling Tigers	0-2
Washington and Lee	1-0	Wooster	1-0
Waynesburg	5-1		

Total Overall Record   520-333-38   .605
Overall Bowl Game Record   7-9-0   .438

RUTGERS

Nickname: Scarlet Knights
Colors: Scarlet
Location: New Brunswick, New
        Jersey

Stadium: Rutgers (23,000)
        Giants (78,000)
First year of football: 1869

Division I Competition

Air Force	1-1	Louisville	3-0
Alabama	0-2	Maryland	3-5
Arizona State	0-1	Massachusetts	2-2
Army	6-12	Navy	2-6-1
Auburn	0-1	Nebraska	0-1
Boston College	1-5	New Hampshire	1-0
Boston University	11-2	North Carolina	2-0
Brown	6-5	Northwestern	1-0
Bucknell	12-4	Notre Dame	0-1
Cincinnati	2-2	Ohio	0-1
Colgate	22-15	Penn State	1-12
Columbia	23-21-5	Pennsylvania	6-9
Connecticut	16-5	Pittsburgh	0-2
Cornell	6-5	Princeton	17-53-1
Dartmouth	0-1	Richmond	4-0-1
Delaware	15-13-3	Syracuse	3-11-1
Georgia Tech	0-1	Temple	8-6
Harvard	3-2	Tennessee	1-1
Hawaii	1-1	Tulane	2-0
Holy Cross	8-11	Virginia	2-3
Kentucky	0-1	Virginia Tech	2-0
Lafayette	41-30-1	West Virginia	2-8-2
Lehigh	43-30-1	William and Mary	6-4
Louisiana State	1-0	Yale	2-11

Other Opponents

Albright	2-0	Brooklyn College	0-1
Alfred	3-0	Catholic	1-1
Bethany (W.V.)	0-1	Detroit	0-1

Dickinson	1-0	Renssalaer Poly	5-0
Drexel	1-0	Rhode Island State	1-0
Fordham	8-5-1	St. Bonaventure	1-0
Franklin and Marshall	3-4-2	St. Johns (Md.)	2-0
George Washington	2-1	St. Lawrence	2-0
Hamilton	4-0	Seton Hall	0-1
Hampden-Sydney	2-0	Springfield	12-1
Haverford	5-9-3	Stevens	30-11-5
Hobart	2-0	Susquehanna	1-0
Jefferson Medical	0-1	Swarthmore	5-9
Johns Hopkins	3-0	Tampa	0-1
Lebanon Valley	1-0	Trinity (Ct.)	1-1
Manhattan	3-3	Tufts	1-0
Marietta	4-0	Union	3-6
Merchant Marine	1-0	Ursinus	9-8
Morgan State	2-0	Vermont	2-0
Muhlenberg	6-0-1	Villanova	5-6
New York	23-18-2	Washington (Md.)	0-1
New York Agric. Col.	1-0	Washington and Jefferson	0-3
New York C.C.	7-0	Washington and Lee	1-0-1
New York Law School	1-0	Wesleyan	1-6
Ohio Wesleyan	1-0-1	West Chester Teachers	0-1
Penn Medical	0-0-1	Western Reserve	1-0
Penn Military Col.	4-1-1	Williams	0-2
Providence	3-1-1	Wooster	1-0

Total Overall Record	466-411-35	.530
Overall Bowl Game Record	0-1-0	.000

SOUTH CAROLINA

Nickname: Gamecocks
Colors: Garnet and black
Location: Columbia, South Carolina

Stadium: Williams-Brice (72,400)
First year of football: 1894

Division I Competition

Alabama	0-7	Florida State	3-9
Appalachian State	5-1	Furman	27-19-1
Army	1-2	Georgia	7-30-2
Auburn	1-2-1	Georgia Tech	7-10
Baylor	1-2	Hawaii	0-2
Cincinnati	2-0	Houston	0-2
Citadel	38-6-3	Iowa State	1-0
Clemson	31-48-3	Kansas State	2-1
Davidson	6-13	Kentucky	1-1-1
Duke	14-24-2	Louisiana State	1-11
East Carolina	2-0	Maryland	11-17
Florida	3-6-3	Memphis State	2-2

Miami (Fla.)	5-6-2	Richmond	1-0
Miami (of Ohio)	2-3	Southern California	1-1
Michigan	1-0	Temple	0-1
Mississippi	5-4	Tennessee	1-7-2
Missouri	0-1	Texas	1-0
Navy	2-3	Tulane	0-3
Nebraska	0-1	Tulsa	1-0
North Carolina	13-33-4	Vanderbilt	1-0
North Carolina State	23-20-4	Virginia	19-10-1
Northwestern	0-1	Virginia Military	1-1
Notre Dame	1-3	Virginia Tech	7-7
Ohio	2-0	Wake Forest	32-20-2
Oklahoma State	1-1	West Virginia	2-5-1
Pacific	2-1	Western Michigan	1-0
Penn State	0-2	Wichita State	1-0
Pittsburgh	1-2		

Other Opponents

Augusta Y.	0-1	Georgia College	1-0
Bingham	5-2-1	Georgia Medical	2-0
Camp Blanding	1-0	Georgia Pre-Flight	0-1
Catholic	1-2	Guilford	4-0
Centre	1-2	Lenoir-Rhyne	1-0
Charleston	7-0	Machinists Mates	1-0
Charleston A.A.	0-1	Marquette	1-0-1
Charleston A.C.	1-0	Mercer	1-1
Charleston C.G.	1-0-1	Newberry	11-1-1
Charleston M.C.	1-0	North Carolina M.A.	2-0
Charleston Y.	0-2	North Carolina M.C.	0-1
Chicago	1-0	Porter	1-0
Columbia Y.	2-0	Presbyterian	12-3
Cumberland	1-0	Ridgewood	0-0-1
Detroit	1-0	St. Albans	1-0
Duquesne	1-1	Sewanee	2-2
Emory and Henry	1-0	Villanova	1-4-1
Erskine	15-1	Washington and Lee	2-3
Fordham	0-1	Welsh Neck	3-0
Fort Benning	0-1	Wofford	15-4
George Washington	1-1	Xavier	1-1
Georgetown	0-1		

Total Overall Record   396-388-38   .505
Overall Bowl Game Record   0-6-0   .000

SOUTHERN MISSISSIPPI

Nickname: Golden Eagles
Colors: Black and gold
Location: Hattiesburg,
        Mississippi

Stadium: Roberts (33,000)
First year of football: 1912

Division I Competition

Alabama	3-18-2	Mississippi State	11-9-1
Appalachian State	1-0	Missouri	0-1
Arkansas State	6-2	Murray State	1-1
Auburn	11-10	North Carolina State	4-3
Bowling Green	1-3	North Texas State	3-3
Brigham Young	1-1	Northeast Louisiana	1-0
Cal State-Fullerton	1-0	Northwestern Louisiana	9-11
Cincinnati	1-3	Pacific	0-1
Citadel	2-0	Richmond	14-2
East Carolina	7-3	San Diego State	1-2
Florida	0-1	Southeastern Louisiana	17-3
Florida State	7-9-1	Southwestern Louisiana	26-8-1
Georgia	1-1	Tennessee	0-1
Hawaii	1-0	Tennessee-Chattanooga	16-3
Houston	0-1	Texas A&M	0-1
Idaho	0-1	Texas-Arlington	10-0
Kentucky	0-1	Texas-El Paso	0-1
Lamar	3-1	Tulane	3-3
Louisiana State	0-1	Utah State	2-1
Louisiana Tech	26-12	Virginia Military	4-0
Louisville	7-3-1	Virginia Tech	2-2
McNeese State	1-0	West Texas State	8-3
Memphis State	14-13-1	William and Mary	0-1
Mississippi	6-18		

Other Opponents

Abilene Christian	9-0	Loyola (La.)	0-4
All-Navy Service Team	0-1	McMurry	2-1
Arkansas A&M	1-0	Marion Military	2-2
Brookley Field	1-0	Meridian College	1-0-1
Carswell A.B.	0-1	Meridian H.S.	0-1
Chamberlain Hunt Acad.	1-0	Millsaps	2-7-5
Clarke Memorial	4-3	Mississippi Col. Frosh	2-0
Copiah-Lincoln A.H.S.	1-1	Mississippi College	0-10
Dayton	2-1	Mississippi Frosh	0-1
Decatur A.H.S.	1-0	Mississippi State Frosh	0-2-1
Delta State	8-3-1	Mississippi State Reserves	1-0
East Texas State	1-2	Mize H.S.	1-0
Ellisville A.H.S.	3-0	Mobile Military Acad.	3-1
Elon	1-0	Mobile Shipbuilders	2-0
Georgia Teachers	1-0	North Dakota State	1-0
Gulf Coast J.C.	1-1-1	Oklahoma City	3-1
Gulf Coast Military Acad.	1-6-3	Parris Island Marines	1-0
Hardin-Simmons	1-0	Pearl River J.C.	3-4
Hattiesburg Boy Scouts	1-0	Perkinston A.H.S.	3-0
Havana	1-0	Poplarville A.H.S.	2-3-1
Hinds J.C.	1-0	Purvis H.S.	1-1
Jacksonville State	2-0	St. Mary's (Tex.)	2-0-1
Jones J.C.	1-0	St. Stanislaus H.S.	1-2
Louisiana College	12-3	Sam Houston State	0-1-1

Seashore Camp Ground	1-0	37th Division	1-0
6th Service Squadron	1-0	Trinity (Tex.)	8-1
Southwest J.C.	0-0-1	Troy State	6-1
Southwestern (Tenn.)	1-1	Tulane Frosh	0-1
Spring Hill	7-9-1	Union	6-2-1
Stephen F. Austin	3-0	Villanova	1-0
Stetson	1-1	Weber State	2-0
Tampa	5-0		

Total Overall Record   364-241-25 .598
Overall Bowl Game Record   1-5-0 ַ.167

SOUTHWESTERN LOUISIANA

Nickname: Ragin' Cajuns   Stadium: Cajun Field (31,000)
Colors: Vermilion and white   First year of football: 1908
Location: Lafayette, Louisiana

Division I Competition

Alabama	0-4	Mississippi State	0-2
Alabama State	6-0	New Mexico State	2-0
Arkansas State	6-11-1	North Texas State	2-2
Auburn	0-1	Northeast Louisiana	13-14
Cal State-Long Beach	1-1	Northwestern Louisiana	34-33-3
Cincinnati	0-4	Pacific	1-2
East Carolina	3-3	Rice	1-2
Florida	0-1	San Jose State	2-1
Fresno State	1-2	Southern Illinois	4-3
Furman	1-0	Southern Mississippi	8-26-1
Hawaii	0-1	Southeastern Louisiana	19-17-3
Houston	2-1	Temple	0-1
Lamar	21-11	Tennessee-Chattanooga	3-4
Louisiana State	0-19	Tennessee State	0-1
Louisiana Tech	29-34-5	Texas-Arlington	6-9
McNeese State	14-18-2	Tulane	0-13
Marshall	0-2	Tulsa	2-2
Memphis State	0-5	West Texas State	2-0
Miami (Fla.)	1-1	Wichita State	1-0

Other Opponents

Abbeville	3-0	Corpus Christi	2-0
Abilene Christian	1-2	Crowley	3-0
Alumni	0-0-1	Delta State	4-1
Arkansas A&M	1-1-1	Doane	1-0
Austin College	2-1	East Texas Baptist	1-0
Cal Poly-Pomona	1-0	East Texas State	2-4
Camp Beauregard	1-0	Fort Benning	1-0
Centenary	3-2	Hardin-Simmons	1-0
Chamberlain-Hunt Mil. Acad.	1-0	Henderson State	1-0

Jefferson	6-4-1	Randolph Field	1-0
Jennings	1-0	St. Charles	8-1
Keesler A.A.F.	0-1	St. Martinville	4-0-1
LaGarde Gen. Hosp.	1-0	St. Norbert	1-0
Lake Arthur	1-0	St. Stanislaus	2-0
Lake Charles	1-0	Sam Houston State	8-5-1
Lake Charles A.A.F.	2-1	Samford	2-0
Lake Charles H.S.	1-0	Santa Clara	2-0
Lenoir-Rhyne	1-0	South Arkansas State	2-1
Lon Morris J.C.	0-1	Southwestern (Tex.)	1-0
Louisiana College	40-16-3	Spring Hill	7-11
Louisiana State (B)	5-5	Stephen F. Austin	16-1-1
Loyola (La.)	4-3-1	Tampa	2-3-1
Mexico Poly	1-0	Trinity (Tex.)	1-3
Millsaps	4-6-1	Troy State	1-0
Mississippi College	1-4-1	Tulane (B)	4-0-1
Morgan City	1-0	27th Engineer Reg.	1-0
New Iberia	2-0	Union	1-0
Ouachita	0-1	Vinton	1-0
Patterson City	3-1	Xavier	0-1
Pensacola N.A.S.	5-2		

Total Overall Record	360-335-30	.517
Overall Bowl Game Record	0-0-0	.000

SYRACUSE

Nickname: Orangemen
Colors: Orange
Location: Syracuse, New York

Stadium: Carrier Dome (50,000)
First year of football: 1889

Division I Competition

Alabama	1-1	Holy Cross	23-5
Arizona	1-0	Houston	0-1
Army	8-9	Illinois	1-9
Baylor	1-1	Indiana	3-4
Boston College	14-11	Iowa	1-1
Boston University	12-3-1	Iowa State	1-0-1
Bowling Green	0-2	Kansas	4-4
Brown	9-3-3	Kent State	1-1
Bucknell	4-0	Lafayette	6-3-1
California	1-1	Lehigh	2-0
Colgate	28-31-5	Louisiana State	0-1
Columbia	11-9-4	McNeese State	1-0
Cornell	11-23	Maryland	14-13-2
Dartmouth	3-6-1	Miami (Fla.)	5-4
Duke	0-2	Miami (of Ohio)	1-0
Florida	1-1	Michigan	4-5-1
Florida State	1-1	Michigan State	3-9

164   College Football Records

Montana	0-0-1	Southern Methodist	0-1
Navy	14-8	Temple	8-8-1
Nebraska	7-5	Tennessee	0-1
North Carolina State	0-4	Texas	1-0
Northwestern	4-3	Texas Christian	0-1
Notre Dame	1-2	Tulane	2-0
Ohio	2-0	UCLA	6-2
Ohio State	1-2	Virginia	2-0
Oklahoma	0-2	Virginia Tech	1-0
Oregon State	5-3	Washington	1-1
Penn State	21-36-5	Washington State	1-0
Pittsburgh	14-24-2	West Virginia	19-13
Princeton	0-5-1	William and Mary	7-0
Richmond	1-0	Wisconsin	2-1-1
Rutgers	11-3-1	Yale	0-11
South Carolina	0-1		

Other Opponents

Alfred	1-0	Niagara	11-0
Allegheny	1-0	North Carolina Pre-Flight	0-1
All-Syracuse	1-0	Oberlin	1-0
Amherst	3-0	Occidental	1-0
Baldwin-Wallace	0-1	Ogdensburg	1-0
Bolling A.F.B.	0-1	Oglethorpe	1-0
Buffalo	0-3-1	Ohio Wesleyan	4-2-2
Carlisle	3-6	Onondaga A.	1-0
Case Tech	1-0	Onondaga Indians	2-0
Cazenovia	3-0	Providence	1-0
Clarkson	15-0	Rensselaer Poly	4-0
Clyde A.A.	0-0-1	Rochester	21-3-1
Cornell (B)	1-1	St. Bonaventure	0-0-1
Cortland State	6-0	St. Johns (N.Y.)	5-5-2
Dickinson	2-0	St. Lawrence	6-0
East Syracuse	2-0	St. Louis	2-0-1
Elmira A.A.	1-0	Scranton	1-0
Fordham	4-2-1	Springfield	1-1
47th Infantry	1-0-1	Susquehanna	1-0
Franklin and Marshall	1-0	Syracuse A.A.	11-7-1
George Washington	1-0	Syracuse H.S.	2-0
Georgetown	1-2-1	Trinity (N.Y.)	0-0-1
Hamilton	10-3	Tufts	4-0
Hobart	25-0	U.S.N. Transport	1-0
John Carroll	0-1	Union	1-6
Johns Hopkins	5-0	Vermont	7-0
McGill	2-0	Villanova	2-1
Manhattan	1-0	Washington and Jefferson	1-2
Mercer	1-0	West Virginia Wesleyan	0-1
Mount Union	1-0	Western Reserve	4-0
Muhlenberg	1-0	Williams	3-4
New York	7-0	Wyoming Sem.	1-0

Total Overall Record   509-354-45   .585
Overall Bowl Game Record   3-5-0   .375

TEMPLE

Nickname: Owls
Colors: Cherry and white
Location: Philadelphia,
      Pennsylvania

Stadium: Veterans (71,640)
First year of football: 1894

Division I Competition

Akron	6-2	Michigan State	1-7-2
Army	0-1	Mississippi	1-0-1
Boston College	3-12-2	Missouri	1-0
Boston University	8-9-1	Northeastern	1-1
Bowling Green	1-1	Oklahoma	1-1
Brown	3-0	Oklahoma State	0-2
Bucknell	16-20-8	Penn State	3-18-1
California	1-0	Pittsburgh	2-12-1
Cincinnati	8-2-1	Rhode Island	11-0
Colgate	1-1	Rutgers	6-8
Connecticut	5-1	South Carolina	1-0
Dartmouth	0-1	Southern Illinois	1-1
Delaware	13-22	Southern Methodist	0-0-2
Drake	8-1	Southwestern Louisiana	1-0
East Carolina	1-2	Syracuse	8-8-1
Florida	2-0	Tennessee	0-1
Florida State	0-1	Texas	0-1
Georgia	0-3	Texas A&M	2-0
Grambling State	1-1	Texas Christian	1-1
Hawaii	1-0	Toledo	1-2
Holy Cross	9-12-2	Tulane	0-1
Indiana	0-1-1	Vanderbilt	1-0
Iowa	0-1	Virginia Military	4-0
Kansas	1-0	Virginia Tech	1-1
Lafayette	8-4-1	Wake Forest	1-0
Lehigh	0-2	West Virginia	11-11
Louisville	3-0	William and Mary	3-1-1
Marshall	1-0	Yale	0-1
Miami (Fla.)	1-0		

Other Opponents

Albright	6-2-1	Carnegie Tech	4-6-1
Bainbridge Training	0-0-1	Central Pennsylvania	5-0
Bloomsburg State	1-0	Centre	2-0
Blue Ridge	1-0	Coatesville	1-0
Brandeis	1-0	Crescent A.C.	1-0
Brooklyn Poly	0-1	Dayton	2-2
Bryn Athyn	0-1	Denver	2-0
Buffalo	1-9	Drexel	2-2
Camden Bus. Col.	1-0	East Stroudsburg	1-1

Eastburn Acad.	3-0	Phila. Normal School	3-0
Fordham	0-4	Phila. Osteopathy	2-0
Franklin and Marshall	0-2	Phila. Team	3-0
Gallaudet	3-1	Pratt Institute	1-4
Geneva	1-0	Providence	1-0
George Washington	0-1-1	Quantico Marines	0-1
Georgetown	1-5	St. Bonaventure	1-0
Gettysburg	4-7-1	St. Francis	0-1
Girard	3-0	St. Johns (Md.)	1-0
Haskell	2-0-1	St. Josephs	6-4-4
Haverford	0-1	St. Mary's (Ca.)	0-1
Hofstra	7-6	Schuylkill	3-2-1
Ithaca	1-0	Schuylkill Navy	1-0-1
Juniata	1-1	Scranton	6-4
Kings Point	5-2-1	Southern Connecticut	1-0
LaSalle	8-1-3	Stevens	0-1
Lebanon Valley	1-2-2	Susquehanna	2-2
Loyola (Md.)	2-2	Swarthmore	2-0
Marquette	2-0	Thiel	3-0
Medico-Chirurgical	3-0	Tioga A.C.	1-0
Millersville	0-1-1	Trenton Teachers	1-6-1
Moravian	0-1	Upsala	1-0
Mt. St. Mary's	1-0	Ursinus	1-5
Muhlenberg	6-7	Villanova	12-13-2
New York	5-0	Washington and Jefferson	3-0-1
New York Agric. Col.	2-1	Washington and Lee	3-0
North Carolina Pre-Flight	0-1	Wayne State	3-0
Penn Military	2-9	West Chester State	0-3
Phila. C. Pharmacy	1-3-1	Western Maryland	1-1
Phila. Dental Col.	7-0	Wyoming Seminary	0-1
Phila. Naval Yard	2-0	Xavier	4-0

Total Overall Record   338-321-52   .512
Overall Bowl Game Record   1-1-0   .500

TULANE

Nickname: Green Wave
Colors: Green and blue
Location: New Orleans,
    Louisiana

Stadium: Louisiana Superdome
(80,100)
First year of football: 1893

Division I Competition

Air Force	3-3	Boston College	7-5
Alabama	10-23-3	California	1-0
Arkansas	0-4	Cincinnati	5-2
Army	2-1-1	Citadel	2-0
Auburn	17-13-6	Clemson	6-4
Baylor	3-3	Colgate	4-1

Colorado	1-0	Penn State	0-1
Columbia	1-0	Pittsburgh	4-3
Duke	2-0	Rice	8-10-1
Florida	6-1ʳ-2	Richmond	1-0
Florida State	1-1	Rutgers	0-2
Georgia	10-13-1	South Carolina	3-0
Georgia Tech	13-35	Southeast Louisiana	1-0
Holy Cross	1-0	Southern California	1-2
Houston	0-2	Southern Methodist	4-3
Illinois	1-0	Southern Mississippi	3-3
Kansas	0-1	Southwestern Louisiana	12-0
Kentucky	6-8	Stanford	1-7
Louisiana State	23-52-7	Syracuse	0-2
Louisiana Tech	7-0	Temple	1-0
Maryland	2-2	Tennessee	1-4
Memphis State	5-3-1	Tennessee-Chattanooga	1-0
Miami (Fla.)	5-6-1	Texas	1-15-1
Miami (of Ohio)	0-1	Texas A&M	5-10
Michigan	0-3	Texas Christian	1-1
Minnesota	0-1	Texas Tech	3-2
Mississippi	27-29	Tulsa	1-0
Mississippi State	22-20-2	Vanderbilt	25-16-3
Missouri	0-0-2	Virginia	4-2
Navy	4-0-1	Virginia Military	5-0
North Carolina	9-3-2	Virginia Tech	3-4
North Carolina State	1-0	Wake Forest	1-0
Northwest Louisiana	5-0	Washington State	1-0
Northwestern	3-1	West Virginia	2-4
Notre Dame	0-8	William and Mary	1-1
Ohio	1-1		

Other Opponents

Alumni	2-0	Mercer	1-0
Birmingham-Southern	1-0	Meridian	2-0
Camp Beauregard	1-0	Millsaps	2-0
Camp Benning	1-0	Mississippi College	9-3
Camp Pike	0-1	Mobile Y.	0-1
Centenary	3-0	New Orleans Gym Club	1-0
Centre	2-3	New Orleans Y.	1-0
Cumberland	0-1	New York	1-1
Detroit	1-2	Pensacola N.A.S.	0-0-1
Drury	1-0	St. Louis	1-0
Fordham	1-1	St. Paul's	1-0
Georgetown	0-1	Santa Clara	1-0
Georgia Pre-Flight	0-2	Sewanee	13-6
Havana	0-1	Shelby Army	1-0
Howard	4-0-1	Shreveport A.C.	0-1
Jefferson	6-0	Southern A.C.	2-1-1
Louisiana College	5-0	Southwestern (Tex.)	1-1
Marion Military Inst.	1-0	Spring Hill	7-0
Marquette	1-0	Tampa	0-1
Memphis Navy	0-1	Vicksburg A.C.	1-0

| Washington (Mo.) | 2-1 | Washington Artillery | 1-0 |
| Washington and Lee | 0-1-1 | | |

Total Overall Record   388-384-38 .502
Overall Bowl Game Record   2-5-0 .286

UNITED STATES MILITARY ACADEMY (ARMY)

Nickname: Cadets
Colors: Black, gold, and gray
Location: West Point, New York

Stadium: Michie (39,867)
First year of football: 1890

Division I Competition

Air Force	9-9-1	Louisiana State	1-0
Arkansas State	1-0	Louisville	0-1
Auburn	2-0	Maine	4-0
Baylor	0-2	Marshall	1-0
Boston College	10-10	Massachusetts	1-0
Boston University	10-0	Miami (Fla.)	0-3
Brown	6-2	Miami (of Ohio)	1-0
Bucknell	3-0	Michigan	5-4
California	4-2	Michigan State	2-0
Cincinnati	1-0	Minnesota	0-1
Citadel	5-0	Mississippi State	0-1
Clemson	1-0	Missouri	1-3
Colgate	16-4-2	Montana	1-0
Colorado	1-1	Navy	38-40-7
Colorado State	1-0	Nebraska	2-3
Columbia	14-4-3	New Hampshire	1-1
Connecticut	1-0	New Mexico	2-0
Cornell	3-2	North Carolina	1-4
Dartmouth	6-1	North Carolina State	1-0
Davidson	3-0	North Dakota	1-0
Delaware	1-0	Northwestern	0-2
Drake	1-0	Notre Dame	8-33-4
Duke	8-4-1	Oklahoma	1-2
Florida	2-1	Oklahoma State	0-1
Furman	5-0	Oregon	0-0-2
Georgia Tech	1-2	Penn State	10-13-2
Harvard	16-19-2	Pennsylvania	12-4-2
Holy Cross	11-3-1	Pittsburgh	6-19-2
Idaho	1-0	Princeton	4-6-3
Illinois	3-3-1	Rice	1-0
Iowa State	1-0	Richmond	1-0
Kansas	1-0	Rutgers	12-6
Kansas State	1-0	South Carolina	2-1
Lafayette	8-1	South Dakota	1-0
Lehigh	7-2-1	Southern California	0-2

Southern Methodist	2-0	Vanderbilt	1-3
Stanford	5-5	Virginia	5-3
Syracuse	9-8	Virginia Military	9-1
Temple	1-0	Virginia Tech	5-1
Tennessee	1-5-1	Wake Forest	3-0
Tennessee-Chattanooga	1-0	Washington State	1-1-1
Texas	0-1	West Virginia	2-1
Texas A&M	1-1	Wichita State	1-0
Tulane	1-2-1	William and Mary	4-0
Utah	3-0	Wyoming	1-0
Utah State	0-1	Yale	12-21-8

Other Opponents

Albright	1-0	Mitchel Field	1-0
Amherst	2-0	Muhlenberg	1-0
Bates	1-0	New York	1-0
Bethany (W.V.)	1-0	New York Volunteers	0-1
Bowdoin	1-0	North Dakota State	1-0
Buffalo	1-0	Ohio Northern	1-0
Carleton	2-0	Ohio Wesleyan	1-0
Carlisle	1-2	Penn Military	1-0
Carnegie Tech	1-0	Princeton Reserves	1-0-1
Centre	1-0	Providence	1-0-1
Chicago	1-0	Rochester	1-0
Coast Guard	1-0	St. Bonaventure	1-0
Coe	1-0	St. John's (N.Y.)	1-0
Colorado College	1-0	St. Louis	2-0
Davis and Elkins	3-0	Sampson N.A.S.	1-0
DeLaSalle	1-0	Schuylkill Navy	1-0
DePauw	1-0	Sewanee	1-0
Detroit	5-0	Springfield	10-0
Dickinson	4-0	Stevens	6-0
Fordham	2-0	Susquehanna	1-0
Franklin and Marshall	5-0	Swarthmore	1-0
George Washington	2-0	Trinity (Ct.)	13-0
Georgetown	1-0-1	Tufts	20-0
Gettysburg	3-0	Union	6-0
Hamilton	1-0	Ursinus	6-0
Hobart	1-0	Vermont	3-0
Kentucky Wesleyan	1-0	Villanova	18-3
Knox	2-0	Wabash	1-0
Lebanon Valley	6-0	Washburn	1-0
Louisville A.A.F.	1-0	Washington (Mo.)	1-0
M.I.T.	1-0	Washington and Jefferson	0-0-1
Manhattan	1-0	Washington and Lee	3-0
Marquette	1-0	Wesleyan	2-0-2
Melville Navy	1-0	West Virginia Wesleyan	1-0
Mercer	1-0	Williams	6-0
Middlebury	3-0		

Total Overall Record	532-282-50	.645
Overall Bowl Game Record	1-0-0	1.000

UNITED STATES NAVAL ACADEMY
(NAVY)

Nickname: Midshipmen   Stadium: Navy-Marine Corps
Colors: Blue and gold   Memorial (30,000)
Location: Annapolis, Maryland   First year of football: 1879

Division I Competition

Air Force	8-9	Mississippi State	0-1
Arkansas	0-2	Missouri	0-2
Army	40-38-7	North Carolina	4-2
Boston College	9-10	North Carolina State	7-1
Boston University	1-0	Northwestern	0-2
Brigham Young	1-0	Notre Dame	9-48-1
Bucknell	9-4-1	Ohio	0-1
California	1-3	Ohio State	0-3
Cincinnati	2-0	Oklahoma	1-0
Citadel	6-0	Penn State	17-18-2
Clemson	0-1	Pennsylvania	20-21-4
Colgate	3-0	Pittsburgh	11-16-3
Columbia	13-9-1	Princeton	12-18-6
Connecticut	5-0	Purdue	2-0
Cornell	9-1	Rice	1-2
Dartmouth	3-0-1	Richmond	1-0
Davidson	3-0	Rutgers	6-2-1
Delaware	1-0	South Carolina	3-2
Drake	3-0	Southern California	1-2
Duke	14-9-5	Southern Methodist	1-5
Eastern Kentucky	1-0	Stanford	1-0-1
Florida State	0-1	Syracuse	8-14
Georgia	2-0	Texas	0-2
Georgia Tech	8-13	Tulane	0-4-1
Harvard	1-1-3	Vanderbilt	1-0-2
Houston	0-1	Virginia	25-6
Illinois	1-0	Virginia Military	6-0
Kent State	1-0	Virginia Tech	7-1
Lafayette	6-4	Wake Forest	1-0
Lehigh	13-5-1	Washington	2-3-1
Maryland	14-5-1	West Virginia	5-1
Miami (Fla.)	2-3	William and Mary	35-4-1
Michigan	5-12-1	Wisconsin	1-1
Minnesota	0-1	Yale	3-5-1
Mississippi	1-0		

Other Opponents

Baltimore A.C.	0-0-1	Bethany (W.V.)	1-0
Baltimore C.C.	1-0	Carlisle	5-1
Baltimore Medical Col.	1-0-1	Colby	3-0

Columbia A.C.	1-0-1	North Carolina Pre-Flight	1-1
Davis and Elkins	1-1	Orange A.C.	0-1
Denison	1-0	Pennsylvania Reserves	1-1
Detroit	1-0	Princeton (B)	1-2
Dickinson	10-1-4	Princeton Frosh	0-1
Elizabeth A.C.	1-0-1	St. Helena	1-0
Fordham	1-0	St. John's (Md.)	18-3
Franklin and Marshall	4-0	St. Xavier	2-0
Gallaudet	4-1	Swarthmore	1-4
George Washington	5-0	Trinity (Ct.)	1-0
Georgetown	13-4-2	USS Utah	1-0
Great Lakes	0-1	Ursinus	2-1
Haverford	1-0	Vermont	1-0
Johns Hopkins	9-3	Villanova	7-2
Loyola (Md.)	3-0	Washington (Mo.)	1-0
Marine Officers	1-0	Washington All-Stars	1-0
Marquette	1-1	Washington and Jefferson	4-1-1
Mercer	2-0	Washington and Lee	2-1
New Jersey A.C.	1-0	West Virginia Wesleyan	7-1-1
New York	3-0	Western Maryland	3-0
New York Naval Militia	1-0	Western Reserve	8-0-1
Newport T.S.	1-0	White Squadron	2-0
Norfolk Navy	1-0	Wooster	1-0

Total Overall Record   520-351-58   .591
Overall Bowl Game Record   3-5-1   .389

VIRGINIA POLYTECHNIC INSTITUTE
(VIRGINIA TECH)

Nickname: Hokies   Stadium: Lane (51,000)
Colors: Orange and maroon   First year of football: 1892
Location: Blacksburg, Virginia

Division I Competition

Air Force	0-1	East Carolina	1-0
Alabama	0-10	East Tennessee State	1-0
Appalachian State	3-0	Florida State	10-14-1
Army	1-5	Furman	3-0
Auburn	1-2-1	Georgia	1-1
Bucknell	0-1	Houston	1-3-1
Cincinnati	0-1	James Madison	1-0
Citadel	2-0	Kansas State	1-1
Clemson	6-13-1	Kent State	1-1
Colgate	1-1	Kentucky	5-10-2
Cornell	0-1	Louisville	2-0
Dartmouth	0-1	Marshall	5-2
Davidson	10-3-1	Maryland	10-14
Duke	4-7	Memphis State	2-3

172   College Football Records

Miami (Fla.)	0-8	Syracuse	0-1
Mississippi	1-1	Temple	1-1
Navy	1-7	Tennessee	2-4
North Carolina	11-8-6	Tennessee-Chattanooga	0-1
North Carolina State	20-16-3	Texas A&M	0-2
Ohio	2-0	Tulane	4-3
Oklahoma State	1-1	Tulsa	1-3
Pennsylvania	1-1	Vanderbilt	3-3
Princeton	0-3	Virginia	33-28-5
Rhode Island	1-0	Virginia Military	49-25-5
Richmond	35-9-4	Wake Forest	20-11-1
Rutgers	0-2	West Texas State	2-0
South Carolina	7-7	West Virginia	9-20-1
Southern Methodist	1-2	William and Mary	38-17-4
Southern Mississippi	2-2	Yale	0-2

Other Opponents

Allegheny	1-0	Morris Harvey	3-0
Bellevue	1-0	Nashville	1-0
Belmont A.C.	1-0	North Carolina SATC	1-0
Buffalo	2-0	Quantico Marines	0-2
Camp Humphreys	1-0	Randolph-Macon	3-1
Catawba	3-0	Roanoke	26-0-2
Catholic	1-0	Roanoke Y.	1-0
Centre	2-3	St. Albans	8-1
Cumberland	1-0	Tampa	2-0
Emory and Henry	5-1	3rd Corps Area	0-1
Gallaudet	1-0	Villanova	5-0
George Washington	10-8	Virginia Med. Col.	0-1
Georgetown	4-4	Virginia Tech Stars	1-0
Guilford	1-0	Washington and Lee	22-20-5
Hampden-Sydney	24-0	Waynesburg	1-0
King	6-0	West Virginia Wesleyan	0-1
Lynchburg	1-0	Western Maryland	2-0
Maryville	1-0		

Total Overall Record   459-324-43   .582
Overall Bowl Game Record   0-5-0   .000

WEST VIRGINIA

Nickname: Mountaineers   Stadium: Mountaineer Field
Colors: Gold and blue   (60,686)
Location: Morgantown, West   First year of football: 1891
         Virginia

Division I Competition

Arizona State	0-1	Boston College	8-5
Army	1-2	Boston University	3-4-1

Bucknell	0-1-2	Oklahoma State	2-0
California	1-2	Oregon	0-2
Cincinnati	6-0	Oregon State	0-2
Citadel	5-1	Pacific	1-0
Colgate	1-0	Penn State	8-41-2
Colorado State	2-1	Pennsylvania	0-5
Dartmouth	0-1-1	Pittsburgh	24-52-1
Davidson	1-0	Princeton	1-1
Duke	0-3	Rice	0-1
East Carolina	4-0	Richmond	21-2-2
Florida State	0-1	Rutgers	8-2-2
Furman	3-1	South Carolina	5-2-1
Georgia Tech	0-1	Southern California	0-1
Hawaii	0-1	Southern Methodist	1-0
Illinois	1-1	Stanford	0-1
Kansas	1-0	Syracuse	13-19
Kansas State	1-1	Temple	11-11
Kent State	1-0	Texas	1-0
Kentucky	8-11-1	Texas Christian	1-0
Lafayette	1-3-1	Texas-El Paso	0-1-1
Lehigh	2-1-1	Texas Tech	1-0
Louisville	1-0	Tulane	4-2
Marshall	4-0	Utah	0-1
Maryland	10-9-2	Vanderbilt	1-1
Miami (Fla.)	1-4	Virginia	10-10-1
Michigan	0-1	Virginia Military	11-0
Michigan State	0-4	Virginia Tech	20-9-1
Missouri	0-2	Wake Forest	2-0
Navy	1-5	William and Mary	15-0-1
North Carolina State	5-4	Wisconsin	0-2
Ohio	10-4	Yale	0-1
Ohio State	1-3	Youngstown State	1-0
Oklahoma	1-2		

Other Opponents

Allegheny	5-1	Duquesne A.C.	0-1-1
Alumni	3-1	Fordham	3-8-1
Bethany (W.V.)	13-0-1	Geneva	4-0
California (Pa.)	5-0	George Washington	17-7
California Y.	1-0	Georgetown	4-7-2
Carlisle	1-0	Gettysburg	2-0
Carnegie Tech	3-2	Gonzaga	1-0
Case Tech	1-0	Grove City	7-0
Catholic	1-0	Haskell	1-0
Centre	3-2	Latrobe Indians	2-2
Connellsville	1-1	Loyola (La.)	0-0-1
Creighton	1-0	Mahoning Cycle Club	0-1
Davis and Elkins	9-2-1	Manhattan	0-2
Denison	0-2	Marietta	16-6-1
Detroit	0-4	Marquette	2-0-1
Drexel	1-0	Monessen Indians	1-0
Duquesne	4-3-1	Morris Harvey	0-0-1

Mt. Pleasant	3-0	Villanova	5-1
New York	1-0	Washington & Jefferson	12-20-2
Ohio Wesleyan	3-0	Washington & Lee	27-6-4
Otterbein	3-0	Waynesburg	16-1
Parkersburg Y.	1-0	West Virginia Wesleyan	29-4-1
Pittsburgh A.C.	1-2-1	Western Maryland	2-0
Pittsburgh Lyceum	1-0	Western Reserve	4-2
Quantico Marines	1-0	Westminster (Pa.)	14-0
St. Louis	1-0	Wooster	1-0
Slippery Rock	1-0	Xavier	1-0
Uniontown Indians	1-0		

Total Overall Record   486-337-40   .586
Overall Bowl Game Record   8-4-0   .667

Appendices

BEST DIVISION I-A OVERALL RECORDS

		Years	W	L	T	Pct.
1.	Notre Dame	96	641	186	40	.762
2.	Michigan	105	648	222	31	.736
3.	Alabama	90	606	213	42	.728
4.	Texas	91	622	227	31	.717
5.	Southern California	95	565	213	49	.713
6.	Oklahoma	90	576	220	50	.710
7.	Ohio State	95	589	233	48	.705
8.	Penn State	98	593	266	40	.682
9.	Tennessee	88	558	251	47	.679
10.	Nebraska	95	592	271	39	.678
11.	Central Michigan	81	426	217	29	.655
12.	Miami (of Ohio)	96	502	258	36	.653
13.	Army	95	532	282	50	.645
14.	Louisiana State	91	517	281	44	.640
15.	Georgia	91	521	294	49	.631
16.	Stanford	91	524	298	48	.630
	Washington	95	490	278	47	.630
18.	Arizona State	71	380	220	21	.629
19.	Minnesota	101	508	301	40	.625
20.	Michigan State	88	463	284	40	.614

BEST BOWL GAME RECORDS
(Minimum of 6 Games)

		W	L	T	Pct.
1.	Miami (of Ohio)	5	1	0	.833
2.	Oklahoma State	7	2	0	.778
3.	Southern California	21	7	0	.750
4.	Kentucky	5	2	0	.714
5.	Penn State	14	6	2	.682
	Houston	7	3	1	.682
7.	Notre Dame	8	4	0	.667
	West Virginia	8	4	0	.667

Iowa	4	2	0	.667
Wyoming	4	2	0	.667
Mississippi State	4	2	0	.667
12. Oklahoma	16	8	1	.660
13. Georgia Tech	14	8	0	.636
14. Arizona State	7	4	1	.625
Texas-El Paso	5	3	0	.625

MOST BOWL GAME APPEARANCES

1. Alabama	37 (20-14-3)	6. Georgia	24 (11-11-2)
2. Texas	31 (15-14-2)	Louisiana State	24 (10-13-1)
3. Southern Calif.	28 (21-7-0)	8. Nebraska	23 (13-10-0)
4. Tennessee	27 (13-14-0)	9. Penn State	22 (14-6-2)
5. Oklahoma	25 (16-8-1)	Georgia Tech	22 (14-8-0)

DIVISION I-A CONFERENCE BOWL GAME RECORDS

	W	L	T	Pct.
1. Mid-American Conference	11	5	0	.688
2. Western Athletic Conference	22	18	2	.548
3. Pacific Ten Conference	54	47	5	.533
4. Southeastern Conference	91	82	8	.525
5. Big Eight Conference	50	46	1	.521
6. Atlantic Coast Conference	41	39	1	.512
7. Pacific Coast Conference	9	10	3	.477
8. Big Ten Conference	32	36	0	.471
9. Independents	66	75	6	.469
10. Southwest Conference	59	71	9	.457

LONGEST DIVISION I RIVALRIES

Games	Schools (Series Leader Listed First)	Record
120	Lafayette-Lehigh (Division I-AA)	66-49-5
107	Yale-Princeton (Division I-AA)	59-38-10
101	Yale-Harvard (Division I-AA)	55-38-8
94	Minnesota-Wisconsin	50-36-8
94	Richmond-William and Mary (Division I-AA)	46-43-5
93	Missouri-Kansas	43-41-9
91	Nebraska-Kansas	67-21-3
91	Texas Christian-Baylor	44-40-7
91	Texas-Texas A&M	63-23-5
91	Pennsylvania-Cornell (Division I-AA)	51-35-5
89	North Carolina-Virginia	51-34-4

89	Miami (of Ohio)–Cincinnati	49-34-6
89	Yale-Brown (Division I-AA)	64-21-4
88	Georgia-Auburn	41-40-7
88	Oregon–Oregon State	41-37-10
88	Harvard-Dartmouth (Division I-AA)	46-38-4
87	Purdue-Indiana	54-27-6
87	Auburn-Georgia Tech	44-39-4
87	Stanford-California	41-36-10
85	Navy-Army	40-38-7
84	Harvard-Brown (Division I-AA)	61-21-2
84	Montana-Montana State (Division I-AA)	48-31-5
84	Penn State-Pittsburgh	41-39-4

DIVISION I-AA FOOTBALL TEAMS

Akron	Lamar
Alabama State	Lehigh
Alcorn State	Louisiana Tech
Appalachian State	McNeese State
Arkansas State	Maine
Austin Peay	Marshall
Boise State	Massachusetts
Boston	Middle Tennessee
Brown	Montana
Bucknell	Montana State
The Citadel	Moorehead State
Colgate	Murray State
Columbia	Nevada-Reno
Connecticut	New Hampshire
Cornell	North Carolina A&T
Dartmouth	North Texas State
Davidson	Northeast Louisiana
Delaware	Northeastern
Drake	Northern Arizona
East Tennessee	Northern Iowa
Eastern Illinois	Northwestern Louisiana
Eastern Kentucky	Pennsylvania
Florida A&M	Prairie View A&M
Furman	Princeton
Georgia Southern	Rhode Island
Grambling State	Richmond
Harvard	South Carolina State
Holy Cross	Southeastern Louisiana
Idaho	Southern Illinois
Idaho State	Southwest Missouri
Illinois State	Southwest Texas State
Indiana State	Tennessee-Chattanooga
Jackson State	Tennessee State
James Madison	Tennessee Tech
Lafayette	Texas-Arlington

Texas Southern
Tulsa
Virginia Military Institute
Weber State
West Texas State
Western Carolina

Western Illinois
Western Kentucky
Wichita State
William and Mary
Yale
Youngstown State

Index

The following are non–division I-A schools and other formal teams that appear as opposition to the schools covered in this book. The NCAA division each following school currently competes within is listed in parenthesis. If no parenthesis follows the school, it no longer fields a football team that competes within the NCAA.

The three non–division I-A football divisions that ensue are abbreviated in parenthesis as follows: (A) Division I-AA; (2) Division II; (3) Division III.

A

Abbeville 162
Abilene (Kansas) 22
Abilene Christian (2) 77, 89, 119, 125, 129, 130, 139, 148, 151, 161, 162
Adams State (2) 69, 77, 79, 80
Adrian (3) 27, 38, 39, 62, 63, 65, 67, 71, 73, 154
Akron (A) 39, 43, 60, 61, 63, 64, 66, 67, 68, 70, 71, 72, 78, 137, 145, 149, 153, 156, 165
Alabama Presbyterian 108
Alabama State (A) 162
Alameda Coast Guard 81, 83, 90, 97
Albany 92, 93
Albany A.C. 93
Albany Navy 81
Albion (3) 38, 39, 62, 63, 65, 66, 73, 154
Albright (3) 49, 51, 55, 147, 158, 165, 169
Albuquerque A.F.B. 89
Albuquerque Athletics 80
Albuquerque Guards 80
Albuquerque Indians 80, 137
Alcorn State (A) 63, 78
Alfred (3) 50, 51, 57, 158, 164
Alfred Holbrook 150
Allegheny (3) 51, 52, 65, 144, 156, 157, 164, 172, 173

Allegheny A.A. 157
Allegheny A.C. 157
Alliance A.C. 94
Alma (3) 39, 62, 63, 65, 67, 71, 73, 154
Altoona 156
Altoona A.A. 156
Amarillo A.F.B. 137
American College of P.E. 69
American Medical 38, 154
American University 10, 115
Ames 41
Amherst (3) 49, 50, 51, 52, 53, 55, 56, 57, 164, 169
Amity 25
Anderson 61
Andover 49, 52, 53
Antioch 43, 67, 146
Appalachian State (A) 6, 11, 13, 15, 60, 147, 159, 161, 171
Arizona Indians 87
Arkansas A&M 67, 119, 161, 162
Arkansas City 28
Arkansas College 79, 151
Arkansas Monticello 151
Arkansas State (A) 21, 23, 61, 63, 64, 72, 77, 79, 103, 106, 111, 113, 127, 137, 141, 145, 150, 161, 162, 168
Arkansas Teachers 119, 151
Arkansas Tech 151
Armour Institute 39, 42, 44, 46
Arrowhead A.C. 94

179

P

Pacific (Oregon) (3) 83, 92, 93, 99, 100
Pacific Fleet 84, 90, 96, 99, 134
Pacific Lutheran (3) 81
Palmyra 51
Panhandle State 80, 130
Panora 21
Pantops 15
Paris A.C. 109
Park Field 113
Park Place Flyers 123
Parkersburg A.A. 70
Parkersburg A.C. 70
Parkersburg Y. 70, 174
Parris Island 153, 161
Parsons 36, 147
Pasadena 95
Pasadena A.C. 95
Pastime A.C. 25, 34
Patterson City 163
Patterson Field 62, 66
Paul's Valley 28
Pawhuska 28
Pawnee Indians 30
Pawtucket C.C. 49
Payne Field 112, 113
Pearl Harbor 92
Pearl River J.C. 161
Peninsulars 38
Penn Medical College 159
Penn Military Institute 11, 55, 159, 166, 169
Penn Reserves 171
Pensacola 96
Pensacola A.C. 103
Pensacola N.A.S. 7, 104, 129, 151, 163, 167
Pepperdine 76, 77, 83, 89, 134, 138
Perris Indians 90, 95
Peru State 20, 27
Philadelphia C. Pharmacy 166
Philadelphia Dental College 166
Philadelphia Naval Yard 166
Philadelphia Normal School 166
Philadelphia Osteopathy 166
Phillips 28, 30, 120, 121, 126, 127, 129
Phoenix Indians 88, 89, 95
Phoenix J.C. 88, 89

Piedmont 153
Pierce C.C. 120
Pillsbury 41
Pittsburg State (Kansas) 22, 24, 64, 72, 120
Pittsburgh A.C. 156, 157, 174
Pittsburgh Academy 157
Pittsburgh Lyceum 174
Pocatello A.C. 141
Polish Seminary 65
Polytechnic 121, 126, 127, 129
Pomona (3) 76, 88, 95, 97, 138, 141
Port Huron Y. 39
Port Royal 7
Port Townsend 96, 99
Porter 160
Portland 77, 82, 83, 89, 92, 93, 100, 134
Portland State (2) 78, 93, 141
Portsmouth 70
Post Field 28
Prairie View A&M (A) 78
Pratt Institute 166
Presbyterian 7, 8, 9, 13, 16, 105, 106, 108, 147, 153, 160
Princeton Seminary 56
Providence 144, 159, 164, 166, 169
Puget Sound (2) 83, 92, 93, 99, 100
Puyallup Indians 99

Q

Q and C R.R. 109
Quantico Marines 16, 38, 62, 65, 68, 72, 82, 116, 144, 151, 166, 172, 174

R

Racine 38
Rainer Valley A.C. 99
Raleigh Academy 13
Randolph Field 123, 125, 126, 163
Randolph-Macon (3) 8, 11, 13, 15, 16, 106, 147, 149, 172
Ream Field 128
Redlands (3) 78, 83, 88, 95, 97, 138